FROM LAST RITES TO BILL OF RIGHTS:

The Miraculous Life and Legacy of James Madison

BY JOE WOLVERTON, II, J.D.
*Constitutional Law Scholar of
The John Birch Society*

WESTERN ISLANDS
PUBLISHING

APPLETON, WISCONSIN

Copyright © March 2025 by Joe Wolverton, II, J.D.
All rights reserved. No portion of this book may be reproduced in any form.

Published by
Western Island
770 N. Westhill Boulevard
Appleton, Wisconsin 54914
www.JBS.org

Cover Design by Lindsey McConnell

Paperback
Library of Congress Control Number: 2025931235
International Standard Book Number (ISBN): 978-0-88279-150-0

Hard Cover
Library of Congress Control Number: 2025935900
International Standard Book Number (ISBN): 978-0-88279-240-8

Printed in the United States of America

Foreword by the Author

James Madison — "the great little Madison" — was one of the greatest and best men of his or any age of American history. He led a life of unalloyed integrity and fervent intellectual endeavor that has few equals, and I am humbled by the opportunity offered me to write a small and ordinary book about such a great and extraordinary man.

Note on Sources and Citations

Unless otherwise attributed, all quotes from James Madison or about him were taken from the physical copies of *The Papers of James Madison*, owned by the author, or from *The Papers of James Madison Digital Edition*, maintained by the University of Virginia Rotunda in Charlottesville, Virginia.

Other works used as source material in the writing of this book are listed within the text or in the "Works Cited" section *infra*.

Archaic spellings/misspellings within quotes are all in the original and have not been corrected.

Apart from these exceptions, every word of this book is from the mind of the author, and he takes full credit for their accuracy and tone.

Table of Contents

Introduction v

Chapter One: James Madison's Birth and Education 1

Chapter Two: James Madison's Moral Obligations 23

Chapter Three: Maintaining Strength
Through Hardship 45

Chapter Four: Avoiding a Repetitive History................. 51

Chapter Five: Reforming a Free Nation 63

Chapter Six: "Miracle" at Philadelphia 85

Chapter Seven: James Madison's Contributions
to the Battle for Ratification: *The Federalist* 93

Chapter Eight: James Madison, Patrick Henry,
and the Ratification Contest in Virginia.................... 109

Chapter Nine: Congressman James Madison
and the Bill of Rights..................................... 121

Chapter Ten: Mr. Madison Goes to Congress 127

Chapter Eleven: James Madison and Thomas Jefferson:
"The Great Collaboration" 151

Chapter Twelve: The Courtship and Marriage of
James and Dolley Madison............................... 173

Chapter Thirteen: The Pen Is Mightier Than the Sword........ 183

Chapter Fourteen: Secretary of State....................... 203

Chapter Fifteen: President James Madison 219

Chapter Sixteen: The Second War of Independence: The War of 1812 227

Chapter Seventeen: Madison's Second Term 243

Chapter Eighteen: Retirement to Montpelier 257

Chapter Nineteen: The Death of James Madison 275

Chapter Twenty: "Madison's Memorial . . . A Free Country Governed by the Rule of Law"................................285

Appendix One: James Madison's Autobiography...............293

Appendix Two: "Vices of the Political System of the United States," April 1787 309

Appendix Three: "Political Observations" 319

Works Cited...347

Selected Quotations from the Writings of James Madison 351

Index..427

Introduction

Of all the illustrious men in the cadre known as the American Founding Fathers, history has bestowed the title "Father of the Constitution" on only one of them—James Madison. During his lifetime, James Madison rejected the accuracy of that appellation, but it is one he unquestionably earned. Madison recognized the momentous nature of the time in which he lived, and profoundly understood the historic significance of his position as a member (some would argue "the" member) of the Convention of 1787 and the concomitant responsibility of forming a functioning, dynamic, restrained government that would best fit the republican genius of the American people.

Physically, James Madison was unimpressive. At just under 5 feet, 4 inches tall, with a weak voice and a somewhat delicate constitution, he did not strike an imposing figure. Madison's life, however, is a lesson in overcoming one's physical impediments and not allowing them to prohibit the intellectual growth and influence one may achieve through self-discipline and honest, consistent study and work. In fact, in this regard, readers would be wise to follow the example of Plutarch and, when reading about one of the "noblest and most estimable characters," use the record of such a man's life "as a mirror and endeavor in a manner to fashion and adorn [their lives] in conformity with the virtues therein depicted" ("Timoleon," Plutarch's *Lives*). The life of James Madison is certainly worthy of such emulation.

Although painfully shy socially, Madison never shied away from taking upon himself the burdens of earnest thought and planning that other people found unbearable. Planning, study, preparation, and critical thinking were the soil in which Madison's inestimable contributions to the cause of American liberty were cultivated.

It is perhaps accurate to declare that Madison earned his place of reverence among the Founding Fathers because he arrived in Philadelphia in May 1787 with a plan—the Virginia Plan. The Virginia Plan was the result of many months of reading and studying the records of republics of the past and analyzing them with a well-focused and critical eye. Madison's focus was on the American people. He knew that any government formed for this country would need to implement the best ideas of the sage political thinkers and philosophers of the past while carefully avoiding the pitfalls that marred the path so many other republics had followed to their eventual demise. The American experiment was novel, and, of necessity, its government would be also.

Madison's early education came at the feet of tutors who, fortunately for him, were energetic, zealous, and eager to quench young Madison's constant thirst for knowledge. One of his early teachers was Donald Robertson, a brilliant but stern professor who followed the old Scottish tradition of "dispensing learning with a burr." At the Robertson school, Madison was expected, as were all young men of his day, to learn Latin and Greek with what by today's standards would be extraordinary proficiency. Records indicate, however, that during his first year under the tutelage of Robertson (1762; Madison was 11 years old), Madison's Latin was too weak to permit enrollment in many of the classes he most sought, so he was compelled to begin his studies in English. In a manner typical of his perpetual quest for self-improvement, he redoubled his efforts to learn Latin and mastered the language so well that years later, while studying international law as secretary of state, he was able to make corrections to the English translations of Latin works by Hugo Grotius, Samuel von Pufendorf, and Emer de Vattel.

One of the primary advantages to being Robertson's pupil was the access it provided Madison to Robertson's small library of what Madison described as "great books." These books included Montaigne's *Essays*, Montesquieu's *The Spirit of the Laws*, and Locke's *Essay Concerning Human Understanding*. It may be said that the number of volumes in this library was small, but it can just as rightly be said that the principles contained therein had an obviously powerful and indelible impact on the fertile and intellectually curious mind of young James Madison. Robertson had supplied Madison with many of the raw materials that, only a few years later, he would use deftly to construct the foundational document of the government of the United States.

To prepare his young son for college, Madison's father employed the services of a young and able Scot—Thomas Martin. Martin was a recent graduate of the College of New Jersey at Princeton, and he brightly reflected much of the intellectual vigor and zeal of the New Light Presbyterians who guided that institution. It is likely that Martin's example and exciting stories of life at Princeton encouraged Madison to depart from the Virginia tradition of young men attending the College of William & Mary for their higher education and to set his sights on Princeton. Of course, the fact that the president of Princeton, John Witherspoon, was a schoolman pressed from the same stern, Scottish mold as Madison's mentor Donald Robertson probably made the decision to attend Princeton an easier one, and likely filled Madison with eager anticipation.

As was the case with Madison's earlier teachers, John Witherspoon played a substantial role in the formation of his character and political thought. Witherspoon was renowned for the keenness of his wit and the ardor of his intellectual enthusiasm; he encouraged the students at Princeton to examine all sides of an issue, to become well-armed in defense of whatever they thought was "right," and to be equally able to logically deconstruct that which they believed to be "wrong." It is easy to see how Madison would thrive in such a milieu, and he expressed such in a letter to his former tutor Thomas Martin: "I am perfectly pleased with my present situation, and the prospect before me of three years confinement, however terrible it may sound, has nothing in it, but what will be greatly alleviated by the advantages I hope to derive from it."

While at Princeton, Madison continued studying natural law and politics by immersing himself in the works of many luminaries of the 15th through 18th centuries, most notably the aforementioned Grotius and Pufendorf, as well as Jean Barbeyrac, Jean-Jacques Burlamaqui,

Thomas Hobbes, Niccolò Machiavelli, John Locke, and Algernon Sidney. It is indisputable that all this exposure to the brightest of the world's political thinkers served as oxygen to the raging fire of intellectual vitality that would define Madison's professional life.

That professional life was one of public service. Madison served as a state legislator in his home state of Virginia, a member of the Continental Congress (also known as the Confederation Congress after March 1781), a member of the House of Representatives, secretary of state under Thomas Jefferson, and president of the United States of America. Despite the upward momentum of his career in public service, though, it can be said that James Madison served his country best as a delegate from Virginia to the Convention of 1787 in Philadelphia. Although the convention was originally styled as a meeting convened to overhaul the apparently faltering Articles of Confederation, Madison arrived in Philadelphia firmly convinced that the only hope of maintaining the freedom America had won at so great a price was to dismantle the malfunctioning infrastructure of the Articles. In its place, the convention needed to construct a new, republican government dynamic enough to perform its necessary duties, yet restrained enough to avoid infringing upon the liberty that was central to the American political heritage. Madison and his fellows were equal to the task. In the summer of 1787, he and representatives from the recently liberated American states convened the meeting that would change the course of history for America and for the entire world.

Four months after beginning their deliberations, the delegates produced the Constitution that created a compact among sovereign states whose common interests would be served by a general government of limited, enumerated powers. A copy of it was sent to all the state legislatures to be ratified. The vote would be yay or nay on ratification, and a supermajority of nine states was needed for passage.

The ratification of the Constitution was a precarious proposition. The large states of Virginia and New York were keystones upon which the arch of union depended. Toward convincing the people of New York to vote for pro-Constitution delegates to the ratifying convention that was to be held, Alexander Hamilton, a young, energetic lawyer from New York, engaged the help of fellow New Yorker John Jay and James Madison in authoring letters to the editors of four New York newspapers, letters that would become classics in political thought—*The Federalist* (also called *The Federalist Papers*).

In his contribution to *The Federalist*, Madison outlined his positions on the danger of factions; the viability and benefit of an extended, commercial republic; the absolute requirement of separation of powers; and the uniqueness of the American situation. He described how a republican government—and only a republican government—would withstand the inherent pressures of self-government that had caused other confederacies to implode.

In *Federalist* No. 10, Madison defined faction as "a number of citizens, whether amounting to a majority or minority of the whole, who are united and actuated by some common impulse of passion, or of interest adverse to the rights of other citizens, or to the permanent and aggregate interests of the community." As for the benefits to be derived from a large, extended republic, Madison declared: "As each representative will be chosen by a greater number of citizens in the large than in the small republic, it will be more difficult for unworthy candidates to practise with success the vicious arts by which elections are too often carried. . . ." As to the indisputable necessity of the separation of the powers of government, Madison summed up lessons he no doubt learned from his study of Montesquieu when, in *Federalist* No. 47, he insightfully recognized that "the accumulation of all powers legislative, executive, and judiciary in the same hands, whether of one, a few or many, and whether hereditary, self-appointed, or elective, may justly be pronounced the very definition of tyranny." Finally, within the first paragraph of *Federalist* No. 39, Madison succinctly observed that "it is evident that no other form [of government other than republican] would be reconcilable with the genius of the people of America or with the fundamental principles of the revolution."

From all his assertions mentioned here, the conclusion can correctly and easily be drawn that Madison was the foremost political thinker of the Founding period, and perhaps the most gifted of all the men charged with building and maintaining the constitutional government of the young American republic. Indeed, Madison drank deeply from the well of history and sated his voracious intellectual appetite on the offerings of the brightest philosophers of his day and the great Greek and Roman historians. This, as well as the lessons learned from his lifelong study of the history of ancient peoples as recorded in the Bible, contributed to the potent admixture that was the creative and forceful philosophy of James Madison.

Timeline of James Madison's Life

March 16, 1751	Born at Port Conway, Virginia
1769-1772	Student at College of New Jersey (Princeton University) (Age 18-21)
1776	Delegate from Orange County to Virginia Convention (Age 25)
1778-1779	Member of Virginia Council of State (Age 27-28)
1780-1783	Representative of Virginia at Continental Congress (Age 29-32)
1784-1786	Representative at Virginia General Assembly (Age 33-35)
1786	Attends Annapolis Convention (Age 35)
1787-1788	Representative of Virginia at Confederation Congress (Age 36-37)
May - Sept. 1787	Delegate to Constitutional Convention in Philadelphia (Age 36)
1788	Delegate at Virginia Ratifying Convention (Age 37)
1788	Co-author (as Publius) of *The Federalist* (Age 37)
1789-1797	Representative at U.S. House of Representatives (Age 38-46)
1789	Sponsors Bill of Rights in First Congress (Age 38)
1794	Marries Dolley Payne Todd (Age 43)
1799	Representative at Virginia General Assembly (Age 48)
1801-1808	Secretary of state under Thomas Jefferson (Age 50-57)
1809-1817	Fourth president of the United States (Age 58-66)
1812-1815	President during the War of 1812 (Age 61-64)
1819	Member of Board of Directors of Univ. of Virginia (Age 68)
1826	Rector of University of Virginia upon Jefferson's death (Age 75)
1829	Delegate to Virginia's Constitutional Convention (Age 78)
June 28, 1836	Dies of natural causes at Montpelier (Age 85)

Chapter 1:
James Madison's Birth and Education

James Madison was born at midnight between March 16 and 17, 1751. His mother, Nelly, was away from home, paying a visit to her mother's house, when the anxiously awaited hour of her son's delivery arrived. James' grandmother's house in Port Conway was some 55 miles from his mother and father's own house in Orange County, Virginia.

Nelly Madison was not yet 19 years old when her eldest son and first child was born, and it was likely her youth that accounted for her desire to be with her own mother when it was time to deliver her first baby.

When the hour of his birth finally arrived, Madison's mother and grandmother were so worried that the sickly looking infant would not survive the night that they called an Anglican priest to attend them at the house and administer last rites to the newborn, just in case the worst should happen and the baby should perish.

James did survive that night and, although notoriously frail—Washington Irving described him as a "withered little apple-john"—would grow up to be one of the most influential men of all the Founding Generation and a man who was generally considered by his contemporaries to be the smartest man in the room, no matter which room he was in.

Like so many of our Founding Fathers, Madison came from a large family; he was the oldest of 12 children: eight boys and four girls. Three of his brothers died as babies, including one who was stillborn. A sister, Elizabeth, and a brother, Reuben, both died as children after drinking contaminated water.

James Madison, Jr. was born in Port Conway, Virginia.

Of those that survived into adulthood, his siblings all earned sound public reputations.

James' brother Ambrose was a captain in the Virginia militia, a successful planter, and overseer of the family's landholdings in Orange County, Virginia. Madison's youngest surviving brother, William (nicknamed "Willey"), also served in the state's military. He went on to become a lawyer, was elected to the Virginia House of Delegates, and achieved "high rank and distinction in the War of 1812" (*White House History*, No. 36, Winter 2014).

As for Madison's sisters, his friend and first biographer, William Cabell Rives, wrote, "His sisters, superadding accomplishments and solid instruction to natural charms married gentlemen of the highest respectability and intelligence, and adorned with their virtues and graces the spheres of life in which they moved."

James Madison: The Boy With Two Birthdays!

Everybody likes birthday parties, and because of a lucky law change, James Madison could have had two! Madison was born in the very year that England adopted a new calendar—the Gregorian calendar. Basically, this is the calendar we currently use (as does the rest of the world).

It is called the "Gregorian" calendar because it was introduced in 1582 by Pope Gregory XIII. The new calendar improved the accuracy of the Julian calendar, the system of counting days adopted in 45 B.C. during the administration of the Roman ruler Julius Caesar.

In fact, the Gregorian calendar was so obviously superior to the centuries-old Julian calendar that it was quickly adopted by most of Europe. England was not, however, among those who switched their official means of marking the passing of the months. It took over 160 years for England to pass a law officially codifying the Gregorian calendar.

The adoption of the new calendar caused a sort of stutter step in the numbering of the days. Under the old calendar (the dates of which are called Old Style, or O.S. for short), March 25 was the first day of the year. Under the Gregorian system, however, January 1 was New Year's Day; thus the day after March 24, 1749 was March 25, 1750, as the new year (1750) had retroactively begun on January 1!

That's a lot of confusing math, but James Madison was born on March 5, 1750 (Old Style), the year the English Parliament passed the law switching measuring methods and changed all legal dates, including birth, marriage, and death dates, so his *official* birthday is March 16, 1751.

Regardless of what label the law put upon the day of her eldest child's birth, Nelly Madison would never need to be reminded of that fearful night her tiny, sickly son survived his first tenuous hours on Earth. Nor would the world forget Nelly Madison's son, for her son who was so often laid low with illness would outlive all his healthier colleagues and go on to earn the appellation "Father of the Constitution."

"Among the Respectable": James Madison's Ancestors

Though they were certainly not aristocrats on a level with the Randolphs or the Lees, the ancestors of James Madison, Sr. and Nelly Madison were solid, successful citizens of their state and their country.

While admittedly James Madison did not descend from particularly, as he called them, "opulent" ancestors, he certainly had his fair share of noteworthy forebears.

Madison's great-grandfather, John Maddison (as they moved farther into the western wilderness, the family would soon drop the second "d"), staked claim to 80 acres of land "a little below the schoolhouse, on the Mantapike Road, where the Church Road crosses," according to Irving Brant in *James Madison: The Virginia Revolutionist*.

It seems a poetic coincidence that the boundaries of the family estate were defined by the schoolhouse and the church, in light of the significant personal and political roles these two institutions would play in Madison's growth and the growth of the country he helped create.

In the next generation, Madison's grandfather, Ambrose, moved his family farther into the western wilderness, a decision that was spurred somewhat by the fact that Ambrose's girlfriend's family was moving west and the relationship between Ambrose and his girlfriend, Frances Taylor, was growing more serious.

Sadly, the pair would part prematurely, as Ambrose died young, leaving Frances, his 32-year-old widow, and his three young children living alone on the edge of the wilderness.

Madison's father, also named James, was one of those three children. Madison's father was known simply as James Madison until his son achieved widespread recognition; then the suffix "senior" was permanently appended to the elder James Madison's name.

In his own description of his genealogy, Madison displays his habitual humility, saying of those who came before him, "In both the paternal and the maternal line of ancestry, they were planters and among the respectable though not the most opulent class."

Such a statement seems to suggest that for Madison, it was more noteworthy to be descended from modest and honorable families than from famous or rich ones.

Speaking of his meekness regarding his relatives, Irving Brant writes that, in Madison, "certainly there was no 'ruling class' consciousness and no social snobbishness." Again, it was enough for Madison—the president, the "Father of the Constitution," the chief sponsor of the Bill of Rights, the major catalyst of the Constitutional Convention of 1787—to know his forefathers were hard-working homesteaders whose tireless efforts to improve their lives and their land left him with a respectable patrimony that provided an opportunity for an education.

As with so many other opportunities that were presented to him, Madison took full advantage of his academic access. Later, he would explain his zeal for learning by saying that the "advancement and diffusion of knowledge . . . is the only guardian of true liberty." For James Madison, liberty required lifelong learning.

Sir Edward Conway: James Madison's Aristocratic Ancestor With a Love of Books

Madison's father's family is not particularly illustrious. On the Conway side—the maternal side—however, there is plenty of family history that merits mention.

According to Brant, one of Nelly Madison's most renowned ancestors was an English nobleman named Sir Edward Conway, and there seems to be much of this forebear in James Madison.

Conway was a noted military commander during the English Civil Wars of the 1640s, but it is another aspect of his life that brought him additional fame and seems to have been handed down to his distant descendant—our own James Madison: he was well-known throughout England for his love of reading and the impressive size of his personal library. According to a biography of Conway published by Oxford University, his collection amounted to more than 15,000 books and manuscripts.

It is little wonder, then, that James Madison was so fond of books and so committed to serious study and regular reading; it was in his genes!

"Knowledge Would Forever Govern Ignorance": Madison's Education Begins

Regarding the importance of education, Madison often counseled his countrymen that "Knowledge would forever govern ignorance: and a people who mean to be their own Governors, must arm themselves with the power which knowledge gives." He also said: "The advancement and diffusion of knowledge is the only guardian of true liberty."

As will be shown in the pages of this biography, Madison practiced what he preached, becoming one of the most learned men of his time. And, although he was taught in his youth by some of the finest tutors—more on them later—he remained devoted until his death to continuing his education and increasing his intellectual strength.

To help counterbalance his constant struggle with poor health, Madison's parents tried to give him every advantage they could afford so that their son's sickliness would not impede his progress. In the end, the most important advantage they gave him was an extraordinary education.

In the tradition of most men and women of the Founding Generation, James' education began at home, where his mother taught him the basics of reading, writing, and arithmetic. She also taught James and all her children lessons on proper behavior and virtue, using the Bible as a textbook. After learning the basics from his mother, young James (nicknamed "Jamie" and "Jemmy") left home to attend the school taught by Donald Robertson. Robertson was 35 years old and had just arrived in Virginia from his native Scotland, where he had graduated from the University of Edinburgh.

From ages 11 to 16, Madison studied at Robertson's school along with about 30 or 40 other pupils each year. Lessons taught included English grammar, composition, literature, the history of England, and the classical histories of Greece and Rome. French was also taught, as well as physics, theology, chemistry, and philosophy. Lessons on the classics required reading Virgil, Cicero, Horace, and Ovid in the original languages and translating them into English. Remarkably, Madison and most boys of his age learned Latin and

Chapter One: James Madison's Birth and Education

Nelly Conway Madison was James' mother. She was his first teacher, teaching him lessons in both academia and behavior.

could read and write in that language before they left school. In fact, the mastery of Latin and Greek was required for entrance into any of the Founding-era universities. Besides Madison, there were many other notable men who studied at Donald Robertson's school, including John Penn, a signer of the Declaration of Independence; John Tyler, governor of Virginia and father of the 10th president; George Rogers Clark, hero of the War of Independence; and John Taylor of Caroline, a United States senator and prolific writer on constitutional subjects.

Robertson's records of his pupils' progress reveal that young James purchased books by Virgil, Horace, Justinian, and Cornelius Nepo. He also borrowed books by Julius Caesar, Tacitus, Lucretius, Eutropius, and Phaedrus that were in Robertson's personal library. To learn Greek, Madison studied works by Plutarch, Herodotus,

Thucydides, and Plato. He also read and took notes on Montaigne's *Essays*, Montesquieu's *The Spirit of the Laws*, and John Locke's *An Essay Concerning Human Understanding*. James was a dedicated and hardworking student. By the age of 12, he was already taking notes in Latin, and his fluency in that language helped him read the works of classic historians and thinkers, all of which influenced his own view of liberty, natural law, and the wisdom of dividing power among different branches of government. Robertson's library provided Madison's first acquaintance with books that would later influence his work in helping to form the government of the United States.

Commenting on the immense influence that Robertson had on his life, Madison wrote in his autobiography, "All that I have been in life I owe largely to that man."

It was while studying under Robertson that Madison began his lifelong habit of keeping a "commonplace book." A commonplace book was the constant companion of many school-age boys and girls in early American history. Students would copy into the book the quotes they wanted to remember, and sometimes they would write their own comments and thoughts on those quotes, as well. The habit of keeping such a book continued throughout the adulthood of these men and women, and many of our most illustrious Founders—from John Adams to George Washington—kept them throughout their lives and considered them great treasures to be handed down to their descendants.

Fortunately, the commonplace book kept by young James has been preserved. In it, we learn that by the time he was 11, Madison was reading very lengthy histories and biographies and making notes on those books in Latin!

Notably, we learn from Madison's commonplace book that the future "Father of the Constitution" made many notes on the value of liberty and the threat posed to it by despotic kings and conspiracies of designing men.

In one such note, he wrote, "'All kings are ravenous beasts,' said Cato. He did not see that the Roman people were as rapacious and oppressive as any tyrant. How could he think, that that was glorious in many men, which was detestable in one?"

Most entries in Madison's commonplace book foreshadow the future of the young scholar. James took copious notes on the proper role of government, the correct character of rulers, and the relationship of the ruled to their rulers.

It is incredible to modern readers to consider the list of students attending Robertson's school with Madison. As detailed above, many of these young men would grow up to be prominent politicians, judges, and statesmen. When they sat together in Robertson's schoolroom, however, they were just pre-teens and teenagers trying to apply themselves to their studies and wondering what life would have in store for them. Little could any of them have imagined the influential parts they would play in the unfolding drama of the American union!

For students of our own time, it may be fascinating to look around at their own classmates, wondering how many of them will grow up to make meaningful contributions to the future of our great country. How many of the young men and women in classrooms around the country will one day see portraits of themselves and their peers hanging on the walls of American History classrooms?

Family as Friends

Finally, before we follow the teenaged James Madison from secondary school in Virginia to college in New Jersey, let us mention his lack of close childhood friends. As was the case with so many of his fellow Founding Fathers, Madison came from a large family and, as such, his brothers and sisters became his best friends and constant companions. Montpelier, the Madison family home, was miles from the nearest house, and James would only see other children at church or reunions of his extended family. He would have been busy with his chores and helping his mother and father with managing the household and family business, leaving him little time to play, in the modern sense of that word.

It wasn't until he enrolled at Princeton that he would make close friends who would become his close confidants and counselors. Some of his Princeton classmates would play integral parts in Madison's professional life, including in those critical moments when he made history.

Even so, for Madison, his mom, dad, and siblings were his lifelong friends and trusted advisors. He appreciated having a built-in group of friends, who just happened to be his family!

Success in Higher Education: Princeton

In August 1769, when he was 17 years old, Madison enrolled at the College of New Jersey (today, it is called Princeton). He was an excellent student, known by his peers as someone who devoted himself more to learning than to any other endeavor. Young James was right to worry about his studies. *Enrolling at* a university didn't necessarily mean one would be *accepted to* the university. All students were required to take an entrance exam. To be formally accepted, James was required to demonstrate "the ability to write Latin prose, translate Virgil, Cicero, and the Greek gospels and a commensurate knowledge of Latin and Greek grammar."

The rest of Madison's fellow future Founders didn't have it any easier at the other Colonial colleges. For example, at Harvard, applicants were required to be able to extemporaneously "read, construe, and parse Tully [Cicero], Virgil, or such like classical authors and to write Latin in prose, and to be skilled in making Latin verse, or at least to know the rules of Prosodia, and to read, construe, and parse ordinary Greek as in the New Testament. . . ." When Alexander Hamilton (one of Madison's co-authors of *The Federalist*) went to King's College (now Columbia University) in New York City, he was required to "give a rational account of the Greek and Latin grammars, read three orations of Cicero and three books of Virgil's *Aeneid*, and translate the first ten chapters of [the Gospel of] John from Greek into Latin." While certainly remarkable to contemporary college-bound students, these high standards were commonplace when Madison was preparing for Princeton.

At Princeton, James found the freshman-year lessons too easy and requested permission from the president of the university, John Witherspoon, to take tests that would allow him to skip the first-year classes and go straight to the classes for sophomores. Witherspoon was surprised to see someone so small and so frail behaving so bravely, but he gave Madison permission to take the exams and skip freshman year if he passed them all.

James attended Princeton University and excelled in his academics.

Djkeddie, CC BY-SA 4.0 via, Wikimedia Commons

In a letter to his former tutor, Thomas Martin, Madison revealed his readiness to apply himself to his studies. "The near approach of the examinations occasions a surprising application to study on all sides," he wrote.

Later in the same letter, Madison sought to reassure his teacher that he would take advantage of the opportunities at Princeton and prepare himself for a prosperous future, no matter how hard the homework and how long the hours of study.

"I am perfectly pleased with my present situation, and the prospect before me of three years confinement, however terrible it may sound, has nothing in it, but what will be greatly alleviated by the advantages I hope to derive from it," Madison declared.

A quick note on Princeton's academic calendar and quality of student life is appropriate here.

The school year lasted about nine months, the first semester running from November until April. Then, scholars would enjoy about a month-long vacation, returning to classes in May to begin the second term. They would then continue studying straight through until the last Wednesday in September.

Life in the dormitory where Madison lived—Nassau Hall—was described by Irving Brant in the first volume of his biography of Madison:

"The students recited, studied, ate, and slept in Nassau Hall, living three in a room. Their nightly talkfests, in which according to well-supported tradition, Madison was a leader in metaphysical discussions, were likely to end, as a college poet (William Paterson) recorded it, with the Scotch burr of President Witherspoon sounding through the halls: 'To bed, lads, to bed.'"

Madison may have graduated from college nearly 250 years ago (in 1771), but judging from Brant's description of Madison's college experience, dorm life hasn't changed much during that time!

"The Minimum of Sleep and the Maximum of Application": James Madison Establishes a Habit of Serious Study

Madison recognized that there were lifelong benefits to be gained by applying himself to doing his best in all of his classes and in learning the important lessons he was being taught.

The habits he developed as a student of Robertson and Martin served him well; he passed all the freshman-year tests and was moved up to the sophomore class. Even that wasn't enough for the eager James Madison, though. He reckoned that if he could pass the freshman-year classes, maybe he could pass the second-year tests, too, and be able to finish college in two years instead of the normal four! Once again, Witherspoon agreed to let James take the tests, and forthwith Madison—along with his friend Joseph Ross, whom he convinced to also try to finish in two years as well—began studying over 10 hours a day to get ready for the second-year exams.

Later, in writing his autobiography, Madison recalled this busy time in his young life as a student, describing it as an "indiscreet experiment of the minimum of sleep and the maximum of

Nassau Hall — James' dormitory.
Djkeddie, CC BY-SA 4.0 via, Wikimedia Commons

application." He pushed himself, he adds, to the limit that his "constitution would bear," limiting his sleep "for some weeks to less than five hours in twenty-four." James knew that he would have to deprive himself of sleep to pass these important exams, but he also believed that the lessons he learned over these many hours would serve him well when he left school and began his career.

Madison was always humble, though. In later years, when asked about his ability to graduate from college in half the time it took most students, he simply said it was not "any extraordinary achievement." It was an extraordinary achievement, though, and it set the course for the rest of his extraordinary life.

School wasn't all study, study, study, however, not even for one as ambitious and motivated as Madison. He was a very popular student while at Princeton. The other young men appreciated his good sense of humor, his loyalty, and his tireless desire for the exchange of ideas and the examination of principles of government and self-discipline. Many of his classmates remarked that "Jemmy" (his nickname as a child and at college) was always a good listener and a trustworthy friend who kept confidences and gave good advice. Yet another remarkable lesson to learn from Mr. Madison.

"Your Sincere and Affectionate Friend": Madison Forges Lifelong Friendships

It was during his first few days at Princeton that James Madison met some fellow students who would become lifelong friends, frequent collaborators, and trustworthy counselors.

First among these new friends was William Bradford. Bradford came from a family of printers in Philadelphia, and, like Madison, was a hardworking and dedicated scholar.

Bradford and Madison remained close, exchanging dozens of letters throughout the more than 25 years of their frequent correspondence. Undoubtedly, their companionship would have lasted many more years had Bradford not passed away at age 40, some 40 years before Madison died at 85 years of age.

Like his friend Jemmy, Bradford (whom Madison called "Billey") went on to contribute to the founding of his country honorably and historically.

During the War of Independence, Bradford served in the Pennsylvania militia, rising to the rank of major. Later, he joined the Continental Army, seeing combat at the Battle of Trenton and camping with George Washington at Valley Forge during the difficult winter of 1776.

After the war, Bradford was appointed attorney general of Pennsylvania. After the ratification of the Constitution in 1789, President Washington named him to be the new country's second attorney general, an office he held until his death in 1795.

In a letter written by "Jemmy" to "Billey" on April 28, 1773, Madison informed Bradford of the lessons their friendship had taught him. "Friendship like all truth delights in plainess and simplicity and it is the counterfeit alone that needs ornament and ostentation,"

Madison wrote warmly. He concluded the letter by calling himself "Your sincere and affectionate friend."

One last word about Madison and Bradford's famous friendship: It is in his letters to Bradford that one gets the first glimpse of young James Madison's nascent ideas about which professional path he would take. In one of these ruminations, Madison reminded Bradford (and himself) of the most important consideration when choosing a vocation. "Nevertheless," the 21-year-old Madison wrote, "a watchful eye must be kept on ourselves lest while we are building ideal monuments of renown and bliss here we neglect to have our names enrolled in the annals of Heaven."

Besides William Bradford, Madison made another close friend during his days at Princeton. This future-famous friend's name was Philip Freneau, the man who would be described years later as the "Poet of the American Revolution."

Freneau graduated from Princeton in the same class as Madison, in 1771. At college, the two scholars collaborated on poems in praise of liberty, and others describing the heroic deeds of notable Greeks and Romans of the ancient world. The pair had more than a love of history in common, as both considered entering the ministry upon graduating from Princeton.

During the early days of America's War of Independence from Great Britain, the talented Freneau penned several articles criticizing the despotism of the British government.

After spending a couple of years in the West Indies, Freneau returned to America and enlisted as a sailor on a patriot privateer ship. While serving on this ship, Freneau was captured by the British and locked up in a prison boat for about six weeks. This experience only served to solidify his commitment to the cause of American freedom.

About eight years after the war ended, Freneau founded the *National Gazette*, a newspaper publishing pro-republican articles. As the editor of this paper, he became a passionate promoter of the policies of his old college friend, James Madison, who was serving in the U.S. House of Representatives.

It was, in fact, a recommendation from Madison that opened the way for Freneau to serve in the State Department under Thomas Jefferson and get the *National Gazette* off the ground. In a letter to Edmund Randolph written on September 13, 1792, Madison described his efforts to find Freneau a position.

"That I wished and recommended Mr. Freneau to be appointed to his present clerkship [in the State Department] is certain," Madison wrote. "But the Department of State was not the only, nor, as I recollect, the first one, to which I mentioned his name and character." Ending the recommendation, he praised his Princeton friend's character: "I was governed in these recommendations by an acquaintance of long standing, by a respect for his talents, and by a knowledge of his merit and sufferings in the course of the Revolution."

High praise indeed from a man as talented as James Madison.

Like Madison, Freneau lived a long life. He passed away at age 80, just four years before his classmate and close friend.

William Bradford and Philip Freneau became two of James Madison's closest friends. Although Madison had no close friends from his childhood, the friends he met at Princeton were fast and faithful.

Madison Relaxes From His Studies

Finally, when James needed a break from studying and wanted to unwind for a while, rather than waste his time with mindless entertainment, often he would go out into the woods near his dormitory (Nassau Hall) and chop wood.

One eyewitness reported that James would pile up the logs, then start swinging his ax with all his might repeatedly for hours, sending wood chips flying everywhere and causing him to sweat profusely!

For him, this strenuous exercise was the best way to relieve stress and clear his mind.

There was no social media for James Madison; there were split logs!

Madison's "Scotch French": James
Tries to Translate for a Visitor to Princeton

Once, before he graduated from college, Dr. Witherspoon asked Madison to serve as an interpreter for a visitor from France. Witherspoon knew that James studied French (and Spanish) at

Donald Robertson's school, and so he reasonably believed that his ever-diligent student would be up to the task of translating.

Things didn't go quite as smoothly as the university president planned, though.

As related by biographer Gaillard Hunt, James' accent was so bad that the French visitor didn't know Madison was speaking French! Describing Madison's facility for French, Hunt writes that "while he was able by hard attention to pick out a few words the Frenchman spoke, the latter was unable to understand a single word of Madison's French" (Gaillard Hunt, *The Life of James Madison*, 14).

This experience likely embarrassed the young scholar, but, as customary for him, setbacks at school were treated by James as incentive for improvement.

After the French fiasco, Madison set about smoothing the rough edges off what he called his "Scotch French" accent.

American Whig Society: In the "Paper War" at Princeton, Madison Sharpens His Persuasive Skills

Perhaps one of the most memorable activities in which Madison participated while at Princeton occurred during his membership in the American Whig Society.

The American Whig Society was founded in 1769 to provide an outlet for students interested in honing their oral and written debate skills. Such a club was right in young James Madison's wheelhouse.

Madison's good friend Freneau joined the American Whig Society, too, and it was there that Freneau first earned a reputation as a talented poet and writer.

As he did with his regular coursework, Madison applied all his time and talents to writing and publishing powerful polemics as a key member of the American Whig Society. Irving Brant confirms the long hours spent drafting and delivering papers for the Whigs. "Since this war [the so-called Paper War between the American Whig Society and its rival, the Cliosophic Society] rose to its climax in 1770-1, the school year in which Madison did two years' work, it is evident that the midnight candles he burned were not all wasted on Watts and Longinus," Brant records.

Unfortunately, the official records of the Whigs and the

James' roommate and good friend, Philip Freneau, who would later be known as the "Poet of the American Revolution."

Cliosophists are believed to have been lost when a fire broke out in Nassau Hall in 1802. The only records we have of Madison's work in the Paper War are copies of his poems included in the history of the society as written by Madison's dear friend and fellow Whig William Bradford.

Although we can't be certain of Madison's early literary efforts to defend the cause of liberty, we do know how he felt about the American Whig Society. In a letter written on January 20, 1827, and included in Volume 1 of *Papers of James Madison*, Madison said he hoped that "the Whig Society in amicable competition with its Cliosophic Rival may continue to receive and reflect the lights which will best prepare its members for a useful life, which alone can promise a happy one."

There is no doubt that the debates and literary battles fought by James Madison as a member of the American Whig Society at Princeton helped the future *Federalist* author, chief sponsor of the Bill of Rights, and president of the United States practice and perfect the talents in persuasive writing and speaking that would serve him and his country very well for decades after his graduation from college.

"Never ... an Indiscreet Thing": Madison's Reputation for Virtue Continues at College

Despite being in very ill health after returning home to Virginia after he received his bachelor's degree from Princeton, Madison reported that he "carried on studying without neglecting a course of reading which mingled miscellaneous subjects. . . ." In other words, he learned to love reading and studying while he was young, and he carried those useful habits with him into adulthood.

Although Madison thought about becoming a lawyer, he says that he "never followed an absolute determination" to enter law school. Rather than decide immediately about his future career, he stayed on at Princeton for an extra six months or so, studying Hebrew and the Holy Bible under the direct tutelage of John Witherspoon.

Being from a family of churchmen (his cousin was the renowned Bishop James Madison) and having been lectured by John Witherspoon in Hebrew and theology while working on his bachelor's degree, James seemed to consider the clergy a worthwhile vocation. And, as was his habit, he went the extra mile in that scholarly and spiritual endeavor, reading and pondering the Old Testament in the original Hebrew language.

It is likely that his close personal relationship with Dr. Witherspoon encouraged young Madison's natural inclination toward virtue and motivated him to more deeply ponder and then later take up his pen in defense of the principles and precepts associated with that most precious of the people's freedoms: religious liberty. For his part, Witherspoon was indelibly impressed by the perseverance, piety, and unwavering personal virtue of his young protégé. In fact, it is from a comment reportedly made by Witherspoon to Thomas Jefferson years after Madison left his presence that the strength of

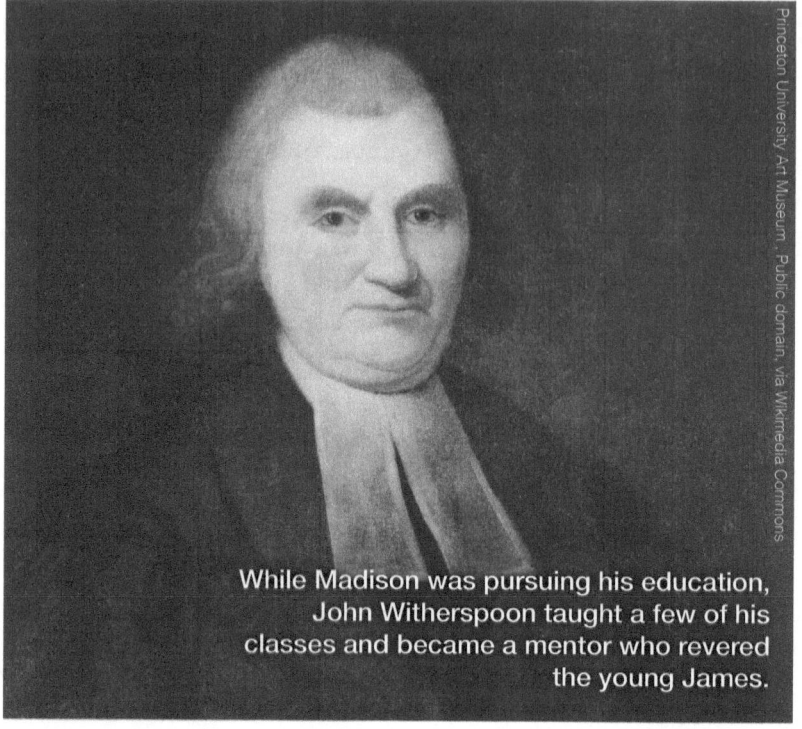

While Madison was pursuing his education, John Witherspoon taught a few of his classes and became a mentor who revered the young James.

Madison's character is mostly fully revealed. Although so many of James' classmates spent hours involved in endless entertainment and in forming clubs for carrying out pranks, Witherspoon told Jefferson that "in the whole career of Mr. Madison at Princeton, he had never known him to do or say an indiscreet thing."

James Madison was the very embodiment of the virtuous citizen who could sustain a republican government. In Madison's case, however, not only could his virtue sustain it, but his intellect and inspiration could help establish it.

From Student to Teacher:
Madison Serves as His Siblings' Tutor

Soon after Madison left Princeton for good in 1772—having graduated in two years, half the time it took most students—he found the Colonies at odds with Great Britain over the right of Americans to continue governing themselves through Colonial assemblies. James Madison jumped into the fray with fervor: "I entered with the prevailing zeal into the American cause, being under very early and strong impressions in favor of liberty." For a while, however, Madison had to put his desire to serve his country on hold.

Just prior to the end of James' college career, his father wrote him and informed him that he would expect James to come back to Montpelier and use his education to tutor his younger siblings.

What James Madison, Sr. didn't know is that James had made plans with his friends to spend the spring and summer after graduation traveling around the northern Colonies of Pennsylvania and New York.

In fact, in a letter written just before he graduated from Princeton, James mentioned to his father that he would "not be able to stay in Virginia more than four weeks at the most." He went on to ask his father to send some money and some clothes.

We don't have a copy of the letter his father sent in return, but in a follow-up letter written by James after his father had instructed him once again that he would be needed as a teacher at home, James accepted his father's instructions, writing, "If you choose rather I should remain in Virginia next Summer, it will be unnecessary" to send the money and clothes up to Princeton.

Thus, James took the long journey home to Virginia, where he would begin teaching his younger brothers and sisters their grammar, their history, and their Latin and Greek, and he himself would begin to study law.

When he returned to his family's home, James was 21 years old. His next-oldest brother was 19, and his other three brothers were 17, 10, and 1, respectively. His three sisters: Nelly, Sarah, and Elizabeth, were 12, 8, and 4 years old.

Although Madison wasn't thrilled about the new responsibility of teaching his siblings, he recognized the right of his father to oversee his family and was grateful that his parents had provided him with such a good education. So, he set about instructing his brothers and sisters "in some of the first rudiments of literature."

This literature, of course, would have included many of the histories of Greece and Rome. Madison set about creating a very disciplined and difficult curriculum for his new students. Every morning, he would sit down with his pupils and they would work through lessons in literature, mathematics, Latin, Greek, and French, and at the end of the lesson on Monday, James would tell his siblings what they would be studying for the rest of the week. He even went so far in his organization of the school to divide the day up into several parts, teaching a different subject in each section.

During the time that James was teaching his siblings, his mother would daily inquire of her children what they had learned in the day's lessons. She was very interested in the education of all her children and wanted them to receive all the instruction necessary to help them become virtuous and active.

In his biography of Madison, William Cabell Rives—who knew Madison personally—wrote that while James was certainly conscientious in his teaching of his brothers and sisters, he was always "recurring with anxious thoughtfulness" of his mother, Nelly. Even when he was very busy, Rives writes, Madison dutifully cared for his mother's "delicate health." One of Madison's cousins wrote that Nelly could "certainly make moments slide away pleasantly" due to her good nature, generosity, and kindness. In 1816, a Frenchman who visited Madison at Montpelier met Nelly, who by then was 86 years old, and reported that she was a "very active woman" blessed with "perfect health" and that she "busies herself with the different occupations" of a mother. Even at a very advanced age, Madison's mother was always busy keeping her home clean and welcoming the many strangers who would come to visit her famous son.

In all things, Madison was a very caring and conscientious son. Rives writes that even after he was older and retired, James was found "personally watching over and nursing [Nelly's] old age with such pious care that her life was protracted to within a few years of the term of his own." Madison and his wife, Dolley, cared for Nelly at Montpelier until she passed away in 1829, at the age of 98.

Chapter 2:
James Madison's Moral Obligations

In a letter written November 9, 1772 to his friend William Bradford, during Madison's time as a tutor to his brothers and sisters, he wrote that the lessons did not "take up so much of [his] time," leaving him plenty of time to read the updates about the ongoing crisis with Great Britain. He asked Bradford if he would be "kind enough to send [him]" all written accounts of the goings-on in Philadelphia, Boston, and other centers of action.

Madison's first position of responsibility in the struggle to place American liberty on a permanent foundation was as an elected member of his county's committee of safety. Despite devoting himself completely to this important obligation, Madison regretted that he could not join the army. He wrote that the "unsettled state of his health and the discouraging feebleness of [his] body" prevented him from enlisting in the ranks of those taking up arms to fight for freedom.

His physical weaknesses did not stop him from playing a significant role in the liberty movement, however. Thanks to frequent letters sent to him from Bradford, Madison was aware of the escalating tension with George III, Parliament, and the American Colonists in Boston. Madison learned of the passage by Parliament of the so-called Intolerable Acts, laws to be imposed on Massachusetts with the intention of punishing the "rebels" who were organizing protests against increasing taxes. These were taxes that, according to the Magna Carta, were not valid against a people who had no say in their imposition.

During a trip to Pennsylvania and New York in the summer of 1774, Madison discovered that the Continental Congress was

William Bradford was a friend who kept James involved in political happenings while he was home in Virginia.

convened to form a united response to the Crown and Parliament of Great Britain. While on that trip, Madison realized that many people in Pennsylvania and New York were reticent to obey the resolutions passed by Congress. The people believed that they should only have to follow their local leaders, and many of them considered the members of the Continental Congress, even those from their own states, to be out of touch with the plight and concerns of the common people.

As he went around visiting friends, Madison would find pamphlets calling for the dissolution of the Congress and complaining about the conduct and quality of the men sent there as representatives. In his travels and during his conversations, he began to appreciate the difficulty Congress was having in setting policies and drafting resolutions that were approved of and heeded throughout the American Colonies.

Madison, taught by his mother to be very patriotic and to respect positions of authority, was surprised by the attitudes he witnessed in Philadelphia and New York City. The situation back home in Virginia was very different. In a letter to Bradford sent on November 26, 1774, Madison reported:

> The proceedings of the [Continental] Congress are universally approved of in this province [Virginia] and I am persuaded will be faithfully adhered to. A spirit of liberty and patriotism animates all degrees and denominations of men. Many publicly declare themselves ready to join the Bostonians as soon as violence is offered them or resistance thought expedient. In many counties independent companies are forming and voluntarily subjecting themselves to military discipline that they may be expert and prepared against a time of need. . . . Such firm and provident steps will either intimidate our enemies or enable us to defy them.

Within two weeks of writing this letter to his friend, Madison was himself elected to represent his home county—Orange County—on its committee of safety. This was a very great honor and an even greater responsibility for 23-year-old James. In his book *American Insurgents, American Patriots*, T.H. Breen describes the duties and the value of the local committees of safety throughout the American Colonies: "For ordinary people, they were community forums where personal loyalties were revealed, tested, and occasionally punished. . . . Serving on committees of safety . . . was certainly not an activity for the faint of heart."

As the conflict with England spread throughout the Colonies, the committees of safety would operate as a sort of shadow government, preparing and training for a time when the king and his officers were gone and the Americans would be able to once again govern themselves. The committees of safety in Virginia and elsewhere claimed their power came from the Continental Congress, not from any English royal grant of authority. By 1775, the crisis had grown serious enough that the committees of safety were charged with administering the government in their counties—this included the raising of troops for the Continental Army as well as for their own state militias. An example of the critical role played by these committees is revealed when we consider that the committee of safety operating in nearby Fairfax County, Virginia, was led by George Washington.

During these early years of the conflict with Great Britain, Virginia counted on the protection of three groups of soldiers: the "regulars," the minutemen, and, as a final line of defense, the militia.

James Madison was a commissioned officer in the militia of Virginia. He was second-in-command to his father, who was the commanding officer of the militia in Orange County. Although he wrote near the end of his life that his poor health prevented him from significant armed service during the War of Independence, in a letter written to Bradford on June 19, 1775, Madison gives a glimpse into his military training with the other members of the militia, informing his friend and fellow patriot of the earnestness of his efforts to become a valuable member of the militia:

> We [the people of Virginia] have as great unanimity and as much of the military ardor as you can possibly have in your government; and the progress we make in discipline and hostile preparations is as great as the zeal with which these things were undertaken. The strength of this colony will lie chiefly in the rifle-men of the Upland Counties, of whom we shall have great numbers. You would be astonished at the perfection this art is brought to. The most inexpert hands reckon it an indifferent shot to miss the bigness of a man's face at the distance of 100 yards. I am far from being among the best and should not often miss it on a fair trial at that distance.

In October 1775, Madison was issued a commission as colonel in the Orange County militia. In the text of that document, the members of the committee of safety for the Colony of Virginia describe the qualities the younger Madison possessed that qualified him for service in the defense of his home.

"We, reposing especial trust and confidence in your patriotism, fidelity, courage, and good conduct, do by these presents constitute and appoint you to be colonel of the militia of the County of Orange; and you are therefore carefully and diligently to discharge the trust reposed in you, by disciplining all officers and soldiers under your command. And we do hereby require them to obey you as their colonel," the commission declares.

While there is no evidence that James Madison ever saw any combat during the War of Independence, he dutifully fell into formation every time his unit practiced and trained for any eventual attack on their county. Madison's contribution to American liberty during the war may not have been on the battlefield, but in his chosen sphere—the executive and legislative branches of the government of Virginia—no one was more valuable to the cause of American liberty or more valiant in its promotion and protection.

A Man of Tenacity

In April 1776, Madison set out on his lifelong career as a statesman and lawmaker when he was elected by his fellow citizens as a delegate to the convention that was called to write a new constitution for the state of Virginia. While serving as a representative at this convention, he joined with his colleagues in unanimously voting to instruct Virginia's representatives at the Continental Congress in Philadelphia to vote in favor of American independence from Great Britain.

Although he was an extraordinarily gifted, highly motivated student and was exceptionally well-read, during his time at the Virginia Constitutional Convention, Madison decided that, "being young and in the midst of distinguished and experienced members of the convention," he would not "enter into the debates," but rather would focus on humbly learning from the wise men in whose company he was honored to be.

While he chose to listen and learn from those with more experience, though, Madison was moved to take an active part in the debates on the "freedom of religion" provision that was to be included in the Virginia Declaration of Rights. For the rest of his long life, James Madison would devote himself to the cause of protecting the freedom of conscience for all Americans. In fact, the text of the religious freedom clause adopted by the Virginia convention for inclusion in that state's Declaration of Rights was almost entirely the work of the 25-year-old Madison. That historic paragraph declares:

> That religion, or the duty which we owe to our Creator, and the manner of discharging it, can be directed only by reason and conviction, not by force or violence; and therefore, all men are equally entitled to the free exercise of religion, according to the dictates of conscience; and that it is the mutual duty of all to practice Christian forbearance, love, and charity, towards each other.

Right to Revolution: "Written in Every American Heart"

Of equal importance in his work as a member of the Virginia convention was Madison's promotion of American independence. On May 15, 1776, he and the other members of the convention voted to instruct the Virginia delegates to the Continental Congress to propose to that body that "the United Colonies" be declared "free and independent states."

Decades later, Madison would point to the Declaration of Independence as the clearest expression of the American conception of civil liberty. "If there be a principle that ought not to be questioned within the United States, it is, that every nation has a right to abolish an old government and establish a new one. This principle is not only recorded in every public archive, written in every American heart, and sealed with the blood of a host of American martyrs; but is the only lawful tenure by which the United States hold their existence as a nation."

Madison Refuses to Pander, Suffers First of Many Political Losses

In 1777, James suffered the first of several electoral setbacks he would experience throughout his long life in public service. When

Chapter Two: James Madison's Moral Obligations

Though successful for his age and reservedness, James would not be chosen for the state legislature due to his integrity and commitment to virtue.

the people of Orange County went to the polls to elect delegates to the state legislature that year, James was not chosen. It was not, however, a lack of qualification that kept him out of the assembly in 1777; it was his commitment to virtue. "It was . . . the usage for the candidates to recommend themselves to the voters, not only by personal solicitation, but by the corrupting influence of spirituous liquors, and other treats, having a like tendency," he recounted regarding his electoral defeat.

Why, then, did James not carry on this kind of campaign? Because, he said, he regarded these practices "as equally inconsistent with the purity of moral and of republican principles and anxious to promote by example the proper reform. . . ." Madison and most of our Founding Fathers believed that if a person wanted power so badly that he was willing to pay for it—or pay others to give it to him—he probably wasn't the sort of person virtuous enough to be given power. Power, Madison believed, was very often abused, and therefore great power should only be given to very virtuous people, people who would not abuse the power of their office, but would honor it by obeying the laws that created it. In this, as in myriad other instances, James Madison chose personal virtue over personal promotion. In the end, although his commitment to upholding "moral and republican principles" kept him temporarily out of public office, it kept him continually clean from the corrupting vices of other, more successful candidates.

In spite of Madison's failure to win a seat in the state legislature, during that same session, the governor of Virginia, Patrick Henry, appointed him to serve on the Council of State. Then, in 1780, during the gubernatorial administration of Thomas Jefferson, Henry's successor, Madison was chosen to serve as a delegate to the Continental Congress, the legislative body for the United States, which became the Confederation Congress (officially referred to as the United States in Congress Assembled) on March 1, 1781, after all 13 states had ratified the Articles of Confederation. Upon taking his seat in Philadelphia, James discovered that, once again, he was surrounded by men of much greater age and experience. In fact, James Madison was the youngest of all the delegates sent to represent the states at the Confederation Congress.

Becoming a Public Servant

In order to prepare himself for this new and important position of national prominence, Madison employed his typical tactic of applying himself assiduously to serious and substantial study of the procedures and policies of the body of which he would be a part. His hard work paid off, as Madison was considered a man of significant skill in building coalitions and reducing recondite issues to easily understood ideas.

Of particular interest to Madison was the study of the financial policies of the Continental Congress. As a result of his study, he came to see that the fiscal condition of the confederation was in terrible shape "owing to the depreciation of the paper currency." As he familiarized himself with the ins and outs of the issue and inflation of paper money, Madison said, he "was led to take on the evil [paper currency] and its causes."

Sometime between September 1779 and March 1780, Madison wrote down his thoughts and published them in a report entitled "Money," which was widely reprinted, bringing deserved attention to the young legislator as a man of keen mind and talent for expressing his thoughts clearly and convincingly.

After being re-elected three times to the Confederation Congress, Madison returned to his native Virginia. The voters of Orange County once again elected him to the Virginia House of Delegates, where he served from 1784-1786. Although James had intended to resume the study of law after leaving the Confederation Congress, he accepted the honor of representing his friends and neighbors in the state legislature. He considered it an "opportunity of pleading in a favorable position the cause of reform in our federal system," which he and others—most notably George Washington—considered to be "in the paroxysm of its infirmities and filling every well informed patriot with the most acute anxieties."

Madison's fervor for repairing the deficiencies of the Articles of Confederation affirms the genuine concern he habitually demonstrated for his country. Where others may have allowed physical infirmities to prevent them from participating in such difficult affairs, Madison persevered, putting the safety and welfare of his country above his own. His dedication to preserving religious liberty was demonstrated during these years as a state legislator, as well.

James Madison's Impressions

James, now 34 years old, began the summer of 1785 at home. The comfortable and calming air of Montpelier was a welcome relief after having spent the winter rubbing shoulders and shaking hands with his fellow delegates at the General Assembly meeting in Richmond. Madison enjoyed his public service, but he always longed for the tranquility of Orange County and the Blue Ridge Mountains.

In January of that year, Madison spent a few weeks at the home of his friend and fellow Virginian Edmund Randolph. Within a couple of years, Randolph would be governor of the Old Dominion and would become the voice presenting the plan of government that came from the fertile and probing mind of Madison. This year, 1785, however, James passed the time at Randolph's house, reading the law and learning all he could from his host, who was renowned as one of the state's finest attorneys.

Upon arriving at Montpelier around the beginning of March, Madison set about reading correspondence sent from his many friends and associates, as well as penning some of his own. The roster of senders and recipients reads like a veritable "Who's Who" of the leading lights of the Founding Generation. First, he fired off a letter to Edmund Randolph, thanking him for his generosity and hospitality and keeping him up to date on events transpiring in Europe, as reported to Madison by Thomas Jefferson.

Next, he opened a letter from the Marquis de Lafayette. In this brief missive, the noble Frenchman and friend of America informed Madison of his efforts to lobby the French Court for greater access for American shipping to the ports of France, and recommended a book that he informed Madison was "worth your reading." The book he recommended was written by Jacques Necker, a French aristocrat and politician, and described his economic theories. It was titled the *Compte Rendu au Roi (The Report to the King)*. Published in 1781, this book was so influential in France that the figures reported therein convinced the government to loan the United States more money to finance the last two years of the war with Great Britain.

The next letter opened by Madison also bore a French return address: that of Thomas Jefferson. In this letter, dated March 18, 1785, Jefferson related to his friend and frequent collaborator the political climate in Paris and the rest of Europe. He confirmed Madison's take on the "character of M. Lafayette," informing him that indeed the young aristocrat was "of unmeasured ambition, but the means he uses are virtuous."

Some of this letter was written in a secret code created by Madison and Jefferson so that they could correspond on sensitive matters without fear of having some of their ideas publicly known. One of the topics touched on by Jefferson using the cipher was the nomination of Madison to serve as ambassador to Spain. Jefferson

Chapter Two: James Madison's Moral Obligations

Not only was Thomas Jefferson an admirable colleague, but he became one of James' dearest friends.

:Mather Brown (painting); A.B. Hall (engraving), Public domain, via Wikimedia Commons

reacted to the news by stating, "I want you in the Virginia Assembly and also in Congress. . . ." He concluded the letter by leaving the choice of where to serve up to Madison, telling him he would be "contented" with whatever decision James made.

Letters then flew fast and furious from the pen of James Madison: Patrick Henry, James Monroe, the Marquis de Lafayette, Thomas Jefferson, Richard Henry Lee, George Wythe (Thomas Jefferson's law tutor), William Grayson, and George Nicholas are but a few of the notable men of the time who received letters from Madison that spring.

James Madison: Champion of Freedom of Conscience

Finally caught up on his correspondence, Madison settled in to begin work on what would become one of his most influential and inspiring contributions to the corpus of Founding documents. On

June 20, 1785, he penned an essay putting forth 15 reasons for opposing a bill in Virginia authorizing the use of public funds to pay "teachers of the Christian religion." This famous letter is called "Memorial and Remonstrance Against Religious Assessments."

Madison biographer Ralph Ketcham described the influence of religion on the young James Madison in the following quote from his invaluable one-volume biography of the Father of the Constitution: "It is not possible to understand the purpose and earnestness of Madison's public life without sensing its connection with the Christian atmosphere in which he was raised."

In order to avoid creating enemies of friends, Madison took great pains to keep his authorship of the "Memorial and Remonstrance" secret. He worried that his involvement in the fight to end state-subsidized religion could bring unwanted confrontation from those with whom he was personally friendly and who believed deeply in the continuation of churches funded by the state government. Both Patrick Henry and Edmund Pendleton were devoted to the perpetuation of the state-sponsorship of the Anglican religion. Henry, in particular, spoke often and passionately about the necessity of taxes being channeled to churches, lest the public morality suffer.

A bill earmarking tax revenue for use by the church was put forward in the Virginia legislature. In light of his authorship of the provision in the Virginia Declaration of Rights that protected religious liberty, those who opposed the use of tax money to support a church asked Madison to write something that would convince his colleagues to vote against the bill.

George Mason received a copy of the "Memorial and Remonstrance" from Madison and had it published and circulated with the goal of defeating the establishment bill. Mason honored Madison's request for anonymity, however, and attributed authorship of the petition to "a particular friend whose name I am not at liberty to mention."

Thousands of copies of the "Memorial and Remonstrance Against Religious Assessments" were printed and distributed in Richmond. Several other opponents of the bill published similar petitions, and legislation that seemed certain to pass just a year earlier was defeated and, in fact, never made it to the floor of the General Assembly for debate.

"One of the Truly Epoch-Making Documents": Madison's "Memorial and Remonstrance"

So persuasive and well-reasoned was Madison's "Memorial and Remonstrance" that one author described the document as "one of the truly epoch-making documents" in American history (Anson Phelps Stokes, *Church and State in the United States*). As for the contents of the petition, the pious and prayerful nature of James Madison shines through. In the first paragraph, Madison laid out what he believed to be the proper boundaries of civil and religious authority, as well as the proper prioritizing of the duties and obligation owed to both:

> The Religion then of every man must be left to the conviction and conscience of every man; and it is the right of every man to exercise it as these may dictate. This right is in its nature an unalienable right. It is unalienable, because the opinions of men, depending only on the evidence contemplated by their own minds cannot follow the dictates of other men: It is unalienable also, because what is here a right towards men, is a duty towards the Creator. It is the duty of every man to render to the Creator such homage and such only as he believes to be acceptable to him. This duty is precedent, both in order of time and in degree of obligation, to the claims of Civil Society.

"Take Alarm at the First Experiment on Our Liberties"

Next, Madison reminded readers of the necessity of a free people to keep their rulers inside the limits of their authority as determined by the people, who are the ultimate sovereigns. Letting leaders roam outside the borders of the consent given by the governed will only end in tyranny, Madison warns:

> The preservation of a free Government requires not merely, that the metes and bounds which separate each department of power be invariably maintained; but more especially that neither of them be suffered to overleap the great Barrier which defends the rights of the people. The

> Rulers who are guilty of such an encroachment, exceed the commission from which they derive their authority, and are Tyrants. The People who submit to it are governed by laws made neither by themselves nor by an authority derived from them, and are slaves.

Building upon that foundation, Madison then turned to placing the responsibility for detecting and defeating tyranny on the shoulders of the people themselves, reminding them that it is never too early to "take alarm" when legislators or presidents begin assaulting their freedom:

> We remonstrate against the said bill ... because it is proper to take alarm at the first experiment on our liberties. We hold this prudent jealousy to be the first duty of Citizens, and one of the noblest characteristics of the late Revolution. The free men of America did not wait till usurped power had strengthened itself by exercise, and entangled the question in precedents. They saw all the consequences in the principle, and they avoided the consequences by denying the principle.

In the next sentence, Madison expressed the optimism, the trust he had in the American people, that they would never fail in their obligation to pass these lessons on to their children. "We revere this lesson too much soon to forget it," he said, sanguinely. What comes through, however, regardless of his misplaced confidence in the virtue of the American people, is that this is yet another in a lengthy list of contemporary ills that could be cured by adherence to the letter and the spirit of the Constitution and the counsel of the Founding Fathers.

"Freedom to Embrace, to Profess and to Observe" Religious Beliefs

Continuing, the third "reason" provided by Madison for rejecting the bill establishing a state religion in Virginia reads like a cautionary tale to modern American politicians who often propose—or at least see the soundness in—imposing sanctions on a particular religion or denomination. He asked his readers rhetorically:

John Locke greatly inspired James' writing of the highly influential "Memorial and Remonstrance Against Religious Assessments."

> Who does not see that the same authority which can establish Christianity, in exclusion of all other Religions, may establish with the same ease any particular sect of Christians, in exclusion of all other Sects? that the same authority which can force a citizen to contribute three pence only of his property for the support of any one establishment, may force him to conform to any other establishment in all cases whatsoever?

He continued along this line in the fourth provision:

> Whilst we assert for ourselves a freedom to embrace, to profess and to observe the Religion which we believe to be of divine origin, we cannot deny an equal freedom to

those whose minds have not yet yielded to the evidence which has convinced us. If this freedom be abused, it is an offence against God, not against man: To God, therefore, not to man, must an account of it be rendered.

Trust Religion to Be Supported by "Ordinary Care of Providence," Not by Government

In the fifth provision of this pamphlet, Madison reminded readers that civil governors are not ministers of salvation and that they are not "competent judge[s] of religious truth." To accept such claims made by civil magistrates, he declared, would be "an unhallowed perversion of the means of salvation."

Next, he described how the "Christian religion" ought to be supported: It is to rely, he insisted, on the "ordinary care of Providence" and not on the generosity of government. Furthermore, to permit government a role in the establishment of religion, Madison wrote, would "weaken in those who profess this Religion a pious confidence in its innate excellence and the patronage of its Author." The Christian religion, he added, has "existed and flourished . . . in spite of every opposition" thrown at it from government. Christians should, therefore, not rely on the opinion of government regarding their religion, but should "trust it to its own merits."

In the seventh article of the "Memorial and Remonstrance," Madison recorded his observation that "ecclesiastical establishments, instead of maintaining the purity and efficacy of Religion, have had a contrary operation." In other words, governments that take upon themselves the right to rule in religious matters have always aimed at its ultimate extinction and the elimination of the faith of its adherents. Madison suggested that lawmakers stay out of the business of approving or disapproving religion and of financially supporting it. He also advised that ministers of the faith should be supported by "the voluntary rewards of their flocks," rather than from the coffers of the government.

"A More Certain Repose From [Their] Troubles"

As he explained in the eighth reason, Madison noted that throughout history, governments have interfered with the practice of religion for one purpose: "to erect a spiritual tyranny. . . ." The usurped power over matters of faith, he averred, have been used by government in "upholding the thrones of political tyranny," and "in no instance have they been seen the guardians of the liberties of the people."

Religion, then, Madison insisted, is a powerful protector of liberty when left free from government intrusion. Any attempt by government to administer in the affairs of faith by taking upon itself the authority to approve and disapprove religion should be seen by those suffering from denial of their right to worship God according to their own conscience as a warning "to seek some other haven, where liberty and philanthropy in their due extent, may offer a more certain repose from [their] troubles."

In another section of the booklet, Madison declared that America has demonstrated to the world that "equal and compleat liberty" promotes and preserves the "health and prosperity of the State." However, when governors consolidate any sort of control over the right of religious exercise, there is a "malignant influence" on the condition of liberty in that place.

"Free Exercise of ... Religion" Is a "Gift of Nature"

Finally, Madison boldly proclaimed that "the equal right of every citizen to the free exercise of his Religion according to the dictates of conscience" is a "gift of nature" and should therefore be "dear to us." The legislature, he warned, must be "bound to leave this particular right untouched and sacred," and "no effort may be omitted on our part against so dangerous an usurpation."

Madison concluded the pamphlet by informing his readers that he and those who support his position are "earnestly praying . . . to the Supreme Lawgiver of the Universe" that lawmakers may be guided "into every measure which may be worthy of his blessing," and thus that they may "establish more firmly the liberties, the prosperity and the happiness" of the people.

Here, in the "Memorial and Remonstrance," we find the faith of James Madison put to paper, and in it we see his sincere supplication to the "Supreme Lawgiver of the Universe" to protect the sacred right of the free exercise of religion in the United States.

As with the other men of the Founding Generation, Madison believed that in society, all men enter on equal condition and retain an equal right to worship according to their own consciences. "While we assert for ourselves a freedom to embrace, to profess and to observe the Religion which we believe to be of divine origin, we cannot deny an equal freedom to those whose minds have not yet yielded to the evidence which has convinced us," he averred. Regarding the proper relationship between government and religion, he wrote, "The preservation of a free Government requires not merely, that the metes and bounds which separate each department of power be invariably maintained; but more especially that neither of them be suffered to overleap the great Barrier which defends the right of the people."

Madison's Personal Religious Beliefs

That James Madison considered himself a Christian throughout his life is clear from his correspondence. Late in his life, in a letter to the Reverend Jasper Adams written in 1832, for example, Madison calls Christianity "the best and noblest religion." And as a much younger man, in a letter written on September 25, 1773 to his dear friend William Bradford, he declares his belief that if men seek to be considered "honorable," they should be "fervent advocates in the cause of Christ."

Besides the letter to Bradford wherein Madison admonishes his friend to take great care in seeing that his name be recorded in the "annals of heaven," there are many other missives and memoranda wherein Madison makes clear the depth of his devotion to his Christian convictions.

In his early works that we still have today, there are detailed and comprehensive notes he took on the Gospels and the Acts of the Apostles. These notes show his thorough and thoughtful examination of these religious texts, as well as his broad knowledge of theology as a whole.

In one of his annotations, he discusses Chapter 17 of the Acts of the Apostles, which talks about the Bereans (inhabitants of the ancient city of Berea in what is now northern Greece). In Acts 17:11, the author describes the Jews in Berea as "more noble than those in Thessalonica, in that they received the word with all readiness of mind, and searched the Scriptures daily whether these things were so." In comments written about this verse, Madison praises the Bereans' behavior "as a noble example for all succeeding Christians to imitate and follow."

In a manner like the Bereans', Madison appears to have engaged in daily and thorough study of the Bible. Below are a few selected examples from his "Notes on Commentary on the Bible" (written between 1770-1773) showcasing how he approached and documented his study of the Scriptures.

It is worth mentioning that Madison's research into religious topics was so extensive and thorough during this time in his life that when the University of Virginia was founded, Thomas Jefferson asked him to create a list of theological authors, both old and new, for the university library's collection. The list Madison provided stands as a lasting tribute to both his scholarly achievements and his deep understanding of the inestimable significance of this vast area of human intellect and belief.

Now, we share a few of Madison's notes from his study of the Holy Bible (particularly the New Testament) that reveal what biographer William Cabell Rives described as Madison's "orthodoxy" and his extraordinary "penetration" of the profound personal application to be derived from a study of the sacred texts.

In his interpretation of the Gospel of St. John, specifically focusing on the scene where Mary Magdalene looks into the tomb and sees two angels dressed in white sitting at the head and feet of where Jesus' body had been, Madison records this meaningful insight: "Angels to be desired at our feet as well as at our head—not an angelical understanding and a diabolical conversation—not all our religion in our brains and tongue, and nothing in our heart and life."

In the same vein, while discussing Acts 9:6, in which Jesus tells St. Paul, who had fallen to the ground from the light shining around him from heaven, "Arise, and go into the city, and it shall be told thee what thou must do," Madison makes a note reminding himself that "It is not the *talking*, but the *walking* and *working* person that is the true Christian." (Emphasis in original.)

In relation to his earnest inquiry into some of the fundamental points of Christian doctrine as gleaned from his study of the New Testament, Madison wrote the following notes:

> "Omnisciency—God's foreknowledge doth not compel but permits to be done." (Acts 2:23)

> "Christ's divinity appears by St. John, ch. XX. v. 28."

> "Resurrection testified and witnessed by the Apostles." (Acts 4:33)

His notes from his study of the Holy Bible made during those years run at least another four pages, and are replete not only with his own insights and observations, but with quotations from William Burkitt's *Expository Notes, with Practical Observations, on the New Testament of our Lord and Saviour Jesus Christ*, published posthumously in London in 1724. When it came to being able to follow the Apostle Peter's injunction to "*be* ready always to *give* an answer to every man that asketh you a reason of the hope that is in you with meekness and fear," Madison's copying down of many of Burkitt's comments into his own notebook demonstrates that he was not content to rely only on his own reading of the Scriptures, but was anxious to fortify his faith with the insights of other learned men of faith.

Atheists, agnostics, and others take glee and gain from attacking the virtue of the Founding Fathers. However, James Madison's faith was so dear to him, so near to his heart and his mind at all times, that in his personal correspondence he frequently reminds his recipient to remain close to God and to act in accordance with the tenets of the Christian faith.

For example, in a letter to his aforementioned friend William Bradford, Madison called the study of "divinity" the "most sublime of all Sciences," and in language both inspired and inspiring, informed Bradford:

> I have sometimes thought there could not be a stronger testimony in favor of religion or against temporal enjoyments, even the most rational and manly, than for men who occupy the most honorable and gainful departments and are rising in reputation and wealth, publicly to declare their unsatisfatoriness by becoming fervent Advocates in the cause of Christ....

Such public proclamations by politicians of their faith in Christ would, Madison declared, make such magistrates a "cloud of witnesses" of the Gospel of Jesus Christ.

Our last selection is from a letter written by Madison to Edward Everett in 1823 wherein he warns Everett that a university where the professors are not Christian would be a place of "irreligious tendencies, if not designs."

In light of such a prediction, one wonders what Madison would think of the classrooms of contemporary American universities, where Christianity is the subject of ridicule, revisionism, and rejection.

It is no exaggeration to claim that to doubt, disparage, or deny the faith of James Madison is an exercise in futility and could only be carried on by someone knowingly and willingly ignoring the absolutely alpine aggregation of evidence against such an allegation. As the selections from his personal commonplace book and correspondence have revealed, Madison was a devout Christian and an able defender of his faith.

His professional pen was no less often employed in the support of Christ and Christianity. Take, for example, an amendment to the Virginia Declaration of Rights authored by Madison sometime in the summer of 1776:

> That religion, or the duty which we owe to our Creator, and the manner of discharging it, can be directed only by reason and conviction, not by force or violence; and therefore, that all men are equally entitled to enjoy the free exercise of religion, according to the dictates of conscience, unpunished and unrestrained by the

magistrate, unless the preservation of equal liberty and the existence of the state are manifestly endangered; And that it is the mutual duty of all to practice Christian forbearance, love, and charity towards each other.

In his notes taken in 1784 on debates of a general assessment bill sponsored by Patrick Henry, Madison writes regarding the essential doctrines of Christianity, "those who reject these, whatever name they take are no *Christian* society." (Emphasis in original.)

In the face of such language written by Madison when he was a legislator, those denying his faith would have to make an impressive display of hermeneutical gymnastics to explain why Madison would seek to enshrine in the law the practice of the Christian religion, going so far as to describe it as a "duty" owed by all.

The foregoing few pages should serve as support for the claim made by Ketcham that "It is not possible to understand the purpose and earnestness of Madison's public life without sensing its connection with the Christian atmosphere in which he was raised."

I would add that it would be equally impossible to understand the life, legislation, and legacy of James Madison without recognizing that, by his own choice from a very young age, he illuminated his mind and his heart with the light of the Gospel of Jesus Christ, He who is the Light of the World.

Despite his personal adherence to the Christian faith, though, Madison was a fervent proponent of the right of all men to enjoy the peaceful practice of their faith, regardless of their theology.

Finally, from the "Memorial and Remonstrance," regarding the ability of the agnostic to provide any sort of valuable service to his (or her) country, he wrote, "Before any man can be considered as a member of civil society, he must be considered as a subject of the Governor of the Universe."

Chapter 3:
Maintaining Strength Through Hardship

It was during his years as a member of the Virginia House of Delegates that James Madison's friendship and correspondence with Thomas Jefferson flourished. Jefferson was serving as the American trade representative in France, taking over for Benjamin Franklin, who resigned in March 1785. His residence in Paris happily provided him with ready access to scores of bookstores and libraries filled with the world's finest written works on the subjects of politics, history, and government. Taking advantage of his friend's generosity and good fortune, Madison asked Jefferson to send him crates full of the best of these books, books he would read, ponder, and pore over during an extraordinarily eventful summer.

During his tenure as a member of the Virginia House of Delegates, Madison took part in several influential meetings, including one at Annapolis, Maryland, aimed at considering potential remedies for the problems afflicting the constitution currently holding the union together. After successfully passing through the trial of the War of Independence, having affirmed thereby their inalienable right of self-government, the 13 former Colonies exercised their sovereignty by making compacts with each other. The first of these agreements was a "firm league of friendship" known as the Articles of Confederation, adopted by the Continental Congress on November 15, 1777 and eventually ratified by all 13 states on March 1, 1781.

The members of this new confederacy established a lawmaking body endowed with power to legislate in several areas of mutual interest, but the states themselves retained the lion's share of sovereign power. This arrangement of authority was set out explicitly in Article II of the document: "Each state retains its sovereignty, freedom, and independence, and every Power, Jurisdiction, and right, which is not by this confederation expressly delegated to the United States, in Congress assembled."

The purpose for forming the confederacy was to unite themselves for their mutual benefit in a "perpetual union," not to surrender their hard-won sovereignty to a despot with the potential to destroy their rights, similar to the monarch they had so recently banished from their shores. To believe there was such an intent would require a suspension of reason and ignorance of the causes and goals of the War of Independence.

Admittedly, the centrifugal forces flinging the states away from the confederacy were more powerful than many anticipated, and the ties that lashed the states together were rapidly loosening. The factors hastening this dissolution are well known. Primarily, the states were concerned with how to enforce an equitable distribution of the obligation to repay the debts incurred to finance the war with Britain. In the vacuum of a suitable settlement, chaos grew, as did an American credibility deficit overseas. This weakened position convinced a majority of the Founding Generation that their newly restored republics were vulnerable to foreign aggression, especially from England.

The Articles of Confederation

To avoid having to fight for freedom every year, the hero of the War of Independence and "Father of His Country," George Washington, hosted a conference at his home, Mount Vernon. The goal of the gathering was to resolve border and trading disputes between Virginia and Maryland. While resulting in no substantial agreement among representatives of the neighboring states, there was a sense that a larger convention—one to which more states would be invited—might have enough clout to solve the pressing issues of common concern, principally that of self-preservation.

The first significant attempt at holding such a meeting with a more expansive agenda was the conference that came to be known as the

Chapter Three: Maintaining Strength Through Hardship

James was heavily involved in the well-being of his fellow citizens, and pushed for revision of the Articles of Confederation.

Annapolis Convention. At Annapolis, Maryland, in September 1786, 12 delegates from five states (Delaware, New Jersey, Pennsylvania, Virginia, and New York) came together for the express purpose of hammering out some workable solutions to the problems of international trade, interstate relations, and the weaknesses of the Articles of Confederation. Looking through the lens of history, we see that the most important product of this mini-convention was the drafting by Alexander Hamilton of a report in which the future Philadelphia delegate and co-author of *The Federalist* proposed to the Confederation Congress that a larger, officially sanctioned meeting be convened in Philadelphia in May 1787 for the purpose of "considering the situation of the United States," including a mandate "to devise such further provisions as shall appear to them necessary to render the constitution of the federal government adequate to the exigencies of the union. . . ."

Congress heeded Hamilton's call and proposed that states send delegates to Philadelphia "for the sole and express purpose of revising the Articles of Confederation." This "business of May next," as Madison described it in a letter, would be the most momentous time of his life and would require all the insight and guidance he could glean from the invaluable trove of books sent by Jefferson.

James Madison took very seriously the task of helping to heal his country's constitutional crises. For weeks before the Annapolis Convention, he devoted every minute of his time to studying the books sent by Jefferson. He would use these books as a guide to the governments—the republican governments—of the past. His study, he trusted, would reveal to him what worked and what failed in the constitutions and confederations whose histories he surveyed. Madison believed that history was a precursor of the future. In the annals of history—particularly that of the Greek and Roman republics of antiquity—he believed he could find the key to inoculating America against the diseases that infected and destroyed past societies. Indeed, it could be said that during this time, he behaved like a coroner, a specialist responsible for examining the lifeless bodies of the self-governing societies of the past, in order to prevent the United States from succumbing to the maladies that shortened the lives of its freedom-loving forerunners.

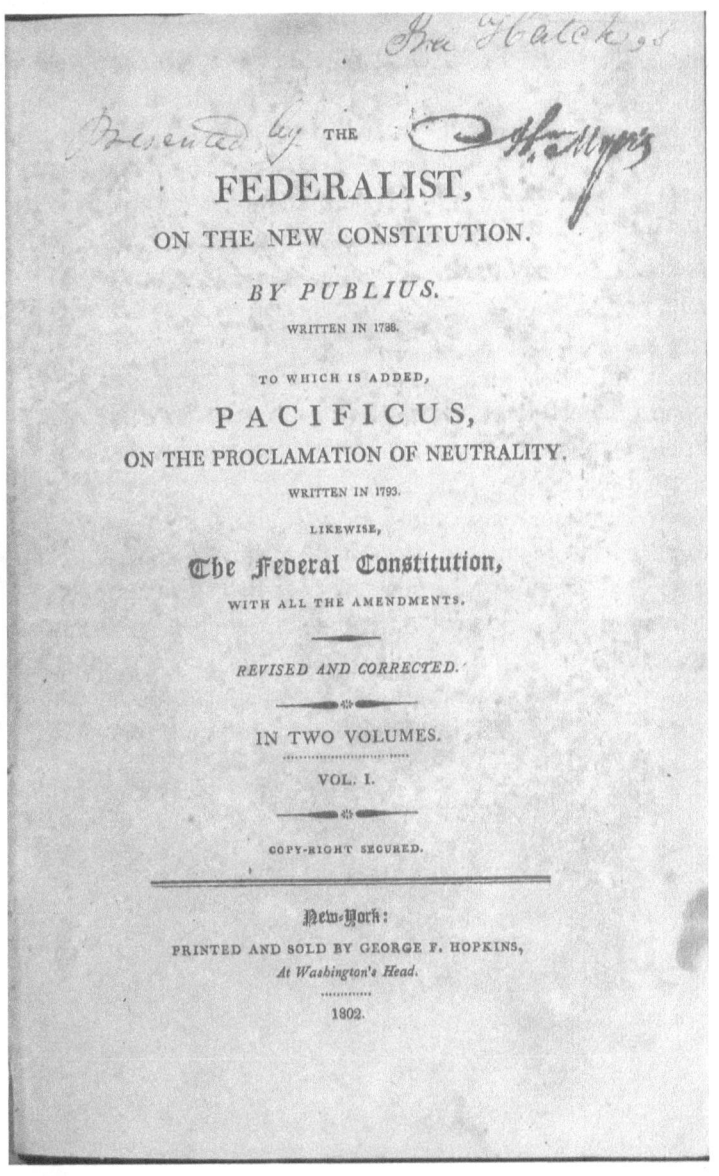

James Madison, Alexander Hamilton, and John Jay composed *The Federalist*, 85 letters written in support of the ratification of the new U.S. Constitution.

Beginning on April 1, 1786 and continuing until June 26 of that year, Madison sketched out what he called his "Notes on Ancient and Modern Confederacies." These are the details he derived of the pros and cons of the unions of sovereign states that had existed or then existed throughout the Western world. The insight he gleaned from this study, he hoped, would be useful in repairing the frayed ties that united the several states into a free and formidable union. Biographers report that as early as 1784, Madison had begun collecting every article, book, essay, and encyclopedia that he could obtain (whether on his own or through the generosity of overseas friends such as Thomas Jefferson) that he believed would "render all such lights of consequence" to his own effort to prevent the confederacy from crumbling and being added to the scrap heap of history. He carefully cataloged all the books he used in his investigation of ancient and modern confederacies, and reports having studiously read and considered the history of at least 20 volumes in various editions. Although it is almost certain that Madison prepared his "Notes on Ancient and Modern Confederacies" for use at the Annapolis Convention, he would turn to that text for information he would use in his speeches at the Philadelphia Constitutional Convention and the Virginia Ratifying Convention, as well as in writing *The Federalist*.

Chapter 4:
Avoiding a Repetitive History

Madison's Knowledge of Ancient History: "First Among Equals"

Madison's study of the various volumes of historical survey revealed that there were definitive patterns in history, and if a country could avoid the causes of downfall, it could almost certainly avoid the effects. As the French philosopher Charles Pinot Duclos wrote:

> We see on the theater of the world a certain number of scenes which succeed each other in endless repetition: where we see the same faults followed regularly by the same misfortunes, we may reasonably think that if we could have known the first we might have avoided the others. The past should enlighten us on the future: knowledge of history is no more than an anticipated experience.

When it came to the classical world, few Founding Fathers were as familiar with the histories of Greece and Rome as James Madison. In fact, Madison was so conversant in the details of classical examples of the establishment and erosion of liberty that historian David J. Bederman described him as "the first among equals insofar as his classical knowledge was concerned."

Bederman's estimation of Madison's grasp of the Greek and Roman worlds is supported by a survey of James' commonplace books. Scores of references to the tales told by the inimitable Latin and Greek chroniclers reveal the influence of Rome and Greece on his understanding of the proven path that leads from liberty to slavery, a path portrayed clearly by the classical historians.

"Experience Is the Oracle of Truth"

His journey through the records of the ancient world provided James with records of behavior that he could apply to his own circumstances. Later, in *Federalist* No. 20, Madison would justify his frequent reliance on the record of ancient historians.

"I make no apology for having dwelt so long on the contemplation of these federal precedents. Experience is the oracle of truth; and where its responses are unequivocal, they ought to be conclusive and sacred," he explained.

Madison buttresses his contributions to *The Federalist* with dozens of references to the history of Rome and Greece, recalling the rise and fall of the Amphictyonic Council (*Federalist* No. 18), the trickery and tyranny of Greek tyrants (*Federalist* No. 43), and Plutarch's warning "that the deputies of the strongest cities awed and corrupted those of the weaker; and that judgment went in favor of the most powerful party" (*Federalist* No. 18). He warned against the dangers of democracy demonstrated by the ancient confederacies (*Federalist* No. 10), and used the demise of the "the turbulent democracies of ancient Greece" as a warning against violence in his own country (*Federalist* No. 14).

Finally, in *Federalist* No. 39, Madison recommended a sound union as the antidote for these political disorders, using Philip II of Macedon's conquest of Greece and Rome's failure to remain free as cautionary tales to be heeded.

"Had Greece, says a judicious observer on her fate, been united by a stricter confederation, and persevered in her union, she would never have worn the chains of Macedon; and might have proved a barrier to the vast projects of Rome," he wrote.

Cicero and Cato: Examples of Virtue and Vigilance

The Founders' Roman heroes lived at a time when the Roman republic was being threatened by power-hungry demagogues, bloodthirsty dictators, and shadowy conspirators. The Founders' principal Greco-Roman heroes were Roman statesmen: Cato the Younger, Brutus, Cassius, and Cicero—all of whom sacrificed their lives in unsuccessful attempts to save the republic—as well as the celebrated Greek lawgivers Lycurgus and Solon.

Cato the Younger was a Roman of sterling reputation who lived from approximately 95 B.C. to 46 B.C. He is described as being "unmoved by passion and firm in everything," even from his youth. He was renowned for finishing whatever he started and for hating flattery. He embraced every worthwhile Roman virtue, and was especially appreciated for his sense of justice and even temperament. As a senator, Cato was always in attendance when the Senate was in session. A no-nonsense legislator, Cato was hated by Pompey and Caesar for his integrity and his refusal to aid them in their corrupt plans to usurp power. Although they imprisoned him, the public clamored for his release and Caesar reluctantly complied.

Unable to squelch Cato's attacks on their corrupt policies, Caesar and Pompey sent him to Cyprus. Finally, Cato aligned himself with Brutus against Caesar, a decision that would eventually cost him his life. George Washington admired Cato so greatly that he ignored a congressional ban on "every species of extravagance" and ordered that Joseph Addison's play about Cato be performed in Valley Forge to boost the troops' morale.

Other Roman heroes very dear to the hearts of the Founders and notable in Madison's study were Brutus and Cassius. Brutus was admired by his contemporaries for his pleasant disposition and virtuous temper. Even those who opposed his attack on Caesar believed that Brutus was motivated by a genuine concern for the republic and not by personal animosity. Marc Antony himself said that Brutus was "the only man that conspired against Caesar out of a sense of the glory and justice of the action; but all the rest rose up against the man, and not the tyrant. . . ."

The most popular Roman hero read and relied upon by Madison was Cicero, upon whom he bestows the honorific title "the Orator" in his commonplace book. Cicero lived from approximately 106 B.C. to 43 B.C. John Adams, in his *Defense of the Constitution*, said of Cicero: "All of the ages of the world have not produced a greater

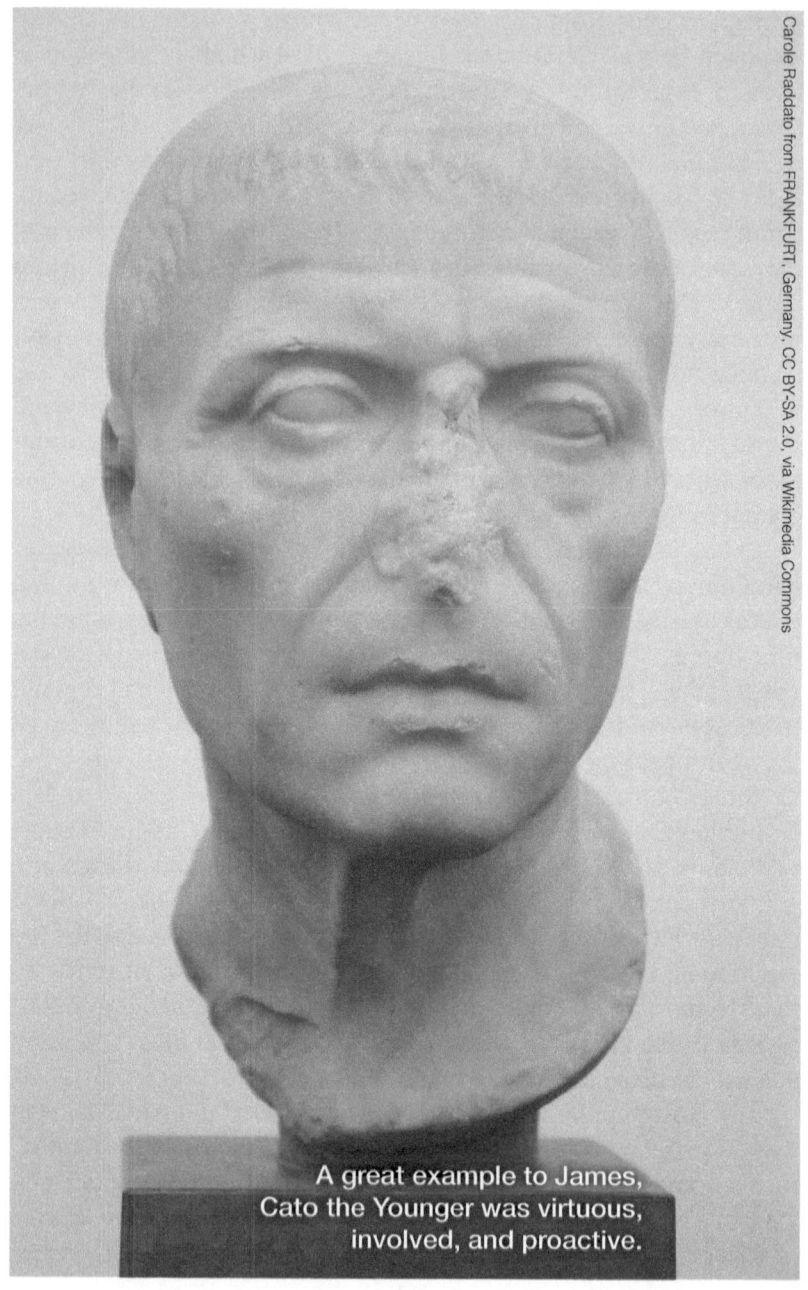

A great example to James, Cato the Younger was virtuous, involved, and proactive.

statesman and philosopher united than Cicero...." First as a lawyer, then as a consul and senator, Cicero boldly defended the republic against the rise of dictators.

Cicero delivered his greatest speeches in defense of the republic against the Catilinarian Conspiracy. The Catilinarian Conspiracy was a plot to overthrow the republic, hatched by aristocrat Lucius Sergius Catiline, with the help of a cabal of aristocrats and disaffected veterans. In 63 B.C., Cicero exposed and thwarted the plot, and Catiline was forced to flee from Rome. For his service in saving Rome, Cicero was given the title "Father of his Country" (*Pater Patriae*) by his countrymen. Like Brutus and Cassius, Cicero's courageous defense of republican liberty in the face of designing conspirators made him a logical model for emulation by our Founding Fathers.

History Teaches Madison of the "Hazards and Difficulties" of Establishing Good Government

Regarding the Greek classics, Madison greatly admired Lycurgus, the lawgiver of Sparta. Lycurgus lived in the ninth century B.C. and reformed the entire Spartan commonwealth. His most important reform was the establishment of a senate equal in authority with the monarchy in matters of great importance. Prior to Lycurgus' innovation, the Spartan government swayed between monarchy and democracy, depending on whether the king or the people had the upper hand. The senate served as a check on the excesses of both king and subjects. The biographer Plutarch called Lycurgus' institutions "in very truth a divine blessing" ("Lycurgus," Plutarch's *Lives*).

In *Federalist* No. 38, Madison rehearses the history of Lycurgus' efforts to establish a mixed form of government in Sparta, then applies those lessons to his own constitutional concerns, explaining that the purpose of studying Spartan constitutional reform is "to admonish us of the hazards and difficulties incident to such experiments, and of the great imprudence of unnecessarily multiplying them."

Another Greek famed for his reform of the law was Solon. Born in Athens about 638 B.C., Solon achieved glory as one of the "Seven Sages of Greece." Around 590 B.C., he was given the task of reforming the Athenian constitution. His improvements included the right of trial by jury and the division of society into several bodies that would balance and check each other in governing Athens. After finishing his constitutional reforms, Solon left Athens for 10 years. While he was away, Pisistratus, his former friend, usurped control of the government and fastened tyrannical controls on the city. Both Lycurgus and Solon appreciated the need for incorporating checks and balances into government, a need that the American Founders understood just as acutely.

James Madison demonstrated the depth of his understanding and appreciation of the life of Solon as a statesman and lawgiver, particularly when it came to creating a constitution that would serve the people well and promote their welfare. In *Federalist* No. 38, he wrote, "And Solon, according to Plutarch, was in a manner compelled, by the universal suffrage of his fellow-citizens, to take upon him the sole and absolute power of new-modeling the constitution." Madison fills that letter (*Federalist* No. 38) with numerous references to the classical world and the lessons he learned from the study of ancient history. Apart from Solon, he applies to his own time and situation the stories of Draco, Lycurgus, Numa, and Brutus among many others.

Many of the lessons Madison learned from his study of the ancients taught him to detect and defeat tyranny, and much of what he read while poring over the annals of the histories of Rome and Greece revealed to him many institutions and distributions of power that promoted and protected the liberty of the citizens of these classical civilizations.

Among the discoveries made by Madison during his study of the history of the ancient world were the crucial contributions made by enlightened men in the crafting of constitutions. In commenting on these contributions, Madison seems to be referring not only to constitutions drafted during the days of classical Athens and Rome, but to the invaluable influence of his own efforts—and those of his colleagues—at the Constitutional Convention of 1787 to place the government of the United States on a firm foundation of republican liberty.

Further on in *Federalist* No. 38, Madison reports "that in every case reported by ancient history, in which government has been established with deliberation and consent, the task of framing

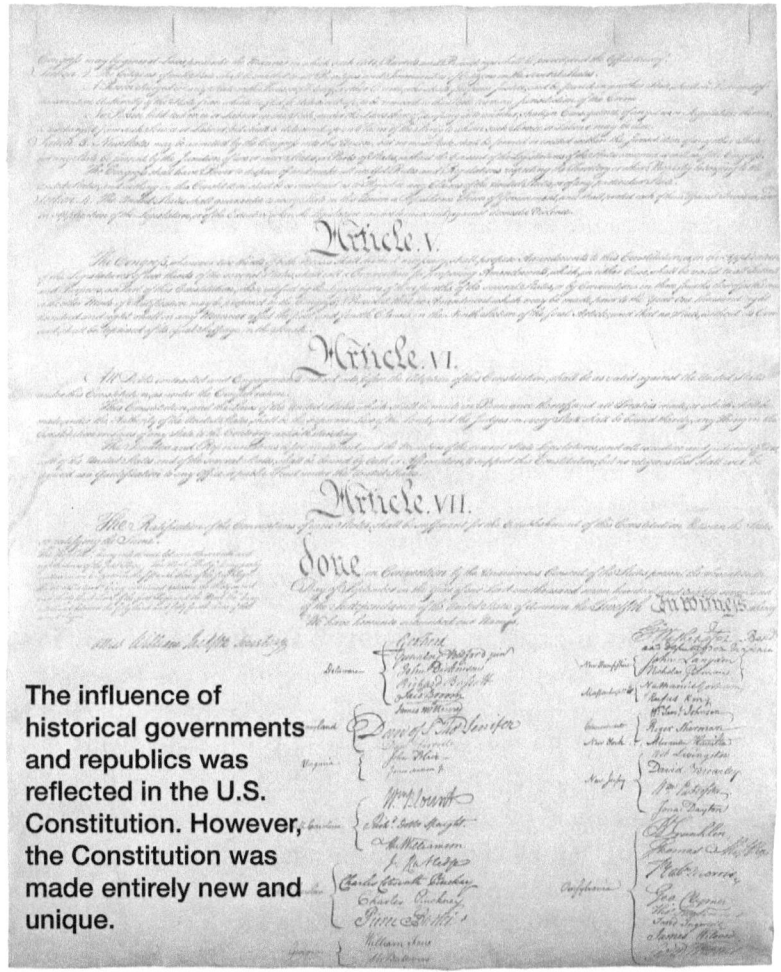

The influence of historical governments and republics was reflected in the U.S. Constitution. However, the Constitution was made entirely new and unique.

National Archives and Records Administration, Public domain, via Wikimedia Commons

it has not been committed to an assembly of men, but has been performed by some individual citizen of preeminent wisdom and approved integrity." Of course, in light of his humility, it is unlikely that Madison was referring to himself, but to a man such as George Washington, whom he famously described as an "indispensable man."

Even in light of the many remarkable results of efforts toward the perpetuation of self-government made by the Romans and Greeks, Madison considered the product of the American Constitutional Convention to be above them all.

"[T]hese lessons teach us . . . to admire the improvement made by America on the ancient mode of preparing and establishing regular plans of government," he wrote.

When it came to working out the form and function of the American government, Madison and his fellow Framers did not simply lay an ancient constitution alongside of a piece of parchment and copy its words, and call it the "Constitution for the United States." No, while this section makes the influence of history on our form of government very clear and undeniable, James Madison made it equally clear that the American Constitution was something new, something novel, and something altogether apart from any ancient charter. To that point, in the preface to his records of the debates at the convention, Madison described the new Constitution as "a system without a precedent, ancient or modern."

"A Candid Examination of History" Teaches Madison How to Detect the "Abridgment of the Freedom of the People"

As Madison spent months scouring the histories of the rise and fall of the Greek and Roman republics recorded by Herodotus, Livy, Tacitus, Sallust, Plutarch, Polybius, and others, he was reminded that the liberties enjoyed by the citizens of those commonwealths were quite often targeted by conspiracies of men determined to enslave the people and establish themselves as tyrants. Madison and his learned contemporaries recognized that the histories of Greece and Rome, as reported by the ancient writers, were rife with evidence of conspiracies in high places to deny liberty to the people.

Surveying the litany of British monarchical abuses, our Founders rightly perceived that the shrouded hand of an evil conspiracy was at work in America and England, just as it had been in the Roman republic they so admired. Madison, in fact, in *Federalist* No. 55 expressed his belief that if state legislators would remain vigilant, they would never "fail either to detect or to defeat a conspiracy of the [federal legislature] against the liberties of their common constituents."

During a speech delivered on June 6, 1788 at the Virginia Ratifying Convention, Madison repeated his earlier warning regarding the collusion of those in power to surreptitiously shrink the sphere of liberty.

"I believe there are more instances of the abridgment of the freedom of the people by gradual and silent encroachments of those in power, than by violent and sudden usurpations," he declared, claiming to have based his belief "on a candid examination of history."

Famed patriot Charles Carroll of Carrollton invoked the record of Roman historian Tacitus when he wrote that the conspiracy of his own time had led America and England to "that degree of liberty and servitude which [Servius Sulpicius] Galba ascribes to the Roman people in the speech to [Gaius Calpurnius] Piso: those same Romans, a few years after that period, deified the horse of Caligula" (letter to Edmund Jennings, August 9, 1771).

History Teaches Madison to Oppose "Largesses" Offered by Tyrants

The equally eminent and historically minded John Adams also applied analogies from the Roman republic to the increasingly open threat to the foundations of English liberty by corrupt legislators. The government of England, he said (quoting Roman historian Sallust), had descended to the level where "the Roman republic was when Jugurtha left it, having pronounced it a 'venal city, ripe for destruction if it can only find a purchaser.'" Sallust was a valuable and oft-cited source of warnings as to the consequences of government corruption and intrigue.

Our Founders heeded these warnings about power elites who used corruption, intrigue, and personal immorality to neutralize public concern and dampen zeal for the protection of liberty. James Madison insightfully noted that most of the tyrants of history masqueraded as friends and protectors of the people, and over time revealed themselves to be power-hungry dictators and shameless demagogues. Alexander Hamilton, an astute student of classical history, devoted his first contribution to *The Federalist* to a warning against tyrants, or "men who have overturned the liberties of republics, commencing as demagogues and ending as tyrants."

Finally, in a letter to Thomas Jefferson written on August 8, 1791, Madison combined his understanding of history and its conspiracies into one sentence, warning that those in the United States government who were then trying to unconstitutionally alter the economic system "will become the pretorian band of the Government, at once its tool & its tyrant; bribed by its largesses, & overawing it by clamours & combinations."

From such statements, it is evident that Madison understood that, throughout the history of the Greek and Roman republics, tyrants were more likely than not to begin their political careers as populists and democrats and to end them as despots. Such demagogues were men of prominence who used their popular support to force their will upon an unsuspecting and trusting populace. As Greek historian Thucydides remarked, "You may rule over anyone whom you can dominate."

A Scholar of Historical Factions

Madison's study of the ancient Greek confederacies revealed to him that almost every one of these republics came to an end as a result of factions among domestic demagogues and foreign allies. Hamilton called these insidious cabals the "Grecian Horse to a republic." Both men worried that such a scheme would eventually destroy the American union. This fear, coupled with a thorough understanding of history, made the Founders vigilant guardians against the rise of such combinations in their own nascent republic.

As he systematically studied the ancient republics and confederacies, Madison noted that conspiracies were rampant among them. Those who were successful in carrying out such evil designs would expose and vehemently rail against similar acts on the part of others, thus painting themselves as guardians of liberty. The source of all this evil was an unquenchable thirst for power and the control of the treasury. Power was the end, and conspiracy was the means commonly used to satisfy the rapacious appetite for dominion.

From Thucydides' *History of the Peloponnesian War*, Madison, as befits a diligent patriot-scholar, learned of a particularly pernicious deception practiced by tyrannically minded conspirators.

42   THE FEDERALIST.

CITIES, or republics, the largest were entitled to *three* votes in the COMMON COUNCIL, those of the middle class to *two*, and the smallest to *one*. The COMMON COUNCIL had the appointment of all the judges and magistrates of the respective CITIES. This was certainly the most delicate species of interference in their internal administration; for if there be any thing that seems exclusively appropriated to the local jurisdictions, it is the appointment of their own officers. Yet Montesquieu, speaking of this association, says, "Were I to give a model of an excellent confederate re-"public, it would be that of Lycia." Thus we perceive, that the distinctions insisted upon were not within the contemplation of this enlightened writer; and we shall be led to conclude, that they are the novel refinements of an erroneous theory.   PUBLIUS.

NUMBER X.

BY JAMES MADISON.

THE SAME SUBJECT CONTINUED.

AMONG the numerous advantages promised by a well constructed union, none deserves to be more accurately developed than its tendency to break and control the violence of faction. The friend of popular governments, never finds himself so much alarmed for their character and fate, as when he contemplates their propensity to this dangerous vice. He will not fail, therefore, to set a due value on any plan which, without violating the principles to which he is attached, provides a proper cure for it. The instability, injustice, and confusion, introduced into the public councils, have in truth, been the mortal diseases under which popular governments have everywhere perished; as they continue to be the favorite and fruitful topics from which the adversaries to liberty derive their most specious declamations. The valuable improvements made by the American constitutions on the popular models, both ancient and modern, cannot certainly be too much admired; but it would be an unwarrantable partiality, to contend that they have as effectually obviated the danger on this side, as was wished and expected. Complaints are everywhere heard from our most considerate and virtuous citizens, equally the friends of public and private faith, and of public and personal liberty, that our governments are too unstable; that the public good is disregarded in the conflicts of rival parties; and that measures are too often decided, not according to the rules of justice, and the rights of the minor party, but by the superior force of an interested and overbearing majority. However anxiously we may wish that these complaints had no

Thucydides was an Athenian orator who realized Philip of Macedon would take over Athens, and was later sentenced to prison for revolting.

These instigators would place their fellow conspirators in leadership positions on both sides of a controversy, constantly inciting the "opposing" factions against one another until the innocent citizens didn't know whom or what to believe.

A companion evil to the conspiracies that contaminated and eventually annihilated the ancient commonwealths was the gradual erosion of liberty by seemingly harmless and legal acts. In Demosthenes' writings, Madison read of how Philip of Macedon—by slow and nearly imperceptible means—dismantled Athenian freedom. Philip was an enemy even to those who fancied themselves his allies. He used "legal" means to subvert the constitution and rob Athens of her liberty. His favorite tactic was to create frivolous diversions and provide luxuries to lull the Athenians into a false sense of security and distract them from noticing his usurpations. Unfortunately, Philip succeeded in gaining control of Athens and in making her formerly freedom-loving citizens slaves to his will. In a letter, Jefferson described such gradual and planned usurpations this way: "Single acts of tyranny may be ascribed to the accidental opinion of a day, but a series of oppressions, begun at a distinguished period and pursued unalterably through every change of ministers, too plainly prove a deliberate and systematic plan of reducing us to slavery."

Chapter 5:
Reforming a Free Nation

A Self-Appointed Emissary
It was with this understanding of the warning signs of impending tyranny and the symptoms of social upheaval, gained from untold hours of determined and dedicated study of history, that James Madison set off for Philadelphia. He was anxious to put to practical use his newfound familiarity with the historical metes and bounds of good government and the necessity of not only the consent of the governed, but their continual concentration on the conduct of those chosen to lead them.

As was habitual for the ever-curious Madison, his journey to Philadelphia was not a direct one. He set off from Montpelier on January 11, 1787, bound for Mount Vernon and a quick visit with General Washington, likely to share with him the results of his recent historical inquiries in preparation for the "plenipotentiary" convention in Philadelphia, a meeting Washington was still not committed to attending.

It is almost certain that the most pressing purpose for Madison's visit to the home of General Washington was to try to convince him to attend the convention. For several months, Madison had been corresponding with Washington, who shared his belief in the necessity of strengthening the union. Madison feared that if Washington didn't attend the convention, many other prominent men—and many Americans—would view the meetings as something less than prestigious.

Madison was hopeful that the general would attend, as he had received a letter from him on November 5, 1786 wherein

Washington expressed his hope "to take the lead in promoting this great [and] arduous work" of keeping the United States together and that an "energetic Constitution" would be drafted that would "restore us to that degree of respectability & consequence, to which we had a fair claim, & the brightest prospect of attaining." While this letter certainly buoyed Madison's hopes that the "Father of his Country" would play a key role at the convention planned for just that purpose, he discovered that Washington did not feel he had to personally attend the convention in Philadelphia in order to play a pivotal part in its successful production of an "energetic Constitution."

A letter sent by Madison to Washington on November 8, 1786, began what would be a steady stream of letters sent to General Washington wherein Madison expressed his sincere belief that Washington's name on the list of delegates to the Convention of 1787 would significantly affect the nation's "opinion of the magnitude of the occasion." Madison was, as always, gracious and respectful, informing Washington that "the ideas by which you ought to be governed will be best decided" by Washington himself, and that Madison and others would respect the general's ultimate decision.

One can only imagine the heartache and genuine grief that James Madison must have felt upon receiving a letter from George Washington dated November 18, 1786 in which the general explained that he had "bid a public adieu to the public walks of life, & had resolved never more to tread that theatre." Furthermore, he informed Madison that even if he wanted to attend the convention in Philadelphia, his "wish for retirement [and] relaxation from public cares, and rheumatic pains which [he began] to feel very sensibly," would prevent him from leaving Mount Vernon. Moreover, he had already informed the Society of the Cincinnati (an organization composed of the officers who were veterans of the War of Independence) that he could not attend their meeting (also to be held in Philadelphia), and he would not want to insult the officers by accepting Madison's invitation while rejecting that of his former fellow soldiers.

James Madison was not one to give in to grief, however. On December 7, 1786 (just weeks before he showed up in person at Mount Vernon on his way to Philadelphia), he wrote again to Washington informing him that "his name could not be spared from the deputation to the meeting in May in Philadelphia" for two reasons: First, "the peculiarity of the mission and its acknowledged pre-eminence over every other public object" should be enough to convince him to attend. Second, "the advantage of having [his] name in the front of the appointment as a mark of the earnestness of Virginia, and an invitation to the most select characters from every part of the Confederacy, ought at all events to be made use of." In other words, Madison let General Washington know that his name had already been published on a list of delegates from Virginia who would be attending the Philadelphia Convention. He then declared that these two reasons should be sufficient to "merit a serious consideration with yourself, whether the difficulties which you enumerate ought not to give way to them." James Madison was small, but he was persistent! And, as we know, his persistence paid off eventually.

Only days before he set out on his journey to Mount Vernon, Madison received another letter from Washington, written

> to excuse my attendance at the meeting on the ground, which is firm & just; the necessity of paying attention to my private concerns; to conformity to my determination of passing the remainder of my days in a state of retirement—and to indisposition; occasioned by Rheumatick complaints with which, at times, I am a good deal afflicted.

Again, Madison wouldn't take no for an answer. On December 24, 1786, he wrote another letter to Washington, professing once again how, without his presence, the Convention wouldn't have the impact that it could and that the fate of the union itself depended on Washington's personal, physical participation at the meeting. Madison predicted that should Washington refuse to attend, "gathering clouds [would] become so dark and menacing" that "our national existence or safety" would be threatened.

Both James Madison and Edmund Randolph tried to convince George Washington to attend the Constitutional Convention.

Madison wasn't the only person trying his hardest to persuade Washington to attend the Constitutional Convention. Edmund Randolph, the governor of Virginia, was writing to Washington, too, and for the same purpose. Finally, on March 28, 1787, Washington sent a letter to Governor Randolph announcing that he would accept his appointment to be a delegate to the convention in Philadelphia, citing as his reason for his change of mind "friends, [who] with a degree of sollicitude which is unusual, seem to wish for my attendance on this occasion."

It is beyond dispute that James Madison was one of those "friends" who pleaded with George Washington to attend the Convention of 1787. It is equally inarguable that had Madison simply stopped imploring Washington in November 1786, after being informed by the general that he would not be present at the convention,

Washington may never have acquiesced to attend. There is no way to estimate, then, the value to our nation's history and the concept of constitutional, republican self-government of James Madison's persistence and his commitment to the cause of American liberty. This tenacity is evident in his many letters to George Washington, letters that humbly and honestly communicated to the general his "indispensable" role in retaining the union of the states and in the crafting of a Constitution strong enough and sound enough to achieve that noble goal.

Preparing and Pondering

Madison stayed just one night at Mount Vernon before resuming his journey to Philadelphia. He stayed in Philadelphia long enough to secure housing to be used while attending the convention that would begin in a couple of months. He then continued on to New York, where he was occupied with the debates in Congress until the convening of the meeting in Philadelphia.

True to form and rather than simply waiting for the convention to start, Madison used his time in New York wisely. He became known as the "Father of the Constitution" because, rather than just showing up at the convention prepared to listen to what others had to say, Madison came with a plan for government that would set the agenda for the convention, setting up the launching pad from which the new constitution and the new federal government would be set in motion.

During his stay in New York in the spring of 1787, James re-read the essay by David Hume called "On the Idea of the Perfect Commonwealth." Such treatises were very influential on the men who would craft the Constitution of 1787. Other modern European and English writers such as James Harrington and John Milton, as well as ancient authors such as Cicero and Plato, had drawn up detailed blueprints for the perfect republic. All warned of the dangers of democracy.

For his part, Plato asks, speaking of democracy, "Is it not the excess and greed of this and the neglect of all other things that revolutionizes this constitution too and prepares the way for the necessity of a dictatorship?"

Cicero, striking a similar note, warns, "No tempest or conflagration, however great, is harder to quell than mob carried away by the novelty of power."

These admonitions served the American statesmen well as they prepared their minds for the difficult and draining days that would precede the Constitution's approval by the delegates of the Convention.

Hume, along with Montesquieu and almost all other political theorists, believed that republics were only possible when confined to small areas. Representation, true representation, was not possible over a vast continental land mass. Madison would digest this discussion, synthesize it, and create an entirely new take on the topic in the days following the Constitutional Convention. For now, however, he was simply soaking up all the accumulated wisdom of the leading lights of statecraft.

Madison reported that during his scholastic sojourn in New York in the spring of 1787, he began to "revolve the subject" of how to construct a central authority for the union that would at once promote and protect liberty and ameliorate the sectionalism that was liable to tear it apart. As usual, he did not just read and ponder the problem, he took detailed notes of his mental exertions and his discoveries in the documents he studied. Madison called the result of this recording of observations and impressions the "Vices of the Political System of the United States." These notes, along with letters written to Thomas Jefferson, Edmund Randolph, and George Washington during this period, contain what one biographer called "the first shoot in his [Madison's] thoughts of a plan of federal government." In fact, these letters, along with his memorandum on the vices present in the political order of the several states, form the basis of what would be distilled very soon thereafter into the Virginia Plan, which Randolph would lay before the delegates in Philadelphia that May.

Although similar in many ways to his "Notes on Ancient and Modern Confederacies," "Vices" was distinct in one signal way: it seemed to be the product of a more settled and determined mind. Whereas "Notes" reads like the unedited notes of a man in a hurry,

"Vices" is well-crafted, well-written, and packed in a way that evinces a more deliberate and specifically tailored approach.

While Madison certainly concluded that the Confederation Congress was unable to compel states to comply with requisitions for funds necessary to finance the effective running of the government of the confederacy, it was the "deficiencies and derelictions" of the state governments that Madison considered the most debilitating defect in the American confederacy. "The evils issuing from these sources," he told Jefferson, "contributed more to that uneasiness which produced the Convention, and prepared the public mind for a general reform, than those which accrued to our national character and interest from the inadequacy of the Confederation to its immediate objects."

His mind was filled with the thought that a new constitution could prevent tyrannies of majorities from denying individuals their basic rights while at the same time provide ample opportunities for the rights of the majority to have appropriate sway in the states, as well as for his concept of a new, constitutionally limited central authority.

It was in the section of "Vices" called "Injustice of the laws of States" where Madison gave full-throated support for his idea that it is "the fundamental principle of republican government, that the majority who rule in such governments, are the safest guardians both of public good and of private rights." And it was this pronouncement that led Madison to conclude that in order to prevent "combinations" from forming among citizens united by "a common interest or passion," a republic would function best if it was spread far and wide, making it nearly impossible for any faction to gain control of the helm of the ship of state. In a large geographical area, there would be so many groups and interests challenging each other, checking each other's growth, that the republic would not only remain free, but would also be free to harness the power of the majority without giving it enough rein to run over the rights and privileges of the minority. This theory would be repeated in *Federalist* No. 10, Madison's first contribution to that seminal set of letters supporting the ratification by the states of the Constitution crafted in Philadelphia over the long, hot summer of 1787.

Creating the United States of America

Madison, a man whose life was lived as a model of personal integrity and virtue, was now intellectually equipped with the fruit of decades and decades of rigorous review and purposeful pondering of the lessons provided by the history of the ancient republics of Greece and Rome, as well as the contemporary confederacies in Europe. Now, he would see his theories thrashed out in public, outside of the safety of his study. On May 2, 1787, Madison left New York City, leaving the work of Congress to those who would not be serving their states at the convention. Exactly three days later, he arrived in Philadelphia, ready and raring to get to the task of establishing a new form of government, one that would permanently bind his beloved American union.

Madison arrived promptly on the date set by Congress for the beginning of the convention. Although there were more than 50 other men expected to show up on that same day, he was the first of all the state delegates to arrive at the appointed time in the appointed place, once again demonstrating his desire to be a leader and an opinion-molder. He was anxious to get down to the business of reforming the government of the United States and felt dispirited by the delay of his fellow delegates' arrival. He worried this could be a sign that the others were not taking the task as seriously as he was.

His fellow Virginians soon arrived in Philadelphia, and the men met together informally to discuss strategy before the convention was officially gaveled to order. The Virginians gathered at an inn near the Philadelphia State House, where the convention was to be held, and discussed details of a plan of government that was the product of the pen and the mind of James Madison. Madison's years of intense investigation of historical and contemporary confederacies would now—finally—be put to practical use. He was eager to share the plan with his fellow representatives of the state of Virginia.

No Wasted Time: Madison Dines With Benjamin Franklin and Other "Principal People"

While waiting for the other states' representatives to arrive in Philadelphia, Madison and the Virginia delegates met regularly at

Chapter Five: Reforming a Free Nation

General George Washington refused the offer to present the Virginia Plan, instead appointing Governor Edmund Randolph to do so.

the home of Benjamin Franklin, beginning on May 16, 1787. In a letter to a friend in France, Franklin reports that "some of the principal people from the several states" dined with him, drinking porter (a dark-brown ale) that "met with the most cordial reception and universal approbation."

The dinners weren't just an excuse to socialize with the great Benjamin Franklin. These like-minded men met to discuss and improve the plan James Madison brought with him to the convention. These working suppers were attended by men whose contributions and constructive criticism would be of invaluable aid to Madison and the cause of constitutional government once the deliberations got underway. While sitting and sipping at Franklin's home, these learned leaders would game-plan, preparing for every possible problem that could crop up and block the road to reform. These sessions would serve the gathered representatives as opportunities to set a sort of schedule for introducing and explaining the Virginia Plan.

Almost immediately upon beginning their conferences, the Virginians unanimously selected General George Washington as their leader. Aside from Franklin, Washington was the most famous man to attend the august confab. Naturally, then, his colleagues felt he was the best man to lead their state in deliberations on the proposed constitution. As leader, it was suggested that General Washington should be the man to present Madison's plan (known to history as the Virginia Plan) to their fellow convention delegates. Washington, with his typical habit of humility, demurred, preferring, he said, that the proposal be presented by the much younger Edmund Randolph, the governor of Virginia. The other men agreed to accept Washington's refusal, and designated Governor Randolph as the man to be the voice of the Virginia Plan when the convention began.

At 36 years old, Madison was by far the youngest of the Virginian delegates, but any one of them would have declared him to be the "intellectual leader of the gathering." Alongside Madison, Washington, and Randolph, two other illustrious Virginians were members of this extraordinary ensemble. George Mason, the oldest of the group, was an accomplished statesman and lawgiver. He was the principal author of the Virginia Declaration of Rights and the Virginia Constitution. A third man named George—George Wythe—was, at 61, one of only six delegates at the convention older than 60. Wythe was the young union's first formal law professor, and counted Thomas Jefferson among his pupils. Wythe was such an influential teacher of students who themselves became influential that he was dubbed "The Teacher of Liberty" and the "American Socrates."

Madison was happy to have Edmund Randolph introduce the Virginia Plan at the convention—if the convention would ever get started! With his frustration reaching a boiling point, Madison was relieved when the requisite number of delegates arrived—a full three weeks after he did. Much to his delight, the other delegates began trickling in from the 12 states (Rhode Island chose not to send delegates to the Constitutional Convention). Although the

Chapter Five: Reforming a Free Nation

Frederick Juengling and Alfred Kappes, Public domain, via Wikimedia Commons

Virginians and Pennsylvanians were present on May 14—the day the convention was scheduled to begin—by May 25, the necessary number of representatives to constitute a quorum had joined their colleagues, and the business of reforming the government of the United States could begin in earnest.

Over the next four months, 55 men would come and go. These respected representatives counted among their number Benjamin Franklin, who at age 81 was the Nestor of the convention, but, despite his global celebrity, rarely participated vocally in the debates that crafted the Constitution. That isn't to say the good doctor wasn't influential, however, as his mere presence was enough to attract attention to his every word. His fame was enough to attach a gravitas to his opinions and observations that was not achievable by most of the younger delegates.

In contrast to Franklin's occasional contributions to the deliberations, James Madison delivered dozens of speeches on scores of subjects. In fact, there was not a single major point of contention upon which he did not discourse, and he was one of the few attendees whose speeches dominated the deliberations. In sum, James Madison spoke over 500 times at the convention. Only James Wilson and Gouverneur Morris were more actively engaged in the debates. No one exceeded Madison's scholarship in every area of import in the field of drafting a document that would be designed to create and control a central authority, however. In a letter describing his good friend's powerful intellect, Thomas Jefferson said that Madison always had "at ready command the rich resources of his luminous and discriminating mind."

A True Leader Among Men

The importance of Madison's contributions to the convention can be neither quantified nor overestimated. There is no exaggeration in the claim that without James Madison's presence, the meeting in which the Constitution was crafted would have produced a very different document, one much less capable of surviving the series of assaults it has suffered since its ratification. In other words, beyond the quantity of his contributions, Madison's ideas were respected for their quality. Each time he spoke, he peppered his participation with examples from history—ancient and modern—and with a depth of insight that derived from his diligent inquiry into the art and science of statecraft. His colleagues, whether they agreed with his position or stood firmly opposed to the young Virginian, learned to expect sober and sincere speeches and grew to respect the man whose personal preparation merited their attention and admiration, if not their deference. So substantial were Madison's speeches and suggestions that John Kaminski, a renowned scholar of the Constitutional Convention, described him as "one of the most important participants in the debates."

"First of Every Assembly":
James Madison and Preparing for Leadership

What set Madison apart from most of the other convention delegates was what set him apart from his peers on almost every other occasion: his preparation. Rather than arriving in Philadelphia with the plan of listening to what the other delegates would say or suggest, he entered the now-historic room at the Pennsylvania State House prepared to present his own proposals, ready to set the agenda rather than to follow it.

This is one of the many lessons historians and students have taken from the life of James Madison. His life and legacy demonstrate that just showing up is not the behavior of a leader; he teaches us that true leaders spend time before all events—important and ordinary—preparing to play a leading role. Leaders are not content to lie back,

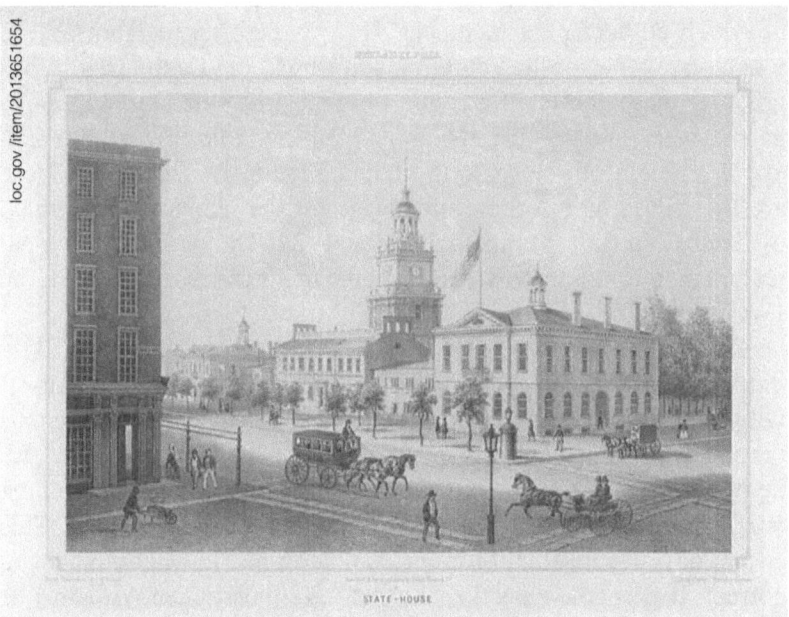

James Madison, along with many other influential men, stood in the Philadelphia State House for countless hours to create a new constitution for the United States.

allowing history to wash over them. Leaders want to wade into that mighty stream and work fearlessly and tirelessly to divert it into channels they have chosen. A leader like Madison studies the issues to be discussed well in advance.

Next, a leader in the mold of Madison doesn't just read material in preparation for his participation; he takes copious and insightful notes on everything he reads so that the lessons learned from his reading might be more readily applied to the problems facing him and his cohorts. And beyond just reading relevant material and taking notes on the contents, he takes time to ponder the content of his study, applying his mind to the task of synthesizing the material until he is conversant in and comfortable with the full spectrum of the associated issues. He can then be confident in his ability to convert these profound points from the theoretical to the practical.

According to Thomas Jefferson, Madison's diligent preparation and "extensive information rendered him the first of every assembly of which he became a member." He was perhaps the shortest, he was certainly one of the youngest, and he was physically fragile, but ignoring these shortcomings and obstacles, he stood strong, spoke persuasively, and applied his ample learning to finding solutions to every problem presented to the convention at Philadelphia. These are the habits of a leader, and these are the habits demonstrated by James Madison in Philadelphia in 1787. They are the principal justification for his endowment with the honorific title "Father of the Constitution."

Throughout the tortuously hot days of the convention, not only did Madison speak on every important issue, but he occupied himself with taking detailed notes on the debates, delegates, and decisions that made history that summer. In order to keep an accurate record, he wrote, he "took a seat in front of the presiding member [George Washington] with other members on [his] right and left hands." This endeavor proved difficult for one so determined to be complete and correct. It was so exhausting, in fact, that biographer William Lee Miller writes that the effort "almost killed" Madison.

In spite of these difficulties and his own fragile health, James Madison was never absent from the convention, showing up every day the meeting was in session and compiling the detailed notes he pledged to write. So committed was he to putting forth his best effort in recording the speeches and votes at the convention that he reports having missed at most "a casual fraction of an hour" of the deliberations. He managed to record every speech delivered by delegates, with the exception of a very few brief ones.

Why, given the amount of extra work it cost him and the extra strain it put on his weak physical constitution, did James Madison shoulder the responsibility of recording the points of every debate and the events of every day at the convention?

Writing sometime between 1830 and 1836, Madison explained his motivation and purpose in preparing his now-famous journal of the Constitutional Convention of 1787:

> The curiosity I had felt during my researches into the history of the most distinguished confederacies, particularly those of antiquity, and the deficiency I found in the means of satisfying it more especially in what related to the process, the principles, reasons, and the anticipations, which prevailed in the formation of them, determined me to preserve as far as I could an exact account of what might pass in the Convention (*Notes of Debates in the Federal Convention*).

In his book chronicling Madison's contributions to the Constitutional Convention of 1787, Miller elaborated on why Madison considered his notes on the convention so crucial:

> Why did he do it? To repeat: because when he started examining those confederacies back in 1786 he had wished they had kept detailed records of their process, principles, reasons and anticipations. So—for the next James Madison—the James Madison of tomorrow—there would be a record. He was ill after August 23 and his notes fell off in quantity and he made some errors, but he kept at it. It was a remarkable performance. In the education of an American one hears about it, but rather takes it for

granted. Madison took notes. (So, in much, much smaller ways, did eight other delegates.) What we know, we know mostly from James Madison.

Here again, the reader is right to admire James Madison. He was very ill, but rather than seeking the sympathy of his colleagues for his maladies or using his sickness as an excuse to stop working, he carried on, committed to compiling a record that would provide some future statesman with the raw data, the daily rundown of the inner workings of a constitutional convention that would give that person a leg up on the lawmaking, an advantage Madison did not have.

Although record keeping was a vital part of Madison's participation at the Constitutional Convention, it was not his primary contribution. He was there as the drafter of the Virginia Plan and as a man convinced that his country needed a stronger central government if the union was to be preserved. Thus, as the days, weeks, and months wore on, the articles of that plan became the primary points of debate among the representatives.

It was not, however, the only plan offered for the convention's consideration. Delegates from the small states feared that Madison's Virginia Plan granted too much influence in the proposed central government to large states like Virginia. Specifically, small state delegates averred that the provision of the Virginia Plan that apportioned representation in the proposed legislative branch according to population would give substantial—even unstoppable—sway to the states with greater numbers of inhabitants.

Fearful of the prospect of being consigned to a second-class category of membership in the new central government, New Jersey delegate William Paterson, offered a competing plan of government, one that preserved the equality of states that existed under the constitution then in effect: the Articles of Confederation. Despite Paterson's persuasive introduction of his proposal, known as the New Jersey plan, it was quickly rejected by the convention. Members resumed consideration of an expanded version of Madison's proposal that was put forward by a committee tasked with drafting a compromise version of the Virginia Plan.

Chapter Five: Reforming a Free Nation

In fear of a new government, William Paterson proposed the New Jersey plan, which remained true to the Articles of Confederation.

The very quick and nearly complete rejection of the New Jersey plan was due primarily to the power of James Madison to take his learning and insight and use them to shine a light on subjects that others found too dim to understand. The speech he delivered on June 19, 1787, made in response to Paterson's passionate presentation of his proposal, is worth reading for its succinct and scholarly description of Madison's view of the proper role of a constitution and the proper relationship between a central government and the state legislatures.

Although Madison himself delivered the speech, he entered it in his notes on the convention as if he were recording the words of a third party. This address is one of the most famous discourses by the Father of the Constitution, delivered at the convention where he began earning that moniker:

Much stress had been laid by some gentlemen on the want of power in the Convention to propose any other than a federal plan. To what had been answered by others, he would only add, that neither of the characteristics attached to a federal plan would support this objection. One characteristic was that in a federal Government, the power was exercised not on the people individually; but on the people collectively, on the States. Yet in some instances as in piracies, captures &c. the existing Confederacy, and in many instances, the amendments to it proposed by Mr. Patterson [Madison misspelled Paterson's name throughout], must operate immediately on individuals. The other characteristic was that a federal Govt. derived its appointments not immediately from the people, but from the States which they respectively composed.

Here too were facts on the other side. In two of the States, Connect. and Rh. Island, the delegates to Cong[res]s. were chosen, not by the Legislatures, but by the people at large; and the plan of Mr. P. intended no change in this particular.

It had been alledged (by Mr. Patterson), that the Confederation having been formed by unanimous consent, could be dissolved by unanimous Consent only. Does this doctrine result from the nature of compacts? Does it arise from any particular stipulation in the articles of Confederation? If we consider the federal union as analogous to the fundamental compact by which individuals compose one Society, and which must in its theoretic origin at least, have been the unanimous act of the component members, it cannot be said that no dissolution of the compact can be effected without unanimous consent. A breach of the fundamental principles of the compact by a part of the Society would certainly absolve the other part from their obligations to it. If the breach of any article by any of the parties, does not set the others at liberty, it is because, the contrary is implied in the compact itself, and particularly by that law of it, which gives an indefinite authority to the majority to bind the whole in all cases. This latter circumstance shews that we are not to consider the federal Union as analogous to the social compact of individuals: for if it were so, a Majority would have a right to bind the rest, and even to form a new Constitution for the whole, which the Gent[lema]n: from N. Jersey would be among the last to admit. If we consider the federal Union as analogous not to the social compacts among individual men: but to the conventions among individual States, What is the doctrine resulting from these conventions? Clearly, according to the Expositors of the law of Nations, that a breach of any one article, by any one party, leaves all the other parties at liberty, to consider the whole convention as dissolved, unless they choose rather to compel the delinquent party to repair the breach.

At this point, the convention turned their substantial talents to trying to come to some sort of compromise, some sort of common approach to solving the question of just representation in a congress that they would propose. On July 17, 1787, a majority of the representatives of the states—both small and large—finally and formally agreed on a compromise that would create a Congress that preserved state equality in one branch—the Senate—while allowing the membership of another branch—the House of Representatives—to be determined according to population. This arrangement was the keystone of the convention, and is known to history as the "Great Compromise."

James Madison didn't think the compromise was "great," however. In fact, he felt defeated, and worried that he would not witness the creation of a more robust central authority capable of controlling the centrifugal forces that were flinging the states into separate orbits. Madison was so dismayed by the development that he wrote to a friend describing the compromise as "imperfect and exceptionable."

The states came to an agreement on just representation within Congress by creating a Senate and a House of Representatives. George Washington was an important contributor to this unanimous decision.

James Peale, Public domain, via Wikimedia Commons

While he may have felt he was denied the opportunity to help establish a new constitution—at least one he believed capable of solving the problems he perceived in the Articles of Confederation—he did not leave the convention sulking in defeat (as Alexander Hamilton had after a plan of his was dismissed summarily by his colleagues). No, even in the face of failure—as he saw it—James Madison proved himself a leader worthy of emulation and celebration.

That there would be something to celebrate is thanks in large part to the influence and presence of George Washington.

On the final day of the convention, the delegates opposed to the Constitution launched their last-minute plan to prevent the document from being unanimously approved by the representatives from the 12 states that sent delegates to Philadelphia that summer—using as their reason the always controversial topic of the appropriate ratio of representation in the House of Representatives.

After listening to the clash between those in favor of the previously agreed-upon apportionment and those who refused to give up the fight for a revised apportionment, Washington waded into the current of controversy, something he was reluctant to do during most of the nearly four months of the Constitutional Convention.

Madison described the event in his *Notes of Debates in the Federal Convention of 1787*:

> When the PRESIDENT [Washington] rose, for the purpose of putting the question, he said that although his situation had hitherto restrained him from offering his sentiments on questions depending in the House, and it might be thought, ought now to impose silence on him, yet he could not forbear expressing his wish that the alteration proposed might take place. It was much to be desired that the objections to the plan recommended might be made as few as possible. The smallness of the proportion of Representatives had been considered by many members of the Convention an insufficient security for the rights & interests of the people. He acknowledged that it had always appeared to himself among the exceptionable parts of the plan, and late as the present moment was for admitting amendments, he thought this of so much consequence that it would give much satisfaction to see it adopted.

In *Miracle at Philadelphia*, historian Catherine Drinker Bowen recorded the effect of Washington's comments: "The General's plea, the General's influence were irresistible. Unanimously, the states agreed."

Chapter 6:
"Miracle" at Philadelphia

Upon arriving at the convention, James Madison had three goals: first, to grant to the central government greater authority than it possessed under the Articles of Confederation; second, to create a bicameral general legislature that would be comprised of representatives of the states apportioned according to population; and, third, to empower the central government to compel states to comply with mandates of the confederated congress.

It is beyond argument that only the first of these goals was completely accomplished at the Convention of 1787. Madison helped shepherd a more capable central government into existence, despite vigorous opposition to a stronger central authority maintained throughout the convention by many of his fellow delegates. Eventually, even the most ardent advocates of absolute state sovereignty came to concede the commendability of a more energetic central authority. This was in no small part the result of Madison's preparation, erudition, and determination.

The futility of forming a coalition sufficient to see his second and third goals brought to fruition did not prevent Madison from continuing to contribute to the articles found in the final version of the Constitution. He was determined not to allow defeat to deter him from working tirelessly to apply his understanding to whatever document he and his colleagues would eventually present to their countrymen. In the final weeks of the convention, Madison aimed his ample faculties at establishing a federal government of three branches that would check and balance each other and be endowed with separate powers, powers that would be walled off from those of the other branches so as to prevent the accumulation of all power into the hands of one or many tyrants.

Organizing a Just Government

On July 21, 1787, Madison rose to discourse on the wisdom of a government comprised of three branches, each of which would be able to check advances toward tyranny in any of the other two. "Experience in all the states had evinced a powerful tendency in the legislature to absorb all power into its vortex," he declared. He then explained that "This was the real source of danger to the American constitutions," and "suggested the necessity of giving every defensive authority to the other departments that was consistent with republican principles."

Here, then, in his advocacy of separated powers that could control excesses in the attempted aggrandizement of the others, Madison put his disappointments behind him and turned his talents and attention to plotting a course that would allow him to arrive at the same destination by another route. In this he was successful.

Having secured this separated and balanced government, Madison teamed up with his frequent ally, James Wilson of Pennsylvania, to design an executive authority with enough power to urge compliance with federal laws by the often recalcitrant states. What would this new executive look like? Would there be a king? Of course not. Americans were only recently rid of the abuses heaped upon them by a monarch who disregarded the consent of the people and any limits on his and Parliament's power.

On this question the delegates at the convention considered many proposals. There were those representatives who pushed for an executive council composed of several members. Others called for an executive of two members, patterned after the consuls of ancient Rome. Unbelievably, there were a few delegates who recommended an executive authority with 30 members!

Originally, Madison (in the Virginia Plan) wanted a federal executive that would be counseled (and checked) by a "revisionary council," a group of advisors "with authority to examine every act of the National Legislature before it shall operate." This was not the choice of the convention's attendees, but Madison's familiarity with the dangers of a powerful executive and the despotism that seemed so often to beset it helped draw historically sound boundaries around any authority that would ultimately be granted to an American executive.

Chapter Six: "Miracle" at Philadelphia

James Wilson joined James Madison to find a healthy balance of governments.

Finally, delegates decided that they preferred a single president. They reckoned that an executive branch composed of a president and several others would prevent the president from possessing the agility he would need as a commander-in-chief. Also, with just one man occupying the office of executive, the states and the people would know precisely whom to hold accountable for any autocratic tendencies of the office.

After determining there would be a single man possessed of the power of the executive, the convention turned to another thorny question: How long should he remain in power? Alexander Hamilton had suggested a president for life. This, nearly all the delegates agreed, would amount to nothing less than an American king, and that would never do. Among the many suggestions for an appropriate term of office for the president were one year (borrowed from the constitution of ancient Rome's single-year term of office for a consul), two years, four years, and as many as 10 years. The arguments for shorter terms were based on the settled opinion that short terms of office were the best means of protecting the people from the tyrannical tendencies of men granted even a modicum of political power.

There were, however, those representatives who, remembering the impotency of the Confederation Congress, which they believed was caused in substantial part by the frequent turnover of members, suggested longer terms as a remedy for that lingering malady. In the end, however, delegates chose to compromise on the executive's term of office, settling on four years as being long enough to lend a sufficient level of stability to the position, yet short enough to thwart the effort of any would-be dictator from consolidating the power necessary to accomplish his evil ends.

Around August 31st, a committee composed of 11 members—one from each state present at the convention on that date—began clearing up any confusion that remained in different parts of the proposed Constitution. James Madison was the representative from Virginia appointed to this committee and helped define the shape of the presidency as it would appear in the approved version of the Constitution.

It was while serving on this committee that Madison pushed through a proposal offered much earlier in the summer by James Wilson, a proposal placing the responsibility for choosing the president on a body of electors selected from among the people. Madison predicted that this organization of electors (today called the "Electoral College") would be the best method for choosing a president; he believed that it would result in a president of remarkable virtue and qualification. The deliberations of this select body of men would be free from "cabal or corruption," and thus their choice of chief executive would likewise be a man of highest personal integrity, not beholden to any particular party or person. Finally, Madison argued that by filtering the election of the president through a body of electors chosen from among the several states, the president would be a man in whom "local considerations would give way to the general." Here he saw the opportunity of strengthening the bond connecting the states in the union by placing a person above the petty pull of sectional bias.

Notably, during the deliberations of this committee—called very inelegantly the "Committee of Unfinished Parts"—Madison proposed a change in the language of the then-working copy of the Constitution to permanently place the power of "declaring war" within the sphere of congressional authority. He argued that a question as significant as whether to embroil the states in a war was best decided by the representatives of the people, rather than by one man, even a man as virtuous as the president was presumed to always be. "The executive," Madison explained, should have "power to repel sudden attacks," but not to declare war. In other words, the president should be able to "repel but not to commence war," as summarized by Roger Sherman of Connecticut.

On September 17, 1787, after nearly four months of often heated contention among the representatives of the 12 states that participated in this "plenipotentiary convention," James Madison recorded in his notes that, "on the question to agree to the Constitution enrolled in order to be signed, it was agreed to, all the states answering ay." With that, one by one, the delegates came forward and signed their names to the historic document that they had drafted together.

In a letter to Thomas Jefferson, Madison made it clear that he appreciated the historical significance of the business just concluded in Philadelphia. "[T]here can be no doubt," Madison wrote, "but that the result [of the convention] will in some way or other have a powerful effect on our destiny."

Once again, Madison's prediction was prescient. It is beyond dispute that the Constitution of the United States of America that was produced in Philadelphia in 1787 would have been very different had James Madison not arrived at that august meeting prepared to craft. This Constitution, by compromise and conviction, was capable of preventing the states—often jealous of each other—from separating into smaller confederacies and enabling them to remain moored together in a union strong enough to survive invasion from abroad and dissension and disagreement at home.

As described above, the two most important figures at the convention—men without whom the Constitution likely would never have been completed—were James Madison and George Washington.

Of the two, the first in preeminence was George Washington. Without a doubt, Washington was the man who, more than any other, when the situation looked dire and it seemed the convention would break up before coming to any worthwhile conclusion, tipped the balance in favor of compromising and constructing the Constitution drafted that summer in Philadelphia.

Following General Washington in degree of influence at the Constitutional Convention was James Madison. As noted above, he prepared tirelessly for months before the convention got underway so as to ensure that the product of that meeting would be—as much as humanly possible—permanent and protective of property and personal liberty and, in general, free from the defects that doomed former free societies. Madison's records of the debates of the convention are an invaluable resource to those committed to coming to a correct understanding of our governing charter.

Accordingly, then, the testimony of these two titans will serve as a summation of how they believed that that historic convention, held over four months in the summer of 1787, was able to inexplicably progress from rancorous to remarkable.

In a letter to the Marquis de Lafayette written on February 7, 1788, General Washington informs his friend and fellow soldier, "It appears to me, then, little short of a miracle, that the delegates from so many different states (which states you know are also different from each other in their manners, circumstances, and prejudices) should unite in forming a system of national government, so little liable to well founded objections."

For his part, in a letter to his best friend, Thomas Jefferson, written just over a month after the convention approved the Constitution, James Madison echoes Washington's assessment of the real reason the Constitution survived the many conflicts at the convention. "The whole of them together formed a task more difficult than can be well conceived by those who were not

The Constitution of the United States was finalized and signed September 17, 1787.

concerned in the execution of it," Madison declares. "Adding to these considerations the natural diversity of human opinions on all new and complicated subjects, it is impossible to consider the degree of concord which ultimately prevailed as less than a miracle," he concludes.

The Fight for Ratification: Madison Becomes "Publius"

Even then, with the Constitution he helped create unanimously approved by all the states present (Rhode Island never participated in the convention, and New York could not officially vote because of the rule requiring a majority of its delegates be present), James Madison didn't stop working to secure the adoption of this document by three-fourths of the states, as required by Article VII of the Constitution. He realized that, given the weight of the names on the roster of those opposed to adopting the Constitution, the real fight to see that document become the law was just beginning! He knew that, if he were to be successful in seeing this Constitution ratified, he would have to employ his extraordinary talents for writing and clear thinking to the task. His only question was, what would be the best means of accomplishing this worthwhile goal?

Chapter 7:

James Madison's Contributions to the Battle for Ratification: *The Federalist*

Between the approval of the Constitution by the delegates at the convention on September 17, 1787 and its ratification by the requisite number of states on June 21, 1788, James Madison joined with Alexander Hamilton and John Jay in writing a series of letters to the editor aimed at convincing the representatives at the New York state ratification convention to approve the new Constitution. These letters were soon collected and published in book form and given the title *The Federalist* (also compiled as *The Federalist Papers*).

When the letters were first printed in New York newspapers, they were signed in the name of a "Citizen of New York." They were soon reprinted in newspapers throughout the 13 states, though, and the authors adopted the pseudonym "Publius." Hamilton chose the pen name from the history of ancient Rome. Plutarch praised Publius for his help in overthrowing the tyranny of the Tarquins and establishing the self-government of Rome for which it became renowned. In his foreword to *The Federalist Papers*, historian Charles R. Kesler explains why Hamilton chose this name from among all the notables of ancient Rome and Greece, and points out the particularly American purpose of the pen name: "He [Alexander Hamilton] chose 'Publius' as the pseudonym, trumping his adversaries' invocation of heroes of the late Roman republic (Brutus

From Last Rites to Bill of Rights: The Miraculous Life and Legacy of James Madison

Alexander Hamilton chose the alias "Publius" when writing *The Federalist Papers*.

and Cato) with a reference to one of the founders and saviors of republican Rome: Publius Valerius Publicola...." Kesler goes on to relate how Publius "firmly established his republic, which endured and expanded for centuries."

It is obvious why Hamilton and Madison would consider Publius an appropriate pseudonym for their papers, as both men wanted to see the American union grow into "an empire in many respects the most interesting in the world" (*Federalist* No. 1). Or, as Madison predicted, "the people of America, knit together as they are by so many cords of affection," could become "fellow citizens of one great, respectable, and flourishing empire" if they could avoid falling into the "gloomy and perilous scene into which the advocates for disunion" were trying to push them.

What would two Americans want their countrymen—many of whom would have been taught the story of Publius in their earliest childhood lessons—to know about their thesis in light of their chosen alias? Kesler suggests an answer: "[Madison] wished to seize a fleeting moment favorable to constitution-making—when the wise and moderate men of the Federal Convention would have their greatest influence—in order to form a just and enduring republic in an extensive land."

Madison genuinely believed that by presenting to the people of America the historical and rational reasons for approving the Constitution he helped craft, he could convince them to do just that, and to unite into a perpetual and powerful republic that would extend across a continent and over many centuries.

The Purpose of Government and John Locke

While it is still unclear when James Madison agreed to participate with Alexander Hamilton in the penning of *The Federalist*, it is certain that without Madison's contribution, the collection would have been much less erudite and much less likely to persuade the people that this new constitution was strong enough to preserve their liberties and well-crafted enough to prevent one or more would-be tyrants from accumulating absolute power.

To this end, then, Madison took up his pen and poured his passion and his intellect onto the pages of *The Federalist*. Of his twenty-nine letters, three have become the most often-cited and often-praised. These are *Federalist* Nos. 10, 14, and 51.

These famous letters will be examined in greater detail below, but, as an outline, in *Federalist* No. 10, Madison lays out his argument in favor of the viability of a large, commercial republic. He proposes that faction would check faction and that in a country as large as the United States, it will be impossible for one faction to gain control of the machine of government. In *Federalist* No. 14, he follows upon his discussion from No. 10, proclaiming not only that republicanism can survive over a territory as vast as the United States, but that the Constitution framed in Philadelphia is perfectly suited toward promoting and protecting that capacity. And in *Federalist* No. 51, he laments that, although government is necessary because men are not angels, that does not mean that the form of the government cannot be constructed in a manner most favorable to self-rule. The best way to achieve this noble end is to separate political power and to position each branch as a foil to the inevitable centralizing tendencies of men possessed of power over their fellow men.

In *Federalist* No. 10, Madison explains that the differences in the faculties of men are the source of the property rights, and that "the protection of these faculties is the first object of government." He elaborates in *Federalist* No. 54 that "government is instituted no less for protection of the property than of the persons, of individuals." (It is interesting at this point to note that one of the first goals of a socialist or communist regime is to eliminate private ownership of property.)

When one compares this view of the purpose of government with John Locke's, there emerges very strong evidence of Lockean influence upon the philosophy of *The Federalist* at a fundamental and integral level. For comparison, let's examine John Locke's opinion on the purpose of government. In his *Second Treatise of Government*, Locke asserts that once a man has entered into civil society, he is assured protection of "his person, actions, possessions, and his whole property. . . ." The protection that man receives from the government is necessary because, upon entering civil society, that man must relinquish "as much of his natural liberty in providing for himself, as the good, prosperity, and safety of the society shall require. . . ."

Chapter Seven: James Madison's Contributions to the Battle for Ratification: *The Federalist*

42   THE FEDERALIST.

CITIES, or republics, the largest were entitled to *three* votes in the COMMON COUNCIL, those of the middle class to *two*, and the smallest to *one*. The COMMON COUNCIL had the appointment of all the judges and magistrates of the respective CITIES. This was certainly the most delicate species of interference in their internal administration; for if there be any thing that seems exclusively appropriated to the local jurisdictions, it is the appointment of their own officers. Yet Montesquieu, speaking of this association, says, "Were I to give a model of an excellent confederate republic, it would be that of Lycia." Thus we perceive, that the distinctions insisted upon were not within the contemplation of this enlightened writer; and we shall be led to conclude, that they are the novel refinements of an erroneous theory. PUBLIUS.

NUMBER X.

BY JAMES MADISON.

THE SAME SUBJECT CONTINUED.

AMONG the numerous advantages promised by a well constructed union, none deserves to be more accurately developed than its tendency to break and control the violence of faction. The friend of popular governments, never finds himself so much alarmed for their character and fate, as when he contemplates their propensity to this dangerous vice. He will not fail, therefore, to set a due value on any plan which, without violating the principles to which he is attached, provides a proper cure for it. The instability, injustice, and confusion, introduced into the public councils, have in truth, been the mortal diseases under which popular governments have every where perished; as they continue to be the favorite and fruitful topics from which the adversaries to liberty derive their most specious declamations. The valuable improvements made by the American constitutions on the popular models, both ancient and modern, cannot certainly be too much admired; but it would be an unwarrantable partiality, to contend that they have as effectually obviated the danger on this side, as was wished and expected. Complaints are every where heard from our most considerate and virtuous citizens, equally the friends of public and private faith, and of public and personal liberty, that our governments are too unstable; that the public good is disregarded in the conflicts of rival parties; and that measures are too often decided, not according to the rules of justice, and the rights of the minor party, but by the superior force of an interested and overbearing majority. However anxiously we may wish that these complaints had no

Federalist No. 10 expresses the importance of the government's responsibility to protect the property of its citizens.

In another section of the *Second Treatise of Government*, Locke reaffirms his belief that "in governments, the laws regulate the right of property, and the possession of lands is determined by positive constitutions. . . ." It seems apparent that in forming a government, men unite for the defense of their property with that of another or many others, and place all under obligation to a constitution. It could be inferred, then, that it is government's first obligation to protect and preserve property and the right to ownership and control of that property.

Madison Recognizes a Faulty System

Although John Locke's defense of the right of property as essential to liberty informed Madison's own writing on the subject in *Federalist* No. 10, the intent of that letter is not just to portray property in its appropriate light as the *sine qua non* of individual and institutional liberty. Rather, Madison aims to convince readers conversant with Montesquieu's maxim that republics only function when confined to small territories that republicanism in fact can be extended over large (even continental) land masses without sacrificing the virtues of a republic, the most desirable form of government.

Although published on November 29, 1787, Madison's description of the political climate in that now-distant day sounds substantially familiar to those of us living in the 21st century:

> Complaints are everywhere heard from our most considerate and virtuous citizens, equally the friends of public and private faith and of public and personal liberty, that our governments are too unstable, that the public good is disregarded in the conflicts of rival parties, and that measures are too often decided not according to the rules of justice and the rights of the minor party, but by the superior force of an interested and overbearing majority.

What does Madison prescribe as the cure for the "might makes right" malady? The Constitution, of course! First, he reveals that the real danger to good government and peaceful populations is the preeminence of factions that try to accumulate absolute power for the purpose of furthering their own agendas and aggrandizing their members. "By faction, I understand a number of citizens, whether amounting to a majority or a minority of the whole, who are united and actuated by some common impulse of passion, or of interest, adverse to the rights of other citizens, or to the permanent and aggregate interests of the community," he declared.

How can we hope to control the selfish subterfuge of factions without simultaneously smothering the flame of liberty? By preventing their formation? No! To prevent the formation of factions would deny liberty to certain men. The solution is not to prohibit factions from forming but to pit them against one another. As Madison asks and answers, "Does [the ability to control factions] consist in the greater security afforded by a greater variety of parties, against the event of any one party being able to outnumber and oppress the rest? In an equal degree does the increased variety of parties comprised within the Union, increase this security."

Next, Madison suggests that by spreading the government over a large area, many of these competing factions would be brought within the boundaries of the country, thus diluting their potential influence and protecting the people from the factions' otherwise tyrannical intent. He asserts that this is the genius of the extended republic, and the management of such a mechanism is the core of the Constitution of 1787.

Here is Madison's clear and, to many, convincing explanation of the faction-phobic quality of a large republic:

> [A] greater number of citizens and extent of territory ... may be brought within the compass of republican than of democratic government; and it is this circumstance principally which renders factious combinations less to be dreaded in the former than in the latter. The smaller the society, the fewer probably will be the distinct parties and interests composing it; the fewer the distinct parties and interests, the more frequently will a majority be found of the same party; and the smaller the number of individuals composing a majority, and the smaller the compass within which they are placed, the more easily will they concert

and execute their plans of oppression. Extend the sphere, and you take in a greater variety of parties and interests; you make it less probable that a majority of the whole will have a common motive to invade the rights of other citizens; or if such a common motive exists, it will be more difficult for all who feel it to discover their own strength, and to act in unison with each other.

"Hence, it clearly appears, that the same advantage which a republic has over a democracy, in controlling the effects of faction, is enjoyed by a large over a small republic,—is enjoyed by the Union over the States composing it," Madison adds. But controlling the consolidating tendency of factions is not the only benefit of spreading the republican principle across a big area.

In *Federalist* No. 10, he explains how a society comprised of a multiplicity of interests and influences will facilitate the finding of representatives endowed with the virtue and wisdom requisite to running a republican form of government. As Madison sees it:

[A]s each representative will be chosen by a greater number of citizens in the large than in the small republic, it will be more difficult for unworthy candidates to practice with success the vicious arts by which elections are too often carried; and the suffrages of the people being more free, will be more likely to centre in men who possess the most attractive merit and the most diffusive and established characters.

In other words, if Americans want to keep the republican form of government that was found in the several states, if they want to keep one party from seizing control of the government, and if they want their elected representatives to be men of the strongest moral fiber and the greatest endowment of wisdom, then they would want the union to stay together, to grow larger, and to be governed according to the outstanding principles and provisions of the Constitution produced by the "Grand Convention" (*i.e.*, the recent constitutional convention).

Exactly one week after *Federalist* No. 10 was published in the *New-York Packet*—a *Federalist*-friendly newspaper—Madison's next letter appeared in the same paper. This was *Federalist* No. 14, defending the preferability of the extended republic he had presented in the previous letter, *Federalist* No. 10.

Madison opened the missive with advocacy of the American union, a cause dear to the heart of the young Virginian:

> We have seen the necessity of the Union, as our bulwark against foreign danger, as the conservator of peace among ourselves, as the guardian of our commerce and other common interests, as the only substitute for those military establishments which have subverted the liberties of the Old World, and as the proper antidote for the diseases of faction, which have proved fatal to other popular governments, and of which alarming symptoms have been betrayed by our own.

Madison knew from letters and from his associations with leading figures of the day that the process of scheduling ratification conventions was not proceeding in an orderly fashion and that there were some—including Patrick Henry in Virginia—who were determined to delay the process for as long as possible.

His correspondence clued him in that those opposed to the ratification of the proposed Constitution in New Hampshire, Massachusetts, and North Carolina, among others, were clinging to the idea that only small territories are capable of maintaining republican, that is to say, representative, government. Therefore, he used this latest contribution to *The Federalist* as an opportunity to challenge that popular premise. The error, as Madison saw it, was that people were confusing democracies with *republics*, and assumed that the natural limitations of the former are identical in the latter. This is not so, he explained:

> As the natural limit of a democracy is that distance from the central point which will just permit the most remote citizens to assemble as often as their public functions

Madison did well to explain the differences between a republic and a democracy.

demand, and will include no greater number than can join in those functions; so the natural limit of a republic is that distance from the centre which will barely allow the representatives to meet as often as may be necessary for the administration of public affairs. Can it be said that the limits of the United States exceed this distance? It will not be said by those who recollect that the Atlantic coast is the longest side of the Union, that during the term of thirteen years, the representatives of the States have been almost continually assembled, and that the members from the most distant States are not chargeable with greater intermissions of attendance than those from the States in the neighborhood of Congress.

In his impressive manner, he used recent community experience to prove his point: Large territories can be governed well and governed by the people through elected representatives without sacrificing any of the advantages of republicanism.

Next, Madison pressed his point by highlighting the superior structural qualities of the proposed Constitution, which were uniquely designed to retain the federal nature of the existing confederacy. These standards are used as a balance against the powers granted to the general government and as a barrier to the central authority's potential power grabs:

> In the first place it is to be remembered that the general government is not to be charged with the whole power of making and administering laws. Its jurisdiction is limited to certain enumerated objects, which concern all the members of the republic, but which are not to be attained by the separate provisions of any. The subordinate governments, which can extend their care to all those other subjects which can be separately provided for, will retain their due authority and activity. Were it proposed by the plan of the convention to abolish the governments of the particular States, its adversaries would have some ground for their objection; though it would not be difficult to show that if they were abolished the general government would be compelled, by the principle of self-preservation, to reinstate them in their proper jurisdiction.

Finally, Madison concluded this contribution to *The Federalist* by assuring readers of the *New-York Packet* (and the scores of other newspapers that would reprint the letter) that the representatives at the Convention of 1787 did not spend the summer cobbling together a constitution from the remnants of Roman or Greek plans of government. Rather, these wise and experienced statesmen sought to draft a governing document that was truly American, with appropriate aspects of all the good governments of history:

But why is the experiment of an extended republic to be rejected, merely because it may comprise what is new? Is it not the glory of the people of America, that, whilst they have paid a decent regard to the opinions of former times and other nations, they have not suffered a blind veneration for antiquity, for custom, or for names, to overrule the suggestions of their own good sense, the knowledge of their own situation, and the lessons of their own experience? To this manly spirit, posterity will be indebted for the possession, and the world for the example, of the numerous innovations displayed on the American theatre, in favor of private rights and public happiness. Had no important step been taken by the leaders of the Revolution for which a precedent could not be discovered, no government established of which an exact model did not present itself, the people of the United States might, at this moment have been numbered among the melancholy victims of misguided councils, must at best have been laboring under the weight of some of those forms which have crushed the liberties of the rest of mankind. Happily for America, happily, we trust, for the whole human race, they pursued a new and more noble course. They accomplished a revolution which has no parallel in the annals of human society. They reared the fabrics of governments which have no model on the face of the globe. They formed the design of a great Confederacy, which it is incumbent on their successors to improve and perpetuate. If their works betray imperfections, we wonder at the fewness of them. If they erred most in the structure of the Union, this was the work most difficult to be executed; this is the work which has been new modelled by the act of your convention, and it is that act on which you are now to deliberate and to decide.

The Resolution

Federalist No. 51, titled "The Structure of the Government Must Furnish the Proper Checks and Balances Between the Different Departments," is another of Madison's famous and forceful additions to *The Federalist* corpus. In this letter, published on February 6, 1788, he once again points to the checks and balances built in to the structure of the Constitution as an effective method of preventing the accumulation of power by one man or group of men whose authority is derived from the Constitution.

Arguably the most famous article within *The Federalist*, No. 51 describes the utmost importance of checks and balances.

Madison begins by describing the separation of powers among the three branches of the federal government as "essential to the preservation of liberty." The three branches would be dependent on each other for the exercise of their enumerated powers, and this dependence would prevent any of them from consolidating all powers of the general government. This will create a climate where power will check power, or, as he explains it, "Ambition must be made to counteract ambition."

It is at this point that James Madison wrote one of the most famous sentences in American political history. Remarking on how the necessity of pitting one power (or power holder) against another is "the greatest of all reflections on human nature," he then reflected on how government itself is necessary because men are by nature greedy for power and loath to relinquish it without a fight. "If men were angels, no government would be necessary. If angels were to govern men, neither external nor internal controls on government would be necessary," Madison lamented.

Then, he laid out the precise constitutional mechanisms that would serve as "auxiliary precautions," backstops to despotism should the power of the people prove insufficient to restrain would-be tyrants:

> This policy of supplying, by opposite and rival interests, the defect of better motives, might be traced through the whole system of human affairs, private as well as public. We see it particularly displayed in all the subordinate distributions of power, where the constant aim is to divide and arrange the several offices in such a manner as that each may be a check on the other—that the private interest of every individual may be a sentinel over the public rights. These inventions of prudence cannot be less requisite in the distribution of the supreme powers of the State.
>
> But it is not possible to give to each department an equal power of self-defense. In republican government, the legislative authority necessarily predominates. The remedy for this inconveniency is to divide the legislature into different branches; and to render them, by different modes of election and different principles of action, as little connected with

each other as the nature of their common functions and their common dependence on the society will admit. It may even be necessary to guard against dangerous encroachments by still further precautions. As the weight of the legislative authority requires that it should be thus divided, the weakness of the executive may require, on the other hand, that it should be fortified. An absolute negative on the legislature appears, at first view, to be the natural defense with which the executive magistrate should be armed. But perhaps it would be neither altogether safe nor alone sufficient. On ordinary occasions it might not be exerted with the requisite firmness, and on extraordinary occasions it might be perfidiously abused. May not this defect of an absolute negative be supplied by some qualified connection between this weaker department and the weaker branch of the stronger department, by which the latter may be led to support the constitutional rights of the former, without being too much detached from the rights of its own department?

Howard Chandler Christy, Public domain, via Wikimedia Commons

The signing of the U.S. Constitution unified the push for a just federal government.

Finally, as he had explained on so many other occasions, Madison pointed to the federal nature of the American union as the surest and safest protection of liberty. The Constitution drafted in Philadelphia, he claimed, would maintain that unique and unrivaled relationship and would be the most reliable restraint on the amassing of all political power by the officers of the federal government:

> In a single republic, all the power surrendered by the people is submitted to the administration of a single government; and the usurpations are guarded against by a division of the government into distinct and separate departments. In the compound republic of America, the power surrendered by the people is first divided between two distinct governments, and then the portion allotted to each subdivided among distinct and separate departments. Hence a double security arises to the rights of the people. The different governments will control each other, at the same time that each will be controlled by itself.

Chapter 8
James Madison, Patrick Henry, and the Ratification Contest in Virginia

Apart from his work writing *The Federalist* letters, in April 1788 Madison was elected by the citizens of Orange County to represent them at the Virginia Ratifying Convention. Also present at the convention were several noted and respected Americans. Patrick Henry, Madison's countryman and the silver-tongued Cicero of his day, was among the heroes of the struggle for independence from the British Crown and was ferociously opposed to the adoption of the proposed Constitution. Henry and others—known to proponents as "Anti-Federalists"—felt obliged to warn the people of the latent threats to liberty they perceived in the product of Philadelphia.

On Monday, June 9, 1788, Patrick Henry rose for the third time at the state convention and addressed the body of 168 delegates gathered in the Richmond Theatre to consider ratification of the newly proposed Constitution. In all, Henry delivered 24 discourses blasting away at the most "objectionable parts" of the Constitution. In this particular speech, he summoned the specter of the "consolidating tendencies" haunting the proposed federal government. The great orator summoned his "poor abilities" to defend and ensure the sovereignty and survival of the state governments. He saw the future and forced his colleagues to look into the grim crystal ball he held:

> If consolidation proves to be as mischievous to this country as it has been to other countries, what will the

From Last Rites to Bill of Rights: The Miraculous Life and Legacy of James Madison

Patrick Henry feared the collapse of the state governments, based on the tyrannical nature of federal governments in other countries.

poor inhabitants of this country do? This government will operate like an ambuscade. It will destroy the state governments, and swallow the liberties of the people, without giving previous notice.

When Madison sat down to draft *Federalist* No. 46, the urgent and eloquent prophecies of the enemies of the Constitution were being published by newspapers throughout the union. The strength and the popularity of these warnings were well-known to all Americans, and especially to Madison, who, in *Federalist* No. 46 addressed himself to those "adversaries of the Constitution" who believed that an "uncontrolled" federal authority eventually would swallow up state governments and assume all state prerogatives.

A Truly Federal Government

In preempting Henry's blow, Madison described a symbiotic relationship of state and federal government that would obviate a clash of powers. He believed that states would maintain their supremacy over the federal government in terms of their sovereignty principally through the effects of the greater attachment of the "affections" of the people to their state governments than to the distant federal authority.

Although history, it seems, has not borne out Madison's confidence in the connections of the people to the state governments, he assumed that the people's devotion to their state legislatures would compel them to resist any effort by agents of the federal government to subordinate states to second-class status. The states and the people, Madison argued, would never submit to such despotic designs. The power of this duo—inherent in the latter and artificial in the former—would prevent Patrick Henry's predicted consolidation of all political power in the federal government.

"What degree of madness," Madison asked incredulously, "could ever drive the federal government to such an extremity," to ambitiously encroach on the state governments? The people, he proposed, would refuse to "cooperate with the officers of the union" attempting to usurp the prerogatives of the states. He genuinely believed that, were the federal government to take such a tyrannical tack, states would combine to block the way, uniting to draw up "plans of resistance."

Besides, like those well-trained weather watchers who can detect the seed of a hurricane in a surging wave, Madison believed that the American people and the several states would notice the "gathering storm" and prevent the precipitation of unchecked power or invasions on the rights of the people.

Why did James Madison place so much trust in his future countrymen? He listed five assumptions upon which his answer to Anti-Federalists' dire predictions was built. First, Madison argued that the people and the states would never elect men to the federal office "ready to betray" the best interests of both the states and the people. Second, it was unthinkable to him that there would be "traitors" in the federal government who would vote to build up and maintain "a military establishment." Third, Madison couldn't conceive that state legislatures would simply sit idly by as the federal government usurped power from the states. Madison believed it was impossible that state governments would tolerate (much less support) a federal behemoth bent on making increasingly despotic demands of the states and the people. Fourth, should the federal government somehow deceive the states and the people and accumulate all power, the people, through the states, would recover their senses and "repel the danger" through a militia mustered and "fighting for their common liberties." These citizen-soldiers would form a popular armed force that Madison believed "could never be conquered." And finally, state governments would form a living, legislative levee, a "barrier against the enterprises of ambition" undertaken by the federal government.

"Promote the Public Happiness":
Madison Promotes the Purpose of the Constitution

Madison could not be convinced that Americans would ever debase themselves to become "subjects of arbitrary power," too lazy to reclaim their hard-won liberty "from the hands of their oppressors." These heirs of the Revolution would never, Madison said, be brought to a state of "blind and tame submission to the long train of insidious measures" that would result in an all-powerful federal authority and the obliteration of the states as sovereign powers.

Madison's defense of the Constitution against the attacks of those opposed to its adoption were not confined to the written word. Despite being stricken with what he called a "bilious fever," Madison personally attended his state's ratifying convention and spoke forcefully and learnedly in support of the Constitution he helped draft. On June 6, 1788, he rose to address his fellow delegates to the Virginia Ratifying Convention and laid out logically and powerfully the reasons why the Constitution under consideration would "promote the public happiness." He called on his convention colleagues not to judge the Constitution according to the claims of those who worked to defeat its adoption, but to "decide this great question by a calm and rational investigation."

Samuel Adams was another Anti-Federalist who opposed the ratification of the Constitution.

Whereas Patrick Henry was a fiery orator (known as the "Lion of Liberty"), James Madison was a man given to calm and rational consideration of every important question presented for his opinion. After appealing to the delegates in attendance to have an open mind and to weigh his words fairly and without prejudice, Madison addressed the complaint made by Henry and others that the Constitution created a consolidated rather than a federal government. He explained, "I conceive myself that it is of a mixed nature; it is in a manner unprecedented; we cannot find one express example in the experience of the world. It stands by itself. In some respects it is a government of a federal nature; in others, it is of a consolidated nature."

This reference to history was a clever gambit by Madison, who was familiar with the recorded history of self-government and confederacies. He wanted to disarm those of his foes who warned that history proved that the powers given (in the proposed Constitution) to the general government would result in the destruction of the states and of individual liberty. Madison accepted his enemies' description of the historical record, then used that tactic to turn history to his favor by showing that the Constitution was something new and unprecedented, and not completely subject to an appeal to the sad story of ancient confederacies.

Next, he explained how the uniqueness of the Constitution would at once preserve the ultimate sovereignty of the people without sacrificing the sovereignty of the state governments they had previously created. The key, Madison said, was the concept of enumerated powers and the ability the states would retain to keep the federal beast inside its constitutional cage. He rose and said:

> Who are parties to it? The people—but not the people as composing one great body; but the people as composing thirteen sovereignties. Were it, as the gentleman asserts, a consolidated government, the assent of a majority of the people would be sufficient for its establishment; and, as a majority have adopted it already, the remaining states would be bound by the act of the majority, even if they

unanimously reprobated it. Were it such a government as is suggested, it would be now binding on the people of this state, without having had the privilege of deliberating upon it. But, sir, no state is bound by it, as it is, without its own consent. Should all the states adopt it, it will be then a government established by the thirteen states of America, not through the intervention of the legislatures, but by the people at large. In this particular respect, the distinction between the existing and proposed governments is very material. The existing system has been derived from the dependent derivative authority of the legislatures of the states; whereas this is derived from the superior power of the people. If we look at the manner in which alterations are to be made in it, the same idea is, in some degree, attended to. By the new system, a majority of the states cannot introduce amendments; nor are all the states required for that purpose; three fourths of them must concur in alterations; in this there is a departure from the federal idea. The members to the national House of Representatives are to be chosen by the people at large, in proportion to the numbers in the respective districts. When we come to the Senate, its members are elected by the states in their equal and political capacity. But had the government been completely consolidated, the Senate would have been chosen by the people in their individual capacity, in the same manner as the members of the other house. Thus it is of a complicated nature; and this complication, I trust, will be found to exclude the evils of absolute consolidation, as well as of a mere confederacy. If Virginia was separated from all the states, her power and authority would extend to all cases: in like manner, were all powers vested in the general government, it would be a consolidated government; but the powers of the federal government are enumerated; it can only operate in certain cases; it has legislative powers on defined and limited objects, beyond which it cannot extend its jurisdiction.

That was the genius of the Constitution: the people ruled through elected representatives who would serve in one house of the federal legislature, and the states retained their authority through their grant of power to choose the legislators who would occupy the other house of Congress.

As for the Congress (and the other two branches of the general government), its powers would be checked not only by the separation of federal powers, but by the influence of the people and the states over those who would wield power in the federal government. Furthermore, this power would be limited and enumerated.

Finally, as he had in *Federalist* No. 46 five months earlier, Madison expressed his belief—his hope—that the Constitution under consideration would make the people of the United States "secure and happy," and that this felicitous condition would persist because the people and the states would be vigilant and diligent, never allowing the general government to overstep the boundaries of its constitutionally enumerated powers:

> If the general government were wholly independent of the governments of the particular states, then, indeed, usurpation might be expected to the fullest extent. But, sir, on whom does this general government depend? It derives its authority from these governments, and from the same sources from which their authority is derived. The members of the federal government are taken from the same men from whom those of the state legislatures are taken. If we consider the mode in which the federal representatives will be chosen, we shall be convinced that the general will never destroy the individual governments.
> . . .

With that, James Madison concluded his zealous defense of the Constitution. He fought back against all the attacks, and he never failed to stand toe-to-toe with the animated Anti-Federalists as they took one shot after another at the "paper on the table," the Constitution of 1787. Madison's performance at the Virginia Ratifying Convention was exemplary. One of the delegates present

THE FEDERALIST

NUMBER XLVI.

The Subject of the laſt Paper reſumed; with an Examination of the comparative Means of Influence of the Federal and State Governments.

RESUMING the ſubject of the laſt paper I proceed to enquire whether the federal government or the ſtate governments will have the advantage with regard to the predilection and ſupport of the people. Notwithſtanding the different modes in which they are appointed, we muſt conſider both of them, as ſubſtantially dependent on the great body of the citizens of the United States. I aſſume this poſition here as it reſpects the firſt, reſerving the proofs for another place. The federal and ſtate of governments are in fact but different agents and truſtees of the people, inſtituted with different powers, and deſignated for different purpoſes. The adverſaries of the conſtitution ſeem to have loſt ſight of the people altogether in their reaſonings on this ſubject; and to have viewed theſe different eſtabliſhments, not only as mutual rivals and enemies, but as uncontrouled by any common ſuperior in their efforts to uſurp the authorities of each other. Theſe gentlemen muſt here be reminded of their error. They muſt be told that the ultimate authority, wherever the derivative may be found, reſides in the people alone; and that it will not depend merely on the comparative ambition or addreſs of the different governments, whether either, or which of them, will be able to enlarge its ſphere of juriſdiction at the expence of the other. Truth no leſs than decency requires, that the event in every caſe ſhould be ſuppoſed to depend on the ſentiments and ſanction of their common conſtituents.

Many conſiderations, beſides thoſe ſuggeſted on a former occaſion, ſeem to place it beyond doubt, that

Federalist No. 46 left an impression of hope for the federal government and the citizens to live in unity and peace.

at those debates said that it was Madison's "plain, ingenious, and elegant reasoning" that was his greatest gift to the deliberations (James Breckenridge, letter to John Breckenridge, June 13, 1788). So impressive was Madison's tireless defense of the Constitution and of that document's peculiar, particularly American construction that guaranteed the perpetuation of individual and political liberty, that a poem was written to praise him:

Maddison among the rest,

Pouring from his narrow chest,

More than Greek or Roman sense,

Boundless tides of eloquence.

In the end, Madison's reasoning proved persuasive and on June 26, 1788, Virginia ratified the Constitution, becoming the 10th state to do so. The delegates voted 89-79 in favor of adopting it. The document declaring the decision of Virginia's delegates was very clear in its conception of the relationship of Virginia (and all her sister states) to the federal government. Virginia declared that if the federal government was ever shown to have "perverted" the powers granted to it in the Constitution of the United States that "the powers granted under the Constitution being derived from the People of the United States may be resumed by them." The document went on to declare that, although Virginia was ratifying "the Constitution recommended on the Seventeenth day of September one thousand seven hundred and eighty seven by the Federal Convention for the Government of the United States," the Ratification Convention was also attaching "Subsequent Amendments" agreed to during its convention and "recommended to the consideration of the Congress which shall first assemble under the said Constitution to be acted upon according to the mode prescribed in the fifth article thereof." Prominent among the recommended amendments was this one: "Each State in the Union shall respectively retain every power, jurisdiction and right which is not by this Constitution delegated to the Congress of the United States or to the departments of the Federal Government."

Chapter Eight: James Madison, Patrick Henry, and the Ratification Contest in Virginia

Raeky, CC BY-SA 3.0, via Wikimedia Commons

Because of James Madison's diligence, Virginia became the tenth state to ratify the U.S. Constitution.

The fight had been close, right down to the wire. Sensing the possibility of defeat, Madison and his allies had privately promised key members of the opposition that if they would provisionally agree to approve the Constitution, then Madison and his fellow Federalists would work to add amendments to the Constitution in the first session of the new Congress, as described in the previous paragraph.

New York was experiencing a similarly close call on the vote to approve or reject the proposed Constitution. Alexander Hamilton predicted that passage would be precarious, so, in a letter written on May 19, 1788, he requested of Madison that "the moment *any decisive* question is taken, if favourable, I request you to dispatch an express to me with pointed orders to make all possible diligence." The message from Richmond arrived in Poughkeepsie—where the New York ratification convention was debating—on July 2, 1788, informing the New York delegates that Virginia voted in favor of ratification.

New York followed Virginia's lead, and ratified the Constitution on July 26, 1788. The vote was swayed, as it was in Virginia, by supporters' promises of pursuing the addition of a bill of rights to the Constitution as soon as the government began functioning.

Virginia recommended 20 such amendments, and many of the other state conventions likewise tied their ratification of the Constitution to the passage of amendments. A version of these proposed amendments would make up a Bill of Rights. It was in the adoption of the amendments of the Bill of Rights that James Madison would once again prove himself a friend of freedom and a competent and convincing statesman. His efforts as a congressman in the First Congress were critical to the adoption of the first 10 amendments to the Constitution, known forever after as the Bill of Rights, and it is indisputable that their form and adoption bear the marks of Madison.

Chapter 9
Congressman James Madison and the Bill of Rights

"There Never Was an Atom of Ill-Will Between Us"
With the Constitution ratified by the requisite number of states, James Madison would finish his term in the soon-to-be-supplanted Confederation Congress and then head back to Virginia for Christmas.

Although he assumed that he would be favored by his fellow citizens of the Old Dominion with an election to some office in the new government, Madison did not take his renown for granted, and resigned himself to having to campaign in order to secure the seat in Congress he would need in order to help the new general legislature get off on the right foot.

He was disappointed in 1788 not to have been elected to the first U.S. Senate (before ratification of the 17th Amendment in 1913, senators were elected by state legislatures), but he knew that opponents of the Constitution in the House of Delegates were committed to preventing him from assuming that important role.

In his autobiography, he refers obliquely to "particular means" used to prevent his election to the newly created United States Senate. He insists that the boundaries of the congressional districts in Virginia were drawn in such a way as to "prevent his election" to the House of Representatives, as well.

Fortunately for Madison (and for the Bill of Rights), his rival in the race to represent Virginia's Fifth District in the First Congress was not a political puppet, but a hero and a man of extraordinary integrity. That man was James Monroe.

From Last Rites to Bill of Rights: The Miraculous Life and Legacy of James Madison

James Madison ran and won against James Monroe for a House seat in the first Congress. Throughout their campaigns and their lives, they remained close friends.

Madison must have been delighted that his political foes had selected James Monroe to challenge him for the House seat. He knew Monroe by reputation, and the two had been friends for several years after being introduced by their mutual friend, Thomas Jefferson.

In a letter to Madison written on May 8, 1784, Jefferson recommended Monroe as a man with whom Madison could confide.

"The scrupulousness of his honor will make you safe in the most confidential communications. A better man cannot be," Jefferson informed his old friend. With such a sound assessment of Monroe's dependability, James Madison knew he needn't worry about being forced into an unsavory season of campaigning, despite the obstructionist efforts of his opponents.

Even with confidence in the strength of Monroe's character, Madison likely could not have predicted how the campaign of 1788-89 would serve to build a bond between himself and James Monroe that would last the rest of Madison's life and tie the two together as they served their country, service that would eventually lead both men to the White House.

"Saved Our Friendship From the Smallest Diminution"

Neither candidate looked forward to traveling around asking for votes. They recognized, however, that the political climate required them to present their positions to the people. There was no worry that there would be any animosity between the two men, however. Both were well known by their fellow Virginians as men of character who would never resort to running negative, nasty campaigns.

In his book *Founding Rivals*, Chris DeRose writes of Monroe's attitude about the necessity of campaigning against James Madison, "Monroe did not have—and would never have had—anything to do with dishonest campaigning, especially against his friend."

But even a clean campaign requires a bit of self-promotion. In a letter written to George Washington on January 14, 1789, Madison referred to political campaigns as "pretensions," but admitted that the situation was such in his home district that in order to be present when the new Congress convened, he would have to consent to travel (he informs Washington, with apparent incredulity, that he had "actually visited two counties") the district and convince his countrymen that he was worthy to represent them in the House of Representatives.

Madison arrived home to Montpelier just a couple of days before Christmas, giving himself very little time to travel and meet the men who would be heading to the polls on February 2 to decide which of the two candidates would represent them when the general government got underway later that year.

In an example of disagreeing without being disagreeable, Madison and Monroe actually campaigned together! The pair appeared together in churches and courthouses around their district, speaking respectfully of each other, focusing on the issues without a single disparaging word spoken by one about the other. In a letter to Thomas Jefferson written on March 29, 1789, Madison described the duo's demeanor and the effect of the campaign: "Between ourselves [Madison and Monroe], I have no reason to doubt that the distinction was duly kept in mind between political and personal views, and that it has saved our friendship from the smallest diminution."

The two remained close throughout the campaign as they traveled miles in the snow, riding together in small coaches. In his biography of Madison, Ralph Ketcham describes some details of the wintry wanderings of Madison and Monroe stumping throughout the district: "On one wintery day they journeyed twelve miles to the church of a 'nest of Dutchmen who generally voted together and whose vote might probably turn the scale.' According to Madison's own account, he and Monroe sat through the service, at which two fiddles provided the music, and afterwards the two candidates kept the people standing in the snow, listening as the constitutional issues were earnestly debated. On the long ride home that night, Madison's nose froze, leaving a scar he bore for the rest of his life."

The debate lasted for hours and the temperatures were frigid, but the audience, Madison reported, "stood it out very patiently—seemed to consider it a sort of fight of which they were required to be spectators."

And what a spectacle it must have been!

There, huddled in a black overcoat, stood the sickly and slight Mr. Madison—coming in at about 5 feet, 4 inches tall—and standing next to him was James Monroe, a powerfully built former front-line soldier who was seven years younger and nearly a foot taller!

Scars and snow, frostbite and friendship—the 1789 campaign to be the first representative of Virginia's Fifth Congressional District was hotly contested by two men who knew how to disagree without being disagreeable. They considered it their obligation to present their views on constitutional issues, not to attack each other, demean each other, or in any way sacrifice virtue on the altar of ambition.

As the votes were tallied on February 2, 1789, Madison won handily. Despite the historically horrible weather, citizens took their suffrage seriously and made it to the polls regardless of the obstacles, and elected James Madison to go to New York, the first home of the new general government.

Chapter 10
Mr. Madison Goes to Congress

"I Well Know Your Object Is the Good of Your Country"
In one of the first letters Madison received after his election to the First Congress, Miles King congratulates him "and our country in being elected as one of the representatives in Congress." After lamenting the loss of Madison in the federal Senate, King adds that he knows that "whatever department you are in, I well know your object is the good of your country."

Madison's service to his country in the First Congress would be delayed, though—as was his service at the Constitutional Convention of 1787—as other members failed to arrive in New York City on the day appointed for the opening of congressional business: March 4, 1789.

Undeterred, Madison took advantage of the postponement, writing letters to his dearest friends: Thomas Jefferson and George Washington.

In the letter to Washington, Madison informed the newly elected first president of the United States about the expected climate in Congress. "It is not yet possible to ascertain precisely the complexion of the new Congress. A little time will be necessary to unveil it, and a little will probably suffice," he reported.

Later in the letter, Madison's character is revealed in his expression of hope for the work to be done by the people's representatives in the House of Representatives and the representatives of the states in the Senate. "Notwithstanding this character of the body, I hope and expect that some conciliatory sacrifices will be made, in order to extinguish opposition to the system [the Constitution] . . . ," he wrote.

Remarkably, a sufficient number of senators and representatives didn't arrive in New York until April 6, over a full month after they were supposed to start work. By that time, Madison was anxious to start shoring up the Constitution and showing his constituents that they chose the right man to represent them.

As the new government got underway, there were many in the Senate and the House who planned to push for a new constitutional convention. They considered James Madison a political foe and were ready to fight him tooth-and-nail to get their way.

That said, even Madison's most obstinate opponents recognized his exceptional character, undeniable good judgment, and unmatched erudition. Fisher Ames, a representative from Massachusetts, was one of those political adversaries whose praise for Madison reads like a roster of the latter's qualifications for leadership:

> He derives from nature an excellent understanding . . . but I think he excels in the quality of judgment. He is possessed of a sound judgment, which perceives truth with great clearness, and can trace it through the mazes of debate, without losing it. . . . As a reasoner, he is remarkably perspicuous and methodical. He is a studious man, devoted to public business, and a thorough master of almost every public question that can arise, or he will spare no pains to become so, if he happens to be in want of information. What a man understands clearly, and has viewed in every different point of light, he will explain to the admiration of others, who have not thought of it at all, or but little, and who will pay in praise for the pains he saves them.

Within a week of the inauguration of George Washington as the first president of the United States (elected under the Constitution of 1787), James Madison was already demonstrating the "devotion to public business" that Ames praised. He immediately embarked on the path to fulfilling the promise he made to many of his friends: to get a bill of rights added to the Constitution as soon as the new national legislature was seated.

Chapter Ten: Mr. Madison Goes to Congress

Although some Federalists—like Fisher Ames—did not politically oppose some of the proposed amendments, they stood against James and their other former political allies with each new proposal that was in any way contrary to their own concept of constitutional purpose.

Madison expected very little opposition to many of the additions he was hoping to be able to shepherd through the First Congress: freedom of the press, freedom of speech, right to a trial by jury, and a right against excessive bail, for example. But many of the most ardent and recalcitrant Anti-Federalists had not abandoned their plan of amending the Constitution to place fetters on federal power. They felt this was essential to retaining the liberty of the people and the sovereignty of the states.

Unfortunately, Madison found keeping his promise a bit harder than he anticipated. Among his colleagues in the First Congress were many of his former foes, men who were elected by constituents concerned about the power granted to the federal government in the Constitution. Many of these men were determined to stall Madison's efforts to pass amendments for a bill of rights that would guarantee personal liberty until they could get enough support for the structural changes they wished to see made to the new Constitution. Thus, they voted against *any* amendment, even those to which they were not politically or philosophically opposed.

Joining these Anti-Federalist congressmen were many representatives who were against any amendment proposed by the Federalists. Although their motives were very distinct, their political positions were aligned and they frequently formed a voting bloc that could have kept most members from adding a bill of rights to the Constitution.

James Madison was not "most members." James Madison was a man whose insight, intellect, and integrity were developed early in his life and were tested regularly and found unassailable. In this most critical contest, Madison would employ his remarkable gifts in a way that would yet again prove him worthy of the respect afforded him by his foes and the trust afforded him by his friends.

"Proper to Be Recommended":
The Road to the Bill of Rights

On June 8, 1789, about a month after he undertook the process of passing a bill of rights, Madison rose and spoke to his fellow congressmen in support of the slate of amendments he believed would strengthen the popular support of the Constitution. His words

Chapter Ten: Mr. Madison Goes to Congress

aoc.gov/explore-capitol-campus/art/washingtons-farewell-address-1796

James proposed the Bill of Rights in the First Federal Congress.

on this occasion would become one of the most famous orations in defense of liberty ever delivered by an American statesman.

Notably, in his book *The Business of May Next: James Madison & the Founding*, William Lee Miller points out that this speech was the third such discourse delivered by James in June in three consecutive years. As Miller reports, Madison made these three declarations on June 6, 1787 at the convention in Philadelphia; June 6, 1788 at the Virginia Ratifying Convention in Richmond, Virginia; and June 8, 1789 in the House of Representatives in New York City. Here is the text of the words spoken by James Madison as he introduced his proposal for an American bill of rights:

> I find, from looking into the amendments proposed by the state conventions, that several are particularly anxious

that it should be declared in the constitution, that the powers not therein delegated, should be reserved to the several states.

Perhaps words which may define this more precisely, than the whole of the instrument now does, may be considered as superfluous. I admit they may be deemed unnecessary; but there can be no harm in making such a declaration, if gentlemen will allow that the fact is as stated. I am sure I understand it so, and do therefore propose it.

These are the points on which I wish to see a revision of the constitution take place. How far they will accord with the sense of this body, I cannot take upon me absolutely to determine; but I believe every gentleman will readily admit that nothing is in contemplation, so far as I have mentioned, that can endanger the beauty of the government in any one important feature, even in the eyes of its most sanguine admirers. I have proposed nothing that does not appear to me as proper in itself, or eligible as patronised by a respectable number of our fellow citizens; and if we can make the constitution better in the opinion of those who are opposed to it, without weakening its frame, or abridging its usefulness, in the judgment of those who are attached to it, we act the part of wise and liberal men to make such alterations as shall produce that effect.

In this same speech, he proposed a list of amendments that he believed seemed "proper to be recommended by congress to the state legislatures." Among those recommendations are found a few that shine a bright light on the moderation of Madison, as well as his genuine love of liberty and concern for its protection and preservation. Madison proposed the following amendments be added to the Constitution, many of which are recognizable to modern Americans as key components of our cherished Bill of Rights:

That there be prefixed to the constitution a declaration—That all power is originally vested in, and consequently derived from the people.

That government is instituted, and ought to be exercised for the benefit of the people; which consists in the enjoyment of life and liberty, with the right of acquiring and using property, and generally of pursuing and obtaining happiness and safety.

That the people have an indubitable, unalienable, and indefeasible right to reform or change their government, whenever it be found adverse or inadequate to the purposes of its institution.

The civil rights of none shall be abridged on account of religious belief or worship, nor shall any national religion be established, nor shall the full and equal rights of conscience be in any manner, or on any pretext infringed.

The people shall not be deprived or abridged of their right to speak, to write, or to publish their sentiments; and the freedom of the press, as one of the great bulwarks of liberty, shall be inviolable.

The people shall not be restrained from peaceably assembling and consulting for their common good; nor from applying to the legislature by petitions, or remonstrances for redress of their grievances.

The right of the people to keep and bear arms shall not be infringed; a well armed, and well regulated militia being the best security of a free country: but no person religiously scrupulous of bearing arms, shall be compelled to render military service in person.

No soldier shall in time of peace be quartered in any

house without the consent of the owner; nor at any time, but in a manner warranted by law.

No person shall be subject, except in cases of impeachment, to more than one punishment, or one trial for the same offence; nor shall be compelled to be a witness against himself; nor be deprived of life, liberty, or property without due process of law; nor be obliged to relinquish his property, where it may be necessary for public use, without a just compensation.

Excessive bail shall not be required, nor excessive fines imposed, nor cruel and unusual punishments inflicted.

The rights of the people to be secured in their persons, their houses, their papers, and their other property from all unreasonable searches and seizures, shall not be violated by warrants issued without probable cause, supported by oath or affirmation, or not particularly describing the places to be searched, or the persons or things to be seized.

In all criminal prosecutions, the accused shall enjoy the right to a speedy and public trial, to be informed of the cause and nature of the accusation, to be confronted with his accusers, and the witnesses against him; to have a compulsory process for obtaining witnesses in his favor; and to have the assistance of counsel for his defence.

The exceptions here or elsewhere in the constitution, made in favor of particular rights, shall not be so construed as to diminish the just importance of other rights retained by the people; or as to enlarge the powers delegated by the constitution; but either as actual limitations of such powers, or as inserted merely for greater caution.

The powers not delegated by this constitution, nor prohibited by it to the states, are reserved to the States respectively.

Chapter Ten: Mr. Madison Goes to Congress

The Bill of Rights presented additional protections not formerly addressed in the Constitution.

Madison's description of the Bill of Rights in this speech as an "impenetrable bulwark against every assumption of power" did not represent, as some biographers have claimed, a politically motivated change of opinion. The fact is that for months, Madison had been expressing his view that, if drafted carefully, a bill of rights could be beneficial to the perpetuation of popular sovereignty and political liberty in the United States.

Some months earlier, on October 17, 1788, while trying to explain his plan to push a bill of rights through Congress, James sent a letter from New York to his friend Thomas Jefferson, who was still in France, serving as an ambassador to that country. In this lengthy letter, Madison laid out his thoughts on the subject of the benefits of a bill of rights:

> It is true nevertheless that not a few, particularly in Virginia have contended for the proposed alterations from the most honorable & patriotic motives; and that among the advocates for the Constitution, there are some who wish for further guards to public liberty & individual rights. As far as these may consist of a constitutional declaration of the most essential rights, it is probable they will be added; though there are many who think such addition unnecessary, and not a few who think it misplaced in such a Constitution. There is scarce any point on which the party in opposition is so much divided as to its importance and its propriety. My own opinion has always been in favor of a bill of rights; provided it be so framed as not to imply powers not meant to be included in the enumeration. At the same time I have never thought the omission a material defect, nor been anxious to supply it even by subsequent amendment, for any other reason than that it is anxiously desired by others. I have favored it because I supposed it might be of use, and if properly executed could not be of disservice.

A few months later, he wrote another letter, this one not addressed to a close friend, but to his fellow citizens of Orange County. His friends were familiar with his firm dedication to timeless principles of liberty, principally to that of the freedom of religious belief and practice, but Madison was equally desirous that those less personally familiar with his views on the inviolability of the right to conscience would have an equal opportunity of learning of it from his own pen. Accordingly, on January 2, 1789, Madison wrote the following brief, but bold, message to George Eve, the presiding minister of the Blue Run Baptist Church, in his home county:

> Being informed that reports prevail not only that I am opposed to any amendmends whatever to the new federal Constitution; but that I have ceased to be a friend to the rights of Conscience; and inferring from a conversation with my brother William, that you are disposed to

contradict such reports as far as your knowledge of my sentiments may justify, I am led to trouble you with this communication of them. As a private Citizen it could not be my wish that erroneous opinions should be entertained, with respect to either of those points, particularly, with respect to religious liberty. But having been induced to offer my services to this district as its representative in the federal Legislature, considerations of a public nature make it proper that, with respect to both, my principles and views should be rightly understood.

I freely own that I have never seen in the Constitution as it now stands those serious dangers which have alarmed many respectable Citizens. Accordingly whilst it remained unratified, and it was necessary to unite the States in some one plan, I opposed all previous alterations as calculated to throw the States into dangerous contentions, and to furnish the secret enemies of the Union with an opportunity of promoting its dissolution. Circumstances are now changed: The Constitution is established on the ratifications of eleven States and a very great majority of the people of America; and amendments, if pursued with a proper moderation and in a proper mode, will be not only safe, but may serve the double purpose of satisfying the minds of well meaning opponents, and of providing additional guards in favour of liberty. Under this change of circumstances, it is my sincere opinion that the Constitution ought to be revised, and that the first Congress meeting under it, ought to prepare and recommend to the States for ratification, the most satisfactory provisions for all essential rights, particularly the rights of Conscience in the fullest latitude, the freedom of the press, trials by jury, security against general warrants &c.

Here again, we see James Madison displaying that depth of character, that trustworthiness, that consistency that makes him a man among men. He was not simply sacrificing his own opinion for selfish gain or in order to be owed a future favor by those whose position he pretended to espouse. He was a man always devoted to extending the blessings of liberty to all his fellow men. He was likewise always devoted to discretion, and to standing unshakably firm in the defense of freedom and in his belief that freedom was made safer and surer by a strong union of the United States.

His contemporaries, even those who disagreed with his position on the Constitution, recognized in him a purity of mind and motive, a paucity of partisanship and petulance, and an abundance of intellect and integrity. This remarkable level of respect is revealed very clearly in a letter written by a state legislator from Winchester, Virginia, and published in a local newspaper:

> Those who know the abilities of Mr. Madison . . . know that his whole life has been devoted to the services of the public, and that he has so conducted himself as to avoid every cause of offence in his public speeches and private conversation to any man or description of men—that envy itself, or the jaundiced eye of faction have never imputed to him interested or corrupt motives. . . .

The sentiments expressed by this anonymous observer remind one of the similar admirable assessment made by John Witherspoon, the president of the College of New Jersey (Princeton) while James was a student there.

The House of Representatives debated Madison's enumerated rights for two months before approving them and sending them on to the Senate for that body's consideration. The 12 amendments were packaged as one single bill rather than individual amendments, thus making their approval an all-or-nothing proposition.

The Bill of Rights: Madison Keeps His Promise

After passing the Senate, the bill was taken up by a conference committee composed of members from both houses of Congress. This committee was tasked with working out a compromise version of the bill that would be acceptable to both representatives and senators. After such a conference report was hammered out by the committee, the final version of the text was then sent back to the House of Representatives and to the Senate for further debate and deliberation.

The conference-report version of Madison's bill of rights did not enjoy a carefree road to approval, however. For weeks, representatives and senators pushed to have this or that provision of the proposal changed or cut from the bill. For example, some congressmen were determined to preserve their states' establishment of a religion and popular (meaning: taxpayer-funded) support for clergymen. Others argued for a clearer line of demarcation between state and federal authority. Elbridge Gerry, Thomas Tucker, and other representatives worried that the amendment reserving all undelegated authority to the states was too vague and would result in accumulation of power by the federal government.

Never defeated, never discouraged, James Madison sat alone for months, waiting for other representatives to show up to conduct the business of the First Congress, just as he had waited two years earlier for delegates to finally arrive at the Constitutional Convention in Philadelphia. And, as in Philadelphia, as he toiled in his rented room, he did not waste his time or idle away his otherwise unaccounted-for minutes. He showed himself ever the leader, ever the statesman by spending hours and days collecting, cataloging, and collating the hundreds of suggested amendments sent in by the state legislatures and ratification conventions. He was determined, at the cost of personal ease and entertainment, to keep the promise he made to his fellow Virginians to propose a bill of rights during the first session of the First Congress. He was equally determined to do all within his personal and political power to protect *explicitly* within the Constitution the natural rights enjoyed by Americans and by all men. This was the caliber of man we appropriately call "The Father of the Constitution."

Throughout it all, James Madison held his own and proved a formidable and fearless ally of the Bill of Rights and the protection of personal liberty. He responded ably to every attack made on the Bill of Rights, and welcomed every opportunity to assure his colleagues that he sought no personal aggrandizement in the approval of his proposal, but that his only intent was to "fortify the rights of the people against encroachments by the government."

His eloquent efforts in this endeavor were successful: On September 24, 1789, the House of Representatives voted 37-14 in favor of the conference committee's version of the Bill of Rights, thus clearing the constitutional two-thirds hurdle. The very next day, the requisite two-thirds of the Senate approved the Bill of Rights (all 12 that were originally offered by Representative James Madison) as contained in the conference report.

This historic roster of protections of personal liberty then moved on to the next step in the approval process. As mandated by Article V of the Constitution, it was then sent to the states for ratification; only after ratification would these proposals become amendments to the Constitution. Article V sets the number of states that must approve a proposal before it becomes an amendment at three-fourths. This threshold was not crossed until December 15, 1791—a full two-and-a-half years from the day James Madison first introduced the measure in June 1789. On that cold day in December, the bill of rights became the Bill of Rights, a seminal and exemplary expression of the sanctity of individual liberty. It comprises a roster of unassailable freedoms that has survived tenaciously to this day.

Regarding his persistence and sincerity during the drafting and ratification of the Bill of Rights and the role he envisioned it would play in the constitutional order of the United States, there is perhaps no better expression than in the preamble to the Bill of Rights, written by Madison. This preamble is rarely read today and is, sadly, completely unknown to most Americans. Its content and tone demonstrate the strength of James Madison's conviction on the vital topics of limited government, individual liberty, and the sovereignty of the states that created the union. The preamble to the Bill of Rights reads, in relevant part:

> The Conventions of a number of the States, having at the time of their adopting the Constitution, expressed a desire,

in order to prevent misconstruction or abuse of its powers, that further declaratory and restrictive clauses should be added: And as extending the ground of public confidence in the Government, will best insure the beneficent ends of its institution. . . .

James Madison's title "Father of the Constitution" was in no small part attributable to his successful shepherding of the Bill of Rights through the rough-and-tumble process of congressional approval and state ratification. It cannot be stressed too strongly that there would be no Bill of Rights were it not for the tireless and fearless efforts of James Madison. As described by Miller in his Madison biography, "[W]ithout his [Madison's] persistence the amendments would not have come before the House, and the Congress, and the nation, in these first days."

The Father of the Constitution, James Madison.

With his promise to see a bill of rights appended to the Constitution fulfilled, James Madison felt he and his colleagues in Congress and earlier at the convention in Philadelphia had managed to found a free government in an historically novel manner and in an age so distant and distinct from the republics of the classical world he studied for so many years.

Perhaps one of the principal differences between the establishment of the governments of Sparta, Athens, Rome, and other ancient societies and the establishment of the American union was the record kept of all the meetings, moments, and men that led to the ratification of this republic's founding charter. In a letter to William Eustis written on July 6, 1819, Madison remarked on the knowledge so commonly possessed by so many of the facts of the Founding.

"The infant periods of most nations are buried in silence or veiled in fable; and the world perhaps has lost but little which it needs regret. The origin and outset of the American Republic contain lessons of which posterity ought not to be deprived; and happily there never was a case in which every interesting incident could be so accurately preserved," he explained.

And Madison knew better than almost anyone the truth of this statement. Not only did he participate in almost every step along the path of perfecting the American union he loved so much, but his notes on the daily drama that unfolded in Philadelphia in 1787 are of inestimable worth to those of us who now live happily in the land of liberty Madison and his fellow Founders worked so diligently to establish upon a firm and lasting foundation.

Our obligation now, of course, is to prevent that foundation from crumbling, living lives worthy of the years of toil and decades of diligence that Mr. Madison hoped would prove profitable to posterity.

"To Increase the Wealth and Strength of the Community": James Madison and Immigration

With the addition to the Constitution of a bill of rights all but assured, within weeks James Madison was called upon once again to employ his substantial talents for taking difficult subjects and simplifying them. This time the issue was the establishment of a national standard for naturalization, the process whereby an immigrant becomes a citizen of the United States.

At the time, each state was setting its own rules for becoming a citizen of the United States. This was problematic for a couple of reasons: First, immigrants would satisfy the citizenship requirements in one state, then move to another state only to have to complete additional steps to be considered a citizen in the new state; and second, Article I, Section 8 of the Constitution very clearly grants to Congress the power to "establish uniform rules for naturalization."

A bill had been proposed covering everything from creating rules for the census to regulations seeking to synchronize the various naturalization procedures. As it worked its way through Congress, James Madison rose to speak on February 3, 1790 to lead his fellow legislators in their efforts to simplify the standards of naturalization, using the opportunity to share with his colleagues not only his understanding of the issue, but his experience as a member of the convention that included the provision in the new Constitution.

Speaking on the benefits of allowing new citizens to join the ranks of Americans, Congressman Madison said:

> When we are considering the advantages that may result from an easy mode of naturalization, we ought also to consider the cautions necessary to guard against abuses. It is no doubt very desirable that we should hold out as many inducements as possible for the worthy part of mankind to come and settle amongst us, and throw their fortunes into a common lot with ours. But why is this desirable? Not merely to swell the catalogue of people. No, sir, it is to increase the wealth and strength of the community; and those who acquire the rights of citizenship, without adding to the strength or wealth of the community are not the people we are in want of. And what is proposed by the amendment is, that they shall take nothing more than an oath of fidelity, and declare their intention to reside in the United States. Under such terms, it was well observed by my colleague, aliens might acquire the right of citizenship,

> and return to the country from which they came, and evade the laws intended to encourage the commerce and industry of the real citizens and inhabitants of America, enjoying at the same time all the advantages of citizens and aliens.
>
> I should be exceedingly sorry, sir, that our rule of naturalization excluded a single person of good fame that really meant to incorporate himself into our society; on the other hand, I do not wish that any man should acquire the privilege, but such as would be a real addition to the wealth or strength of the United States.

Notably, Madison said nothing of immigration. The Constitution did not grant any power over immigration to the federal government, so under the clear language of the Tenth Amendment, that power was retained by the states and the people.

Naturalization, the subject under consideration that day in the winter of 1790, is the process of becoming a citizen of the United States. Immigration is the act of coming into one of the states from another country. Establishing rules for how one could legally enter a state from a foreign country was the responsibility of each state's legislature. When an immigrant sought to stay in a state and become a citizen of the United States, that's when Madison's methods, should they become law, would be applied.

It is little wonder that Madison spoke so passionately and powerfully on the subject of naturalization. During the debates on the Constitution just a couple of years earlier, he had warned in *Federalist* No. 42 that "The dissimilarity in the rules of naturalization has long been remarked as a fault in our system," and that the proposed Constitution would remedy this "defect."

As he did in the case of the Bill of Rights, James Madison went to Congress committed to curing the ills of the former constitution (the Articles of Confederation) and making laws for his country that would make it more organized, more orderly, and thus freer and more prosperous.

Just weeks after Madison delivered his speech on the need for a standard list of requirements for becoming a citizen, Congress passed the bill. It was soon thereafter signed into law.

"No Further Meaning and No Further Power": James Madison on the "General Welfare" and "Necessary and Proper" Clauses

Just two years after fighting to enforce the strict adherence by the federal government to the enumerated powers granted to it in the Constitution regarding immigration and naturalization, James Madison was once again called to stand as sentry, protecting the people from potential violations of the Constitution.

In February 1792, the House of Representatives was considering a bill that would exempt New England cod fishermen from paying

Public domain, via Wikimedia Commons

The United States Congress was not intended to have further power than that stated in the Constitution. Though Congress has a responsibility for the public's welfare and happiness, it is not exclusively up to them to decide what is in the best interest of the people.

a tariff on salt. Alexander Hamilton, serving as secretary of the Treasury, was one of the principal supporters of the bill, and the Senate had already passed it.

On February 6, 1792, Congressman James Madison rose to announce his view of the measure, not using his opinion as the standard by which it should be judged, but comparing the provisions in the bill to the powers granted to Congress. This way, he could know whether to vote for or against the bill, regardless of the intent of its sponsors.

Madison opened his speech by declaring that there are some members of Congress who believe that the Constitution grants to them "a power by virtue of which they may do anything which they may think conducive to the 'general welfare.'"

He was referring to the clause in Article I, Section 8 of the Constitution that grants to the legislative branch the power to "provide for the common defense and general welfare of the United States."

Explaining his position on this key clause of the Constitution, Madison illuminated the intended interpretation, the interpretation held by those who wrote and ratified the Constitution. "I, sir, have always conceived—I believe those who proposed the constitution conceived; it is still more fully known, and more material to observe, those who ratified the constitution conceived, that this is not an indefinite government deriving its powers from the general terms prefixed to the specified powers," he said, "but, a limited government tied down to the specified powers, which explain and define the general terms."

Next, Madison explained that it wouldn't make sense to assert that Congress can do anything it insists would help "the general welfare," and then go on and make a list of the things the Congress is authorized to do!

"It will follow, in the first place, that if the terms be taken in the broad sense they maintain, the particular powers, afterwards so carefully and distinctly enumerated, would be without meaning, and must go for nothing," he said.

"It would be absurd to say, first, that Congress may do what they please; and then, that they may do this or that particular thing," he added.

Madison then proceeded to instruct his colleagues in Congress that if they accept the premise that they are allowed to spend money on anything that they classify as good for the "general welfare," then there is nothing they cannot do!

To be very clear, though, he went on to list the sorts of unconstitutional programs and policies Congress might create if the only restriction was making sure the general welfare was being promoted, warning:

> If Congress can apply money indefinitely to the general welfare, and are the sole and supreme judges of the general welfare, they may take the care of religion into their own hands; they may establish teachers in every state, county, and parish, and pay them out of the public treasury; they may take into their own hands the education of children, establishing in like manner schools throughout the union; they may assume the provision for the poor; they may undertake the regulation of all roads other than post roads; in short, every thing, from the highest object of state legislation, down to the most minute object of police, would be thrown under the power of Congress.

Just two weeks prior to delivering this speech in Congress, Madison had expressed the same sense of congressional power in a letter to his friend Edmund Randolph. "If Congress can do whatever in their *discretion* can be *done by money*, and will promote the *general welfare*, the Government is no longer a limited one possessing enumerated powers, but an indefinite one subject to particular exceptions," Madison told Randolph.

On that day in February 1792, though, there stood James Madison on the floor of the House of Representatives, in his familiar occupation, fighting to keep the federal beast from roaming outside of its constitutional cage.

(Consider Madison's list. Curiously, every one of the unconstitutional things Madison warned that Congress would do if they were empowered to do anything they considered necessary for the "general welfare," Congress has done and is still doing to this very day.)

Three days later, the House of Representatives passed the bill, and it was signed into law by the president on February 16, 1792.

Some eight years later, James Madison expressed a similar concern over the attempt by Congress to assume unenumerated powers based on the clause of Article I Section 8 granting that body power to "make all laws which shall be necessary and proper for carrying into execution the foregoing powers. . . ."

This time, though, Mr. Madison was not a U.S. congressman, but was serving in his home state of Virginia as a delegate to its General Assembly. In this capacity, he issued a statement challenging Congress's usurpation of power, reminding the federal legislature of the legitimate scope of the "Necessary and Proper Clause." Madison's statement is known as the "Report of 1800." That report declares the following regarding the constitutional role of the Necessary and Proper Clause:

> The plain import of this clause is, that Congress shall have all the incidental or instrumental powers, necessary and proper for carrying into execution all the express powers; whether they be vested in the government of the United States, more collectively, or in the several departments, or officers thereof. It is not a grant of new powers to Congress, but merely a declaration, for the removal of all uncertainty, that the means of carrying into execution, those otherwise granted, are included in the grant.
>
> Whenever, therefore a question arises concerning the constitutionality of a particular power; the first question is, whether the power be expressed in the constitution. If it be, the question is decided. If it be not expressed; the next enquiry must be, whether it is properly an incident to an express power, and necessary to its execution. If it be, it may be exercised by Congress. If it be not; Congress cannot exercise it.

Having fought valiantly to protect the Constitution and to restrain the federal government with the chains forged by that document, James Madison would soon find himself facing difficult challenges both to it and to the peace and prosperity of the United States. This time, he would be serving in the administration of his dear friend and fellow Virginian, Thomas Jefferson, elected in 1801 to be the third president of the United States.

It's worth reading about the history of this dynamic duo, James Madison and Thomas Jefferson.

Chapter 11
James Madison and Thomas Jefferson: "The Great Collaboration"

James Madison and Thomas Jefferson first became acquainted in 1776, while both were serving in the Virginia House of Delegates. Many years later, Jefferson recalled that "Mr. Madison came into the House in 1776, a new member and young: which circumstances, concurring with his extreme modesty, prevented his venturing himself in debate. . . ." James was 25 years old when he entered into the arena that would be his lifelong vocation: public service. Jefferson was a more seasoned statesman, but he could perceive in the demure delegate from Orange the probing and insightful mind that would be of great value to both men in the almost half a century of their friendship.

Madison's admiration of his older friend (Jefferson was eight years his senior) and fellow Founding Father was never in question, and was mentioned by him regularly in his correspondence. In a letter to Nicholas Trist, written in 1826, he tenderly expressed his fondness for Jefferson after Jefferson's death:

> He [Thomas Jefferson] lives and will live in the memory and gratitude of the wise and good, as a luminary of science, as a votary of liberty, as a model of patriotism, and as a benefactor of human kind. In these characters, I have known him, and not less in the virtues and charms of social life, for a period of fifty years, during which there was not an interruption or diminution of mutual confidence and cordial friendship, for a single moment in a single instance.

Great friends and colleagues, Thomas Jefferson and James Madison first met while serving as delegates in the Virginia Legislature in 1776.

Public domain, via Wikimedia Commons

During Madison's time as a member of the Virginia Council of State mentioned above, he and Jefferson—then serving as the state's governor—began spending significant amounts of time together, consulting on important matters such as Virginia's political policy.

Two Mighty Minds

Of course, as the primary penman of the Declaration of Independence, Thomas Jefferson was already renowned throughout the union. James Madison's reputation, however, was as yet undistinguished. Together, the two men would go on to accomplish extraordinary achievements that would change the history of the world. Madison quickly earned the respect of his colleagues, developing a reputation for having, as Jefferson later wrote in his autobiography, "at ready command the rich resources of his luminous and discriminating mind. . . . [Madison's] extensive information rendered him the first of every assembly of which he became a member."

These two great men certainly belonged to a mutual admiration society, but it was not founded on flattery. Their friendship of nearly half a century was built firmly on the concepts of liberty, self-government, and republicanism held so dear by both men. Like two instruments in the grand symphony that is the United States of America, Madison and Jefferson played separate parts, but played them in great harmony and with great skill. In a speech delivered in 1839, during a jubilee celebration of the ratification of the Constitution, former President John Quincy Adams described the melodious effect of these two great instruments of American liberty:

> Mr. Madison was the intimate, confidential, and devoted friend of Mr. Jefferson, and the mutual influence of these two mighty minds upon each other, is a phenomenon, like the invisible and mysterious movements of the magnet in the physical world, and in which the sagacity of the future historian may discover the solution of much of our national history not otherwise accountable.

"Pains are Lessened by Communication with a Friend"

The second letter written from Madison to Jefferson (the first letter is referred to in the second, but has never been found) touched upon the difficulties faced by the Colonies in their efforts to restore the liberty they enjoyed before the usurpations and abuses of the British Crown and Parliament. Typical of the mind of James Madison, he informed Jefferson:

> Our army threatened with an immediate alternative of disbanding or living on free quarter; the public treasury empty; public credit exhausted, nay the private credit of purchasing Agents employed, I am told, as far as it will bear, Congress complaining of the extortion of the people; the people of the improvidence of Congress, and the army of both; our affairs requiring the most mature & systematic measures. . . .

Later in the letter, Madison, also in a manner typical of his tenor and devotion to plain speaking, ascribes much of the source of the tenuous state of the "revolution" to the predominance of politics and the deterioration of principles among the representatives of the people. He wrote:

> Congress from a defect of adequate Statesmen more likely to fall into wrong measures and of less weight to enforce right ones, recommending plans to the several states for execution and the states separately rejudging the expediency of such plans, whereby the same distrust of concurrent exertions that has damped the ardor of patriotic individuals, must produce the same effect among the States themselves.

It was their shared commitment to be statesmen and "patriotic individuals" that brought James Madison and Thomas Jefferson together in 1776 and kept them close throughout the decades of dedication to their country and to common causes. After the American victory over Great Britain in the War of Independence, James Madison found himself a frequent ally and nearly constant philosophical analogue to Jefferson.

It should be noted that these two sons of Virginia and builders of the American union were not political collaborators only. They were, in fact, close personal friends who would support the other in each man's attempts to pass legislation or push his countrymen toward greater virtue, individual liberty, and sounder political union.

One of the first, although not the most famous, examples of Madison and Jefferson riding to each other's defense came when Madison proposed resolutions in the Confederation Congress aimed at strengthening that body's authority to enforce critical wartime measures in the face of recalcitrance on the part of state governments.

After the Confederation Congress approved a plan to "improve the public credit," the representatives appointed Alexander Hamilton, Oliver Ellsworth, and James Madison to form a committee to draft a letter to the state governments explaining the purpose of Madison's resolutions, as well as encouraging them to participate in the effort to bolster the credit of the confederation.

Oliver Ellsworth was part of a committee that helped write a letter explaining the purpose of Madison's bills to strengthen the Confederation Congress's authority.

Madison served as chairman of this committee. While his correspondence with Jefferson and others reveals that he considered Congress's plan to be flawed, Madison did what he seemed always to do: placed his personal preferences to the side, promoting instead that which he considered to ensure "justice, good faith, and national honor."

The message the committee presented to Congress, penned by Madison, is called "Address to the States," and is filled with the author's genuine esteem of his countrymen and his earnest allegiance to the lofty principles of liberty and law embraced by all patriotic Americans. In the name of calming the seas of government, Madison would not now choose to collect political capital by pointing out his perception of the plan's defects.

The "Address to the States" proclaims:

> Let it be remembered finally that it has ever been the pride and boast of America, that the rights for which she contended were the rights of human nature. By the blessing of the Author of these rights on the means exerted for their defence, they have prevailed against all opposition and form the basis of thirteen independant States. No instance has heretofore occurred, nor can any instance be expected hereafter to occur, in which the unadulterated forms of Republican Government can pretend to so fair an opportunity of justifying themselves by their fruits. In this view the Citizens of the U.S. are responsible for the greatest trust ever confided to a Political Society. If justice, good faith, honor, gratitude & all the other Qualities which ennoble the character of a nation, and fulfil the ends of Government, be the fruits of our establishments, the cause of liberty will acquire a dignity and lustre, which it has never yet enjoyed; and an example will be set which can not but have the most favorable influence on the rights of mankind. If on the other side, our Governments should be unfortunately blotted with the reverse of these cardinal

and essential Virtues, the great cause which we have engaged to vindicate, will be dishonored & betrayed; the last & fairest experiment in favor of the rights of human nature will be turned against them; and their patrons & friends exposed to be insulted & silenced by the votaries of Tyranny and Usurpation.

Almost immediately, as Madison had predicted, the finance plan, as well as Madison's defense of it, came under fire, even from his fellow Virginians. There was one notable Virginian, however, who defended James Madison, the Virginian who knew the heart of Madison was always in the right place. That Virginian was, of course, Thomas Jefferson.

On May 7, 1783, Jefferson wrote to Madison that, whereas he was "not a little concerned" about key provisions of the plan to finance the war, he considered Madison's contributions to that proposal to be the "one palatable ingredient at least in the pill we are about to swallow." Doubtless to reassure Madison of the sincerity of his commitment to pushing the Virginia state legislature to accede to the plan put forth by the Confederation Congress, Jefferson reported that he "waited a fortnight in the neighborhood of Richmond that [he] might see some of the members" of the Virginia General Assembly.

Alternately serving each other and the cause of liberty as proposer and promoter would become regular practice for the two titans of American freedom. In fact, the two tag-teamed each other in 1783, when James Madison left the Confederation Congress for Virginia and Thomas Jefferson left Monticello for Princeton, New Jersey, where he served as a representative of his constituents at the Confederation Congress.

"A Catalogue of My Wants":
Madison Asks Jefferson for Books From Europe
One of the most historically significant among the benefits of Madison and Jefferson's friendship and correspondence is the invaluable assistance to Madison of the crates of books sent by Jefferson in the two years prior to the Constitutional Convention

of 1787. In August 1784, Jefferson arrived in France to serve as a representative of the United States. In March 1785, he replaced Benjamin Franklin as the head of that delegation. While in France, Jefferson regularly mailed Madison boxes of books on every subject that he believed would be of interest to his friend. In fact, he told Madison he would be happy to send him any books that were "old and curious or new and useful."

In a letter written to Jefferson on April 27, 1785, Madison took him up on his offer, sending his scholarly shopping list ("a catalogue of my wants" as Madison described it) to Jefferson, asking his friend to send him "treatises on the ancient or modern federal republics, on the law of nations, and the history, natural and political, of the new world," as well as "such of the Greek and Roman authors, where they will be got very cheap, as are worth having, and are not on the common list of school classics." Madison went on for paragraphs, requesting a variety of written material: books, essays, encyclopedias, historical surveys, etc.

In a letter written on September 1, 1785 (the seemingly lengthy delay was attributable to the "speed" of 18th-century communication), Jefferson informed Madison, "I have at length made up the purchase of books for you, as far as it can be done for the present. The objects which I have not yet been able to get, I shall continue to seek for. Those purchased, are packed this morning in two trunks, and you have the catalogue & prices herein inclosed."

The books sent to Madison from Jefferson were of inordinate value. As the eminent historian Adrienne Koch wrote in her book *Jefferson and Madison: The Great Collaboration*, "Certainly [Madison's] reading in the history of political theory, including the law of nature and nations, could hardly have been so comprehensive without the contents of the treasured boxes Jefferson shipped to him from France." Madison expressed the joy these books brought to him in a letter to Jefferson sent on March 18, 1786: "Since I have been at home I have had the leisure to review the literary cargo for which I am so much indebted to your friendship," he wrote. "The collection is perfectly to my mind."

"Some Observations on the Subject": Jefferson on the Constitution

While the books sent from Thomas Jefferson were fundamental in helping James Madison formulate his proposals for the Constitutional Convention of 1787 and fixed in his mind the timeless principles of liberty upon which any product of that convention must be built, he was unable to keep Jefferson informed of how the lessons he learned from these books played out in the day-to-day goings-on of the convention as he and all members had agreed to abide by a secrecy rule. Nearly all delegates present at the convention in Philadelphia agreed with the secrecy provision, which mandated "That no copy be taken of any entry on the journal during the sitting of the House, without leave of the House. That nothing spoken in the House be printed, or otherwise published or communicated without leave."

Despite his relationship with Jefferson, Madison would not break the rule. He would not break faith with his fellow delegates, considering his word a bond that could not be broken. Accordingly, his first report to Jefferson on the events that transpired at the Constitutional Convention that summer was contained in a letter written on October 24. This letter is an important contribution to the corpus of contemporary accounts of the debates and deliberations of the delegates to the Constitutional Convention of 1787. In fact, writing of Madison's letter, Adrienne Koch claims, "No better brief summary is available of the major principles considered by the delegates to the Convention." While the entire, lengthy letter is worth reading, it suffices this biography to include the following selections, demonstrating the moments of the convention considered most noteworthy to its most engaged participant: James Madison.

"It appeared to be the sincere and unanimous wish of the Convention to cherish and preserve the Union of the States," Madison began. Then, he set out the four most important issues faced by the delegates in Philadelphia:

"[The] ground-work being laid, the great objects which presented themselves were..."

1. To unite a proper energy in the Executive and a proper stability in the Legislative departments, with the essential characters of Republican Government.
2. To draw a line of demarkation which would give to the General Government every power requisite for general purposes, and leave to the States every power which might be most beneficially administered by them.
3. To provide for the different interests of different parts of the Union.
4. To adjust the clashing pretensions of the large and small States.

Madison then admitted to Jefferson that while each one of those subjects was difficult to deal with, the "whole of them together formed a task more difficult than can be well concieved by those who were not concerned in the execution of it."

He explained that, given the presence at that convention of prominent and persuasive men of such diverse interests and distinct and dearly held political opinions, "it [was] impossible to consider the degree of concord which ultimately prevailed as less than a miracle." But prevail it did, and Madison's determined, unrelenting, informed, and inspired leadership in the long, hot months of deliberation was rewarded when his countrymen gave him the title "Father of the Constitution."

The Pacificus-Helvidius Debates of 1793-1794

Within five years of the publishing of *The Federalist* (and four years of the ratification by the states of the Constitution), the co-authors of those seminal and influential essays on American political theory and constitutional interpretation were back at their desks once again, writing letters to the editors of newspapers. This time, however, James Madison and Alexander Hamilton were not allies working to persuade others to commit to their common constitutional cause, but opponents, striving through their letters to reveal each other's perceived constitutional misdeeds to the American people. This episode in American history is known as the "Pacificus-Helvidius" debates, named for the pen names adopted by Alexander Hamilton and James Madison, respectively.

Chapter Eleven: James Madison and Thomas Jefferson: "The Great Collaboration"

In the earliest days of the Republic, the precise balance of powers between the legislative and executive branches in the arena of foreign affairs was unsettled. The Constitution, many argued, wasn't clear on the point, and the various views on the matter created controversy. George Washington issued the Neutrality Proclamation of 1793 after France declared war on Holland and Great Britain. According to Washington's way of thinking, it was in the best interest of the country to avoid war at all costs, and he did not want the belligerents to be unsure of the official American position.

While certainly laudable, some of Washington's colleagues considered the Neutrality Proclamation to be hostile to the French, as the Treaty of Alliance signed by France and the United States in 1778 prohibited peace treaties and commercial agreements between the United States and England.

Thomas Jefferson was among the most vociferous of the officials calling out Washington for allegedly violating the prior agreement. Some of the opposition, including Jefferson and Madison, believed that the advice and consent of the Senate should have been sought before President Washington issued any declaration of the official American position on any topic touching upon foreign affairs.

Alexander Hamilton was one of the first president's most ardent advocates, however. And that's where the trouble started. Just weeks after the Neutrality Proclamation was published, Hamilton wrote a letter defending the document. Then, beginning in June 1793, he wrote an essay almost once a week, under the pen name "Pacificus," in support of President Washington's administration and his policies. After the seventh Pacificus letter was published on July 27, 1793, Thomas Jefferson wrote a now-famous letter to James Madison, pleading, "my dear sir, take up your pen. . . ." Madison took up his pen, and on the 24th of August, 1793, responded to Hamilton's Pacificus essays using the pseudonym "Helvidius."

In the first letter, Madison wrote that the first Pacificus essay "may prove a snare to patriotism," and warned that Hamilton advocated principles "which strike at the vitals of the country's constitution." Later in the essay, Madison recommended that in all questions concerning the correct conduct of federal officials, Americans must

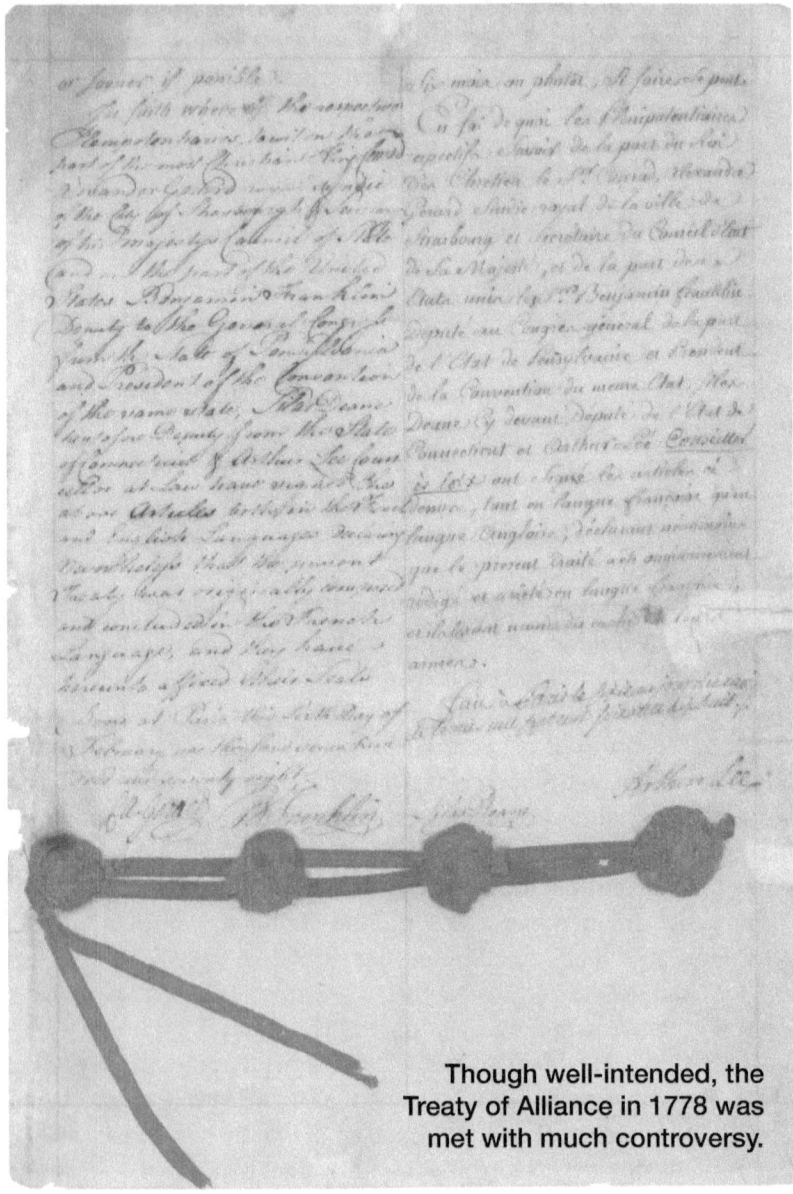

Though well-intended, the Treaty of Alliance in 1778 was met with much controversy.

Benjamin Franklin, Public domain, via Wikimedia Commons

be guided by "our own reason and our own constitution." And, in a statement that once again proves how prescient he was, Madison wrote that the power to declare war (war with France, in this case) is "of a legislative and not an executive nature." He continued on that subject:

> Those who are to conduct a war [the executive branch] cannot in the nature of things, be proper or safe judges, whether a war ought to be commenced, continued, or concluded. They are barred from the latter functions by a great principle in free government, analogous to that which separates the sword from the purse, or the power of executing from the power of enacting laws.

Madison was so strident in his insistence that the power to make war not be placed in the presidency, that his next letter ("Helvidius" No. 2) began with the bold pronouncement that if any president were to presume the war-making power, "no ramparts in the constitution could defend the public liberty or scarcely the forms of republican government."

(In the modern era, notably, it is typically the president who initiates the commitment of American troops to combat zones and who orders the military might of the United States of America to deploy here or there to fight this or that foreign foe. Congress is rarely involved in that decision, with the exception of allocating money to supply the armed forces with requisite equipment, ammunition, and other necessary supplies.)

Continuing on the same subject, Mr. Madison once again made a clear and constitutionally sound statement: "Until war be duly authorized by the United States, they are actually neutral when other nations are at war, as they are at peace (if such a distinction in terms is to be kept up) when other nations are not at war." Finally, he explained in "Helvidius" No. 4 why Americans must remain vigilant, keeping close watch over the actions of their elected representatives. To an equal degree, though, Americans must be familiar with the powers granted to those representatives lest they usurp constitutional powers that are not enumerated in that document. Regarding the duty of Americans to learn for themselves and enforce on their elected leaders the limits of federal power set out in the Constitution, Madison wrote:

> It is also to be remembered, that however the consequences flowing from such premises, may be disavowed at this time, or by this individual, we are to regard it as morally certain, that in proportion as the doctrines make their way into the creed of the government, and the acquiescence of the public, every power that can be deduced from them, will be deduced, and exercised sooner or later by those who may have an interest in so doing. The character of human nature gives this salutary warning to every sober and reflecting mind. And the history of government in all its forms and in every period of time, ratifies the danger. A people, therefore, who are so happy as to possess the inestimable blessing of a free and defined constitution cannot be too watchful against the introduction, nor too critical in tracing the consequences, of new principles and new constructions, that may remove the landmarks of power.

Now, it must be understood that while the two men—once collaborators, now combatants—were writing and disagreeing with each other, there was not a sense that either of them undertook to embarrass or personally insult the other. They knew each other well and they respected each other even more. They simply supported opposing views on a question of constitutional ambiguity and took to the press to attempt to persuade the public.

"A Warm Attachment to the Union": The Virginia and Kentucky Resolutions

The next joint venture entered into by James Madison and Thomas Jefferson was the writing of the Virginia and Kentucky Resolutions. They considered a trio of bills passed in 1798 by Congress and signed by President John Adams to be anathema to American liberty and beyond the scope of the powers granted to the federal government in

Chapter Eleven: James Madison and Thomas Jefferson: "The Great Collaboration"

the Constitution. The laws causing Madison and Jefferson so much concern were known collectively as the Alien and Sedition Acts.

After suffering years of French and British warships attacking American commercial vessels and forcing American sailors to join the enemy navies, and fearing that agents of the French government would seek to establish surreptitious influence over the government of the United States, President John Adams signed the Alien Friends Act, the Alien Enemies Act, and the Sedition Act. These laws were intended to prevent any European power from insinuating itself into the halls of American government.

A peace treaty with England put President Adams' mind somewhat at ease regarding relations with Great Britain. He worried, though, that France's refusal to regard the United States as any sort of military threat might result in all-out war with that country. It

President John Adams felt uneasy because of the French government's disdain and lack of respect for the governments and militaries of America and Great Britain.

also didn't help ease the president's mind that France resented the friendly relations between England and the United States.

Accordingly, Adams and his congressional allies enacted the Alien and Sedition Acts to, in their view, protect the country from the pernicious influence of any French foreign agents residing within the United States.

For his part, James Madison was no friend of the French government. He regarded Paris's insults to American envoys as despicable, and viewed the intrigues of French foreign ministers as incompatible with principles of peace and contrary to long-established laws of nations. Regardless, Madison described Adams' reaction to France's contemptuous and arrogant attitude as "vile insults and calumnies, . . . most abominable and degrading," and not at all conducive to peace. Furthermore, he considered the Alien and Sedition Acts to be violative of the Constitution in that they were an exercise by the federal government of authority not granted to it by that document.

Additionally, Madison believed that the enforcement of the acts in question would prevent citizens from considering themselves completely free to exercise the fundamental rights of speech and assembly guaranteed in the First Amendment. He feared that in trying to stand firm in the face of the French, the president and the Congress were denying Americans their most precious civil liberties. On that subject, he observed in a letter to Thomas Jefferson that "it is a universal truth that the loss of liberty at home is to be charged to the provisions against danger, real or pretended, from abroad." Madison saw the arena of American relations with other nations as ripe for abuse, explaining to Jefferson:

> The management of foreign relations appears to be the most susceptible of abuse, of all the trusts committed to a Government, because they can be concealed or disclosed, or disclosed in such parts & at such times as will best suit particular views; and because the body of the people are less capable of judging & are more under the influence of prejudices, on that branch of their affairs, than of any other.

Chapter Eleven: James Madison and Thomas Jefferson: "The Great Collaboration"

Popular Graphic Arts, Public domain, via Wikimedia Commons

The first four presidents of the United States formed a solid foundation for the country with their hard work and genuine interest in the well-being of its citizens.

The act that finally convinced Madison to take up his pen and draft a proposal for consideration by the Virginia state legislature was the arrest of Samuel Jordan Cabell, who represented Thomas Jefferson's home district in Virginia. In May 1797, a grand jury returned a presentment of libel against Cabell (incidentally, as a delegate to the Virginia Ratifying Convention, Cabell voted against ratification of the Constitution). What was his crime? He sent a letter to constituents criticizing the administration of John Adams. For this effrontery to his authority, Adams charged Cabell with "endeavoring at a time of real public danger to disseminate unfounded calumnies against the happy government of the United States."

In response, Madison and Jefferson met on at least two occasions at Monticello (Jefferson's home), agreeing to author a pair of proposals opposing the Alien and Sedition Acts. One of the proposals (to be written by Jefferson), known as the Kentucky Resolutions, would be put forth by friendly state legislators in Kentucky, and the other would be similarly submitted to the General Assembly of Virginia. Madison was the author of the other proposal, the Virginia Resolutions, although his identity was not, for obvious reasons, revealed at the time of the measure's consideration by Virginia state lawmakers.

The text and tone of the Virginia Resolutions are typical of the moderate mien of James Madison—sharp, but sincere; courageous, but considerate. More than anything, the resolutions recite Madison's concept of the correct constitutional relationship between the states and the federal government. Madison's opinion on the subject carries more weight than even that of his cohort, Jefferson, as Madison was present every day in Philadelphia and was an active advocate both at the Constitutional Convention and in *The Federalist*. As fitting for the Father of the Constitution, Madison started by noting that the Virginia Resolutions "doth unequivocally express a firm resolution to maintain and defend the Constitution of the United States." He next stated that the Virginia General Assembly "most solemnly declares a warm attachment to the Union of the States, to maintain which it pledges all its powers. . . ."

Then, Madison began his concise rehearsal of the creation of the Constitution by the states, including the establishment in that document of a federal government, a general government that would serve as the agent of the states. In this regard, the Virginia Resolutions read:

> That this Assembly doth explicitly and peremptorily declare, that it views the powers of the federal government, as resulting from the compact, to which the states are parties; as limited by the plain sense and intention of the instrument constituting the compact; as no further valid than they are authorized by the grants enumerated in that compact; and that in case of a deliberate, palpable, and dangerous exercise of other powers, not granted by the said compact, the states who are parties thereto, have the

Madison and Jefferson collaborated often. On one of these occasions, the pair wrote proposals opposing the Alien and Sedition Acts.

right, and are in duty bound, to interpose for arresting the progress of the evil, and for maintaining within their respective limits, the authorities, rights and liberties appertaining to them.

By "interpose," Madison meant that the states should "stand between" the people and any act of tyranny committed by the federal government. States, explained Madison, have a responsibility to restrain the government of the United States, to keep the federal beast inside its constitutional cage, so to speak. This responsibility is not to be taken lightly, as it is only through the vigilance of the states that the federal government can be kept within the boundaries drawn around its powers by the delegates to the Constitutional Convention of 1787. Madison's proposal then went on to express "deep regret, that a spirit has in sundry instances, been manifested by the federal government, to enlarge its powers by forced constructions of the constitutional charter which defines them."

It is worth noting of the Virginia Resolutions that, once again, we find the Founders (in this case, one of the Founding Fathers' varsity teams!) providing a key to solving a contemporary problem, the problem of a federal government that has grown too large and too powerful. In the end, the state governments of both Virginia and Kentucky passed their respective resolutions, but other states did not follow suit, leaving the lasting solution to the problem of federal overreach for a later generation to discover.

"The Harmony of Our Political Principles": Madison and Jefferson See Key Subjects in the Same Light

In his final letter to James Madison, Thomas Jefferson revealed much of not only his admiration, but his affection for his compatriot, colleague, and confidant. In his letter of February 17, 1826, Jefferson touched on various subjects of common interest—chiefly the management of the University of Virginia—but devoted most of his missive to putting into print his fraternal feelings for Madison:

> [T]he friendship which has subsisted between us, now half a century, and the harmony of our political principles

> and pursuits, have been sources of constant happiness to me thro' that long period. And, if I remove beyond the reach of attentions to the University, or beyond the bourne of life itself, as I soon must, it is a comfort to leave that institution under your care, and an assurance that they will neither be spared, nor ineffectual. [I]t has also been a great solace to me to believe that you are engaged in vindicating to posterity the course we have pursued for preserving to them, *in all their purity*, the blessings of self-government, which we had assisted too in acquiring for them. If ever the earth has beheld a system of administration conducted with a single and steadfast eye, to the general interest and happiness of those committed to it, one which, protected by truth, can never know reproach, it is that to which our lives have been devoted. To myself you have been a pillar of support thro' life. [T]ake care of me when dead, and be assured that I shall leave with you my last affections. (Emphasis in original.)

In a letter written one week later (February 24, 1826)—one that turned out to be one of the last written by James Madison to Thomas Jefferson—Madison echoed his friend's assessment of the benefit of their half-century friendship, not only to each other, but to the country they both loved and to which they had devoted so many decades of their lives. The last paragraph of the letter is reserved by Madison for expressing to Jefferson his tender regard for their lifelong collaboration and close friendship. With obvious affection and admiration, he wrote:

> You cannot look back to the long period of our private friendship & political harmony, with more affecting recollections than I do. If they are a source of pleasure to you, what ought they not to be to me? We can not be deprived of the happy consciousness of the pure devotion to the public good, with which we discharged the trusts committed to us. And I indulge a confidence that sufficient evidence will find its way to another generation,

to ensure, after we are gone, whatever of justice may be witheld whilst we are here. The political horizon is already yielding in your case at least, the surest auguries of it. Wishing & hoping that you may yet live to increase the debt which our Country owes you, and to witness the increasing gratitude, which alone can pay it, I offer you the fullest return of affectionate assurances.

Chapter 12
The Courtship and Marriage of James and Dolley Madison

As strong, lasting, and inspirational as James Madison's partnership with Thomas Jefferson was, it was nothing when compared to the love, friendship, and fidelity he shared with his devoted wife, Dolley. The story of their courtship and marriage is rarely told today, but it is worthy of relating and emulating. "[H]e hopes that your Heart will be calous to every other swain but himself." Those words, written in a letter to Dolley Payne Todd from her friend Catharine Cole on June 1, 1794, reveal a romantic side to James Madison that we rarely read about in other biographies and history textbooks.

There are good reasons for the lack of coverage of the lovesick, fawning follower in most descriptions of the relationship of James and Dolley. First, in the 18th century, the intimate details of courtship and marriage were just that: intimate. Public displays of affection and casual sharing of the correspondence between a man and a woman approaching marriage or already married were considered impolite and indecorous. Second, privacy in personal matters was thought to convey respect for the holy and cherished—something a courtship and a marriage were widely believed to be. So sacred were these relationships and the correspondence and convictions associated with them that Martha Washington destroyed General Washington's letters to her upon his death.

Thankfully, many of the love letters exchanged by James and Dolley (and their trusted intermediaries such as Catharine Cole) remain extant. They provide unique insight into the sights and sounds of a middle-aged, famous, influential, and committed bachelor and the young, beautiful, widow with whom he seems to have fallen instantly in love.

George G. Milford, Public domain, via Wikimedia Commons

Dolley Payne Todd

There was much to love about Dolley Payne Todd. She was described as vivacious and even-tempered, qualities that attracted many men to her. Stories are told of how men would line up outside her father's house just to take a turn trying to appeal to the eldest of John Payne's four daughters.

In 1790, some four years before she would meet the future president and her future second husband, Dolley married an up-and-coming Pennsylvania lawyer named John Todd. Todd was a Quaker, like Dolley, and the two made a very good pair. Soon, two children—John Payne and William Temple—were born to the couple. The young family was growing, and life for the Todds seemed sweet and settled.

Sadly, their lives were soon shattered by the fatal effects of the yellow fever epidemic that devastated Philadelphia. Over five thousand people were killed within four months in 1793, including Dolley's husband, John, and their three-month-old son, William Temple Todd. Even Dolley's extended family was struck hard by the yellow fever outbreak, as her husband's parents also perished. Caring for his parents was likely what kept John himself in a weakened state, so weak that he succumbed to the worst of the disease's attacks.

All told, nearly 20,000 people fled Philadelphia to avoid the ravages of the deadly plague. By the end of the epidemic, Dolley, then a widow of 25, and her young child were left nearly penniless. Unfortunately, Dolley was legally obligated to pay her late husband's debts. Soon, though, the bequests left to her in her husband's and father-in-law's wills were paid to the young widow, and she was able to turn her attention to the successful arrangement of her finances and the education of her son. At this point in the story, Dolley walked into the law office of the man who would introduce her to James Madison—Aaron Burr.

This wasn't the first time Dolley had met Mr. Burr, the charming congressman from New York. While in Philadelphia, he lived in her mother's boarding house, and thus became acquainted with Dolley and her late husband. There is some evidence that Dolley and Aaron Burr were close, though not necessarily in a romantic way. While sorting out schooling for her son, Dolley drew up a will of her own, naming Aaron Burr as the sole guardian of John Payne should she die before she remarried.

In the 18th century, young widows typically remarried rather quickly in order that they might have a household to care for and, if they had children, so that those children could be provided for and protected. Dolley was certainly a young widow, and by all accounts, she was very attractive, as well. According to Ralph Ketcham's biography of Madison, Dolley's friend Elizabeth Collins described how "gentlemen would station themselves where they could see her pass." In light of this fascination with her friend, Elizabeth scolded Dolley, "Really Dolley, thou must hide thy face, there are so many staring at thee."

From Last Rites to Bill of Rights: The Miraculous Life and Legacy of James Madison

James Madison and Dolley Payne Todd married soon after they met.

There is no doubt that Dolley was now financially stable and available. It seems no exaggeration to assert that she was one of the most sought-after young women in Philadelphia in 1794. She was not the only eligible single person in the city that summer, though. Congressman James Madison was also unmarried (and at 43, it was assumed he would stay that way). Enter Aaron Burr, Dolley Madison, and a lifelong love affair and happy marriage.

Meeting "The Great Little Madison"

Sometime in May 1794, James Madison asked his old schoolmate Burr (the two had attended the College of New Jersey together) to introduce him to the young widow everybody talked about—Dolley Payne Todd. Burr graciously obliged.

"Thou must come to me. Aaron Burr says the great little Madison has asked to be brought to see me this evening," Dolley wrote to her friend. Judging from the way she described him, it is unlikely that this was her first time meeting "the great little Madison." Madison traveled frequently to Philadelphia, and on at least one occasion made a trip there with Dolley's uncle, Isaac Coles, a member of Congress. In fact, Ketcham records that later in his life, Madison credited Coles with having introduced him to Dolley.

Little is known about what happened on James and Dolley's first date. As described above, such events were not to be shared casually with anyone other than the couple's closest friends and family. Ketcham recounts in his biography that Dolley wore a "mulberry-colored satin dress, a silk kerchief at her neck, and a tiny cap." James dressed up for the date, too, wearing, according to the same biography, "his new 'Round Beaver' hat." The two made quite a well-dressed pair, and they must have hit it off quite well as they would be married fewer than four months later!

On September 15, 1794, James Madison, Jr. and Dolley Payne Todd were married in the home of George Steptoe Washington, General George Washington's nephew and ward. When the Reverend Alexander Balmain pronounced the couple man and wife, thus began a marriage, a partnership, and a life of wedded bliss that would last forty-two years. In a letter written to her friend on the day

Aaron Burr's introduction of Dolley and James resulted in a full love and lifelong marriage.

she exchanged vows with James, Dolley wrote that she was uniting in holy matrimony "to the man who of all others I most admire." She added that her marriage to James would bring to her "everything that is soothing and grateful in prospect."

Life as Dolley's husband apparently suited James, as one friend reported that marriage had made Madison "much more open and conversant than I had ever seen him before." Others saw a subtle but welcome change in demeanor come across the new husband. One dinner guest of the Madisons described his host as "an incessant humorist" adding that the company all delighted in hearing James' stories "and his whimsical way of telling them."

James and Dolley were happy and hospitable. They were in love with each other, and looking forward to the life they would begin at home in Virginia as soon as James' public duties were at last at an end.

The Madisons' Family Life
For about two years after their wedding, the Madisons lived in Philadelphia while James served as a congressman representing his home district of Orange County, Virginia. They lived at the home of another renowned son of the Old Dominion: James Monroe. Monroe was overseas serving as the ambassador to France and had graciously offered his friend the use of his house while he was away.

Madison, eager to get back to his own home—Montpelier—retired from Congress early in 1797, and he and Dolley left immediately for the Blue Ridge Mountains and the lush green grass of Virginia. Arriving at home, the Madisons settled in along with Dolley's son, John Payne Todd (now five years old), and Anna Payne (Dolley's little sister), and began improving the property and socializing with neighbors and relatives. Dolley was yet a young woman (she was only 29, some 16 years younger than her husband), and she quickly acquired a reputation as a charming hostess, throwing delightful dinner parties at her new Virginia home.

Although James and Dolley had no children of their own, Montpelier was always home to children of relatives. In fact, judging from the letters written by the Madisons and the biographies written about them, there were more than 20 children—mostly nieces, nephews, and young distant relations—running around Montpelier year in and year out. Though they were not parents of their own children, James and Dolley were certainly caring guardians of the many children who lived in their home.

While living and working at their estate, the Madisons welcomed many famous Virginians to their home, including Thomas Jefferson, who in turn hosted the Madisons at Monticello twice a year until his death. Visitors enjoyed the convivial spirit always present at Montpelier. There are scores of letters written by guests of the Madisons describing the pair as friendly and fun. Of particular note in this regard is the memoir of her time at Montpelier written by Dolley's niece, Mary Cutts. Mary's account of the joy that James and Dolley shared as husband and wife and as best friends brings these two historical figures into full and living color:

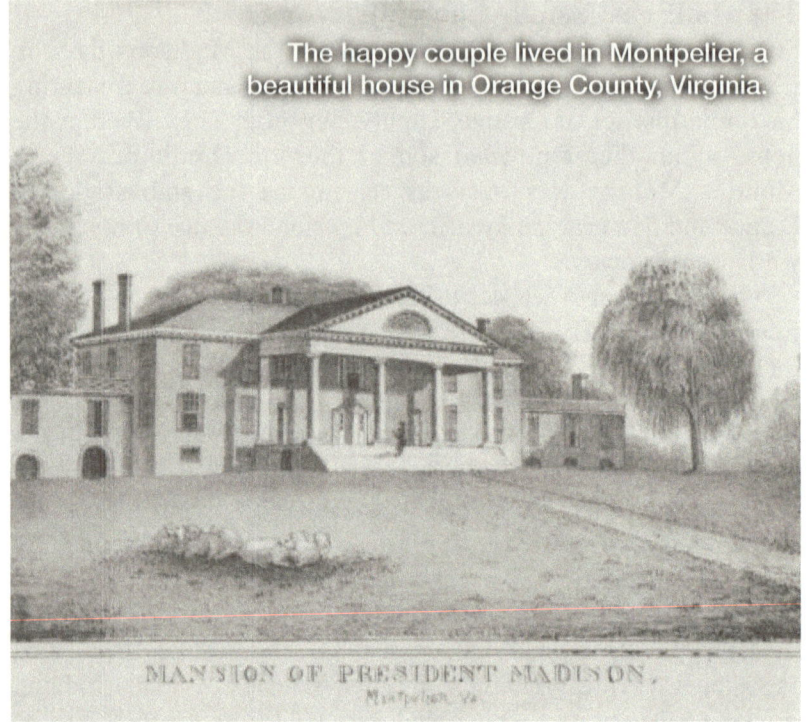

Yale University Art Gallery [1], Public domain, via Wikimedia Commons

Mr. Madison dearly loved and was proud of his wife, the ornament of his house—she was his solace and comfort, he could not bear her to leave his presence, and she gratified him by being absent only when duty required. No matter how agreeably employed she was her first thought and instinct seemed to tell her when she was wanted—if engaged in conversation, she would quickly rise and say, 'I must go to Madison.' On his return from riding round the plantation she would meet him at the door with refreshment in her own hands.

Years later, a regular visitor to Montpelier described a day she spent there in the company of James and Dolley:

> Mr. and Mrs. Madison would in private sometimes romp
> and tease each other like two children, and engage in antics

James and Dolley left for Washington, D.C., and the great Mr. Madison became the fourth president of the United States.

Martin Falbisoner, CC BY-SA 3.0 , via Wikimedia Commons

that would astonish the muse of history. Mrs. Madison was stronger as well as larger than he. She could—and did—seize his hands, draw him upon her back, and go around the room with him.

In every demonstrable way, James and Dolley were devoted to each other, devoted to their friends and family, and devoted to maintaining the mirth and magic of their courtship throughout the decades of their marriage.

James Madison Is Called to Serve His Country . . . Again

A life away from politics, spent in the repose and relative ease of their bucolic Montpelier, was not to last, however. In 1800, Thomas Jefferson was elected president of the United States, and he called on his friend and fellow Virginian, James Madison, to serve as the secretary of state in his administration. James would answer the call to serve, despite his sincere desire to remain the "squire of Montpelier." Setting aside James' own interests for those of his country, he and Dolley headed for Washington, D.C. They were away from their beloved country home for many more years than they had anticipated in 1800, as James would serve his country not only as President Jefferson's secretary of state, but also as president of the United States from 1809-1817.

Chapter 13:
The Pen Is Mightier Than the Sword

As demonstrated already, it was James Madison's pen and preparation that set him above his peers. At no time did he use that pen more often and on a greater range of subjects than during his years as the leader of the Republicans in the House of Representatives. During these years, not only did Madison fulfill his promise to deliver a bill of rights, but he regularly published the bountiful harvest of his many years of hard work and hours upon hours of reading and pondering the words of the wisest writers in history, including specific and frequent references to Aristotle, Thucydides, and Pliny.

Madison learned, as described in an earlier chapter, that lessons from history could be applied to the challenges facing the young United States. He believed that by familiarizing his countrymen with the causes and effects of historical events, the good examples could be followed and the actions that led to destruction could be avoided. "[I]t is universally admitted that a well instructed people alone, can be permanently a free people," Madison wrote. He added that such endeavors should be "favorite objects with every free people," because of the ability of the lessons of history to "throw that light over the public mind which is the best security against crafty and dangerous encroachments on the public liberty."

For that very purpose—to share with his fellow Americans the lessons he had learned from years of diligent study and pondering over the stories from the history of the world—Madison took up his persuasive pen and began to write essays aimed at providing a view on key concepts of liberty, a view different from that put forth in a number of policy reports written by Secretary of the Treasury Alexander Hamilton.

Madison's essays are regarded as a prototype of party platforms that would become the norm in later years, after the establishment of two major political parties, as he would make clear for his fellow Americans the significant and substantial differences between the so-called Jeffersonian Republicans and those pushing for a more powerful central government that could exercise a grander scope of implied powers.

Even in this endeavor, Jefferson contributed in some degree, informing Madison in a letter written to him in March of 1791, "When I get my library open you will often find a convenience in being close at hand to it."

So as not to bring unwelcome attention to Jefferson—who was then serving as secretary of state in the George Washington administration—and to not even tacitly require that the Republicans throughout the country defend the positions he would take in these explanatory essays, Madison published nearly all of them anonymously. He wrote at least 18 essays between November 1791 and December 1792. These essays were published in newspapers around the country, particularly in those papers where the editors were philosophically allied to Madison, Jefferson, and the Republican cause.

The *National Gazette*, published by Madison's college friend Philip Freneau, was the principal vehicle for the publication of these essays, which proved so popular that within a year the *Gazette* had over 1,700 subscribers! Each of the essays was devoted to expounding on some principle of government and freedom that Madison considered critical to the preservation of liberty and the union of the states.

In light of Madison's exceptional skill in seeing patterns in history, several excerpts from these essays will be included here with the hope that the counsel shared therein might be of use to his modern countrymen. It is unfortunate that these essays are rarely noted in most biographies of James Madison. They are full of the learning and wisdom acquired by James Madison over decades of study and

Chapter Thirteen: The Pen Is Mightier Than the Sword

The *National Gazette* published many of James' essays.

application, and are uniquely germane to our own time and political situation. For that reason if for no other, these letters deserve to be brought to the reader's attention and the counsel provided in them merits publication and pondering.

"Population and Emigration"

One of Madison's first essays, published anonymously in the *National Gazette*, was entitled "Population and Emigration," in which he enlightened readers on the benefits of permitting immigrants into the United States and of free trade with foreign nations. "Freedom of emigration is due to the general interests of humanity. The course of emigrations being always, from places where living is more difficult, to places where it is less difficult, the happiness of the emigrant is promoted by the change," Madison explained.

He wrote later in this essay that "freedom of emigration is favorable to morals," because those who leave the lands of their birth to settle in the United States will eventually have children, and those children will grow up in a country where virtue is promoted and vice scorned. In his essay, then, Madison taught that, when immigrants come to improve their lives and the lives of their families, and when they adopt the virtues of their new home and contribute meaningfully to the well-being of the United States immigration is good for both parties.

The principles and recommendations published by Madison in this letter echoed the message he delivered in Congress in 1790 during debate on Congress's first effort to establish a standard set of qualifications for becoming a citizen of the United States of America. (Madison's speech on that occasion is found in Chapter 10.)

About a month after his first essay was published, he submitted his next letter. This time, his focus was the nature of the union and whether the United States was a consolidated government or a compact among sovereign states.

"Consolidation"

Madison opened this essay by admitting that, "not without reason," there is much said "against the consolidation of the states into one government." He went on to name two dangerous consequences of converting the United States into one consolidated government. First, we would see the "accumulation of powers into the hands [of the president], as might by degrees transform him into a monarch." Then, as the presidency accumulates power, it increases the "splendor and number of its prerogatives" and thus attracts people with "ambition too powerful for sober execution of the elective plan. . . ."

In other words, if the power of the states is consolidated unconstitutionally into the hands of the federal government, then the president will likely become the seat of most of that usurped power. Next, the power, pomp, and prestige of that office would entice people who want that power and luxury to seek the presidency, rather than people who wish to act according to the boundaries of presidential power established in the Constitution.

The second ill effect of the consolidation of the United States into one all-powerful central government would be that the states would be "abolished" and the Congress would never truly know "the voice nor the sense of" the citizens of the entire country, thus preventing "a faithful discharge of its trust," the obligation congressmen have to represent the will of the people they represent.

Finally, if the state governments and their authority were dissolved, the federal government would assume all political power and would leave the federal government "to that self directed course which, it must be owned, is the natural propensity of every government." Once again, were it applied to our own day, the wisdom and counsel of James Madison written about 225 years ago could solve many of the serious problems plaguing the modern United States.

"Public Opinion"

Madison's next paper dealt with the power of the people in a republic. He declared in the opening sentence that "Public opinion sets bounds to every government, and is the real sovereign in every free one." However, in a large country such as the United States, it may be difficult to determine the "real opinion" of the people. He then wrote that in such a country, the public opinion might be "counterfeited" for the purpose of increasing "the authority of the government" and that such false reporting would be "unfavorable to liberty." Then, as he always does after diagnosing the disease, Madison prescribed a cure.

He suggested that "a circulation of newspapers through the entire body of the people, and Representatives going from, and returning among every part of them" would be "favorable to liberty." It is crucial that reliable information be made available to all the people so that the government might be kept within its proper bounds and liberty might be protected.

Madison then restated the benefits and admitted the detriments in expanding a republic over a large geographic area, something political philosophers for centuries insisted would be impossible. Demonstrating a deftness of thought and clarity of description, he revealed how the trouble the wise men of the ages detected in big self-governing societies might also be a problem for the United States:

> The larger a country, the less easy for its real opinion to be ascertained, and the less difficult to be counterfeited; when ascertained or presumed, the more respectable it is in the eyes of individuals. This is favorable to the authority of government. For the same reason, the more extensive a country, the more insignificant is each individual in his own eyes. This may be unfavorable to liberty.

"Government"

On New Year's Eve 1791, Madison submitted to the *National Gazette* an essay entitled simply "Government." In this paper, Madison set out the reasons a republican form of government is superior to all others. In monarchies, he noted, there are two dangers: first, "the eyes of a good prince cannot see all that he ought to know"; and second, "the hands of a bad one will not be tied by the fear of combinations against him." Aristocracies are better than monarchies as they are generally "tempered by the facility and the fear of combinations among the people." This is only true in a small country, however. In a large country such as the United States, aristocracy is "intolerable." Finally, in defense of republics,

Madison wrote, "A republic involves the idea of popular rights." In other words, the people rule through elected representatives who are oath-bound to protect the sacred liberties of the people they serve.

He then went on to explain how a republic can be protected from the terrors of tyranny:

> To secure all the advantages of such a system, every good citizen will be at once a centinel over the rights of the people; over the authorities of the confederal government; and over both the rights and the authorities of the intermediate governments.

"Charters"

Madison's next essay is a powerful pronouncement of the true source of American liberty. In most countries, he wrote, "charters [constitutions] of liberty have been granted by power." In the United States, however, we have a "charter of power granted by liberty." How beautifully simple and how simply beautiful! In the United States, the people do not derive their liberty from the power of their rulers; rather the rulers derive their power from the liberty (the consent) of the people. The American Revolution, Madison said, made it possible for us to "look forward with joy, to the period, when it [despotism] shall be despoiled of all its usurpations, and bound for ever in the chains, with which it had loaded its miserable victims."

What is the price we as Americans must pay for our liberty? Madison wrote that all the principles included in our Declaration of Independence and in our Constitution are secured in proportion to "the vigilance with which they are guarded by every citizen in private life, and the circumspection with which they are executed by every citizen in public trust." Here again, we find in Madison's words the wisdom necessary to preserve our republic and the liberty we enjoy under the Constitution. We, the people, must remain vigilant and virtuous, while those who are elected to political office must restrain their use of power according to the limits enumerated in the Constitution.

Later in this essay, Madison made a similar, though more direct, point regarding the obligation placed upon citizens of the United

States to be responsible for retaining their unique federal system of self-government. He wrote:

> Being republicans, they must be anxious to establish the efficacy of popular charters, in defending liberty against power, and power against licentiousness: and in keeping every portion of power within its proper limits; by this means discomfiting the partizans of anti-republican contrivances for the purpose.

Next, Madison warned what would happen should the people of the United States fail to perform their role of watchmen, protectors of liberty, and guardians of the limits of constitutional powers. "The most systematic governments are turned by the slightest impulse from their regular path, when the public opinion no longer holds them in it," he explained. Simply put, if Americans fail to force the federal government to remain within the constitutional bright lines limiting its powers, then they will easily stray from the path of liberty onto the path that leads to its destruction by despots.

Madison closed this essay with a powerful, persuasive appeal to the American people to protect with "holy zeal" the liberty they enjoy:

> How devoutly is it to be wished, then, that the public opinion of the United States should be enlightened; that it should attach itself to their governments as delineated in the great charters [the Declaration of Independence and the Constitution], derived not from the usurped power of kings, but from the legitimate authority of the people; and that it should guarantee, with a holy zeal, these political scriptures from every attempt to add to or diminish from them. Liberty and order will never be perfectly safe, until a trespass on the constitutional provisions for either, shall be felt with the same keenness that resents an invasion of the dearest rights.

Fewer than six days passed between the publication of Madison's essay on charters and his next piece, "Parties."

Chapter Thirteen: The Pen Is Mightier Than the Sword

James' essays were alluring and engaging. His knowledge and integrity truly shaped the United States.

"Parties"

To begin his examination of the danger of parties, Madison admitted that they are "unavoidable." He suggested, therefore, that the focus of the people "should be to combat the evil" that they present to our political peace, and listed a few ways that Americans can reduce the influence of parties.

The first policy Madison proposed is to establish "political equality among all." This is a recitation of the "self-evident" principle put forth in the Declaration of Independence that "all men are created equal." This equality is one of opportunity, of course, not one of outcome. An attempt by government to guarantee equality of outcome would violate one of Madison's warnings against "violating the rights of property," thus actually working to increase the influence of parties rather than reduce it.

Next, Madison described something that we today call "crony capitalism." Crony capitalism is the manipulation of the law to the benefit of a small group of citizens by burdening another group, typically through taxation. It is what amounts to corporate welfare, and it should be avoided with a zeal equal to that of the shunning of "entitlements" paid to people by the federal government out of taxes taken from laborers. Americans can limit the expansion and exercise of power by parties by "abstaining from measures which operate differently on different interests, and particularly such as favor one interest at the expense of another."

Since the creation of political parties cannot be avoided, Madison advised devising a system whereby parties check and balance each other, preventing any one of them from becoming too powerful. This is the republican way, Madison insisted. Without this checking of one party's power by another party's power, false distinctions are created "by favoring an inequality of property" and by "establishing kings, and nobles, and plebeians." This, Madison said, is not the republican way.

It is apparent from this essay that Madison perceived immense danger in the growth of political parties among a free people. In this article, he echoed the warning he wrote some three years earlier in *Federalist* No. 10, wherein he declared:

Chapter Thirteen: The Pen Is Mightier Than the Sword

42 THE FEDERALIST.

CITIES, or republics, the largest were entitled to *three* votes in the COMMON COUNCIL, those of the middle class to *two*, and the smallest to *one*. The COMMON COUNCIL had the appointment of all the judges and magistrates of the respective CITIES. This was certainly the most delicate species of interference in their internal administration; for if there be any thing that seems exclusively appropriated to the local jurisdictions, it is the appointment of their own officers. Yet Montesquieu, speaking of this association, says, "Were I to give a model of an excellent confederate republic, it would be that of Lycia." Thus we perceive, that the distinctions insisted upon were not within the contemplation of this enlightened writer; and we shall be led to conclude, that they are the novel refinements of an erroneous theory. PUBLIUS.

NUMBER X.

BY JAMES MADISON.

THE SAME SUBJECT CONTINUED.

AMONG the numerous advantages promised by a well constructed union, none deserves to be more accurately developed than its tendency to break and control the violence of faction. The friend of popular governments, never finds himself so much alarmed for their character and fate, as when he contemplates their propensity to this dangerous vice. He will not fail, therefore, to set a due value on any plan which, without violating the principles to which he is attached, provides a proper cure for it. The instability, injustice, and confusion, introduced into the public councils, have in truth, been the mortal diseases under which popular governments have every where perished; as they continue to be the favorite and fruitful topics from which the adversaries to liberty derive their most specious declamations. The valuable improvements made by the American constitutions on the popular models, both ancient and modern, cannot certainly be too much admired; but it would be an unwarrantable partiality, to contend that they have as effectually obviated the danger on this side, as was wished and expected. Complaints are every where heard from our most considerate and virtuous citizens, equally the friends of public and private faith, and of public and personal liberty, that our governments are too unstable; that the public good is disregarded in the conflicts of rival parties; and that measures are too often decided, not according to the rules of justice, and the rights of the minor party, but by the superior force of an interested and overbearing majority. However anxiously we may wish that these complaints had no

James warned against the dangers of political parties without checks and balances in *Federalist* No. 10.

> Complaints are every where heard from our most considerate and virtuous citizens, equally the friends of public and private faith, and of public and personal liberty, that our governments are too unstable; that the public good is disregarded in the conflicts of rival parties; and that measures are too often decided, not according to the rules of justice, and the rights of the minor party, but by the superior force of an interested and overbearing majority.

In his essay "Parties," however, it seems evident that Madison considered it more dangerous to violate the right of property in any misguided effort to create "artificial distinctions" among the people. The right of a person to own property, improve property, and benefit from the fruit of his efforts is, to James Madison, vital to the maintenance of a self-governing society. Equally, the violation by government, politicians, or political parties of that right is fatal to freedom.

"Universal Peace"

Here is another piece very applicable to more modern times. Madison's essay expresses hope in its identification of the types of war and the means of eliminating it, or limiting its frequency.

First, he wrote that "war contains so much folly, as well as wickedness" that Americans should try everything to avoid it. In another letter written a few years later, he echoed this sentiment, writing, "Of all the enemies to public liberty war is, perhaps, the most to be dreaded, because it comprises and develops the germ of every other [enemy of liberty]." Madison went on to suggest a way to reduce the zeal of some ambitious men for the waging of war:

> [W]hilst war is to depend on those whose ambition, whose revenge, whose avidity, or whose caprice may contradict the sentiment of the community, and yet be uncontrolled by it; whilst war is to be declared by those who are to spend the public money, not by those who are to pay it; by

those who are to direct the public forces, not by those who are to support them; by those whose power is to be raised, not by those whose chains may be riveted the disease must continue to be hereditary like the government of which it is the offspring. As the first step towards a cure, the government itself must be regenerated. Its will must be made subordinate to, or rather the same with, the will of the community.

What wise counsel! If, as Madison insists, war is an enemy to liberty, the best way to defeat that enemy is to keep the government under the watchful eye and complete control of the people whose sons and daughters would be sacrificed by the prosecuting of the war. This exercise of dominion is critical, Madison explained, because war is declared by people who will profit from it, but is fought by people who will suffer from it. Therefore, we cannot let the former segment of society be set free from the control of the latter, lest we see the waging of perpetual war and the ruination of liberty.

There is, Madison instructed, another type of war: war waged because the people demand it. This type of war is more difficult to control; Madison insisted that the way to "remedy" this disease is by "establishing permanent and constitutional maxims of conduct, which may prevail over occasional impressions, and inconsiderate pursuits." While the people are sovereign in the United States and in all free societies, sometimes the people's passions will lead them to make decisions that are not in the best interest of protecting life, liberty, and property. At these times, the limits on power placed in the Constitution are reliable resources for reducing the damage that could be done by rashly reacting to perceived slights by engaging in deadly combat.

Five days after this essay's publication, on February 4, 1792, Madison wrote another essay expanding themes he first wrote about in *The Federalist* and in his studies on ancient and modern confederacies. This time, his topic was one vitally important to all Americans: "The Government of the United States."

"The Government of the United States"
First, Madison laid the foundation of all free governments: separation of powers. "Power, being found by universal experience liable to abuses, a distribution of it into separate departments, has become a first principle of free governments," he wrote, repeating his position put forth in *Federalist* No. 51. Next, he praised those systems of government that are "modelled on a partition of their powers into legislative, executive, and judiciary, and a repartition of the legislative into different houses." But even among governments where power is divided among different branches, he said, the American federal system is worthy of higher praise:

> The power delegated by the people is first divided between the general government and the state governments; each of which is then subdivided into legislative, executive, and judiciary departments. And as in a single government these departments are to be kept separate and safe, by a defensive armour for each; so, it is to be hoped, do the two governments possess each the means of preventing or correcting unconstitutional encroachments of the other.

This is an echo of the point he made in *Federalist* No. 39: "The local or municipal authorities form distinct and independent portions of the supremacy, no more subject, within their respective spheres, to the general authority than the general authority is subject to them, within its own sphere."

Madison then predicted the benefit to the world that the U.S. Constitution would be if not "marred in the execution." The Constitution of the United States "may prove the best legacy ever left by lawgivers to their country, and the best lesson ever given to the world by its benefactors," he declared.

Therein lies the key. Can we, as the benefactors of this marvelously crafted Constitution, make sure that the government remains restrained by the statutes of the Constitution? Or will we see our praiseworthy country reduced to a historical relic by our failure to follow its formula for maintaining freedom?

Then, to drive the point home about the "palladium of constitutional

> ## THE FEDERALIST.
>
> Would they not act with more consistency, in urging the establishment of the latter, as no less necessary to guard the union against the future powers and resources of a body constructed like the existing congress, than to save it from the dangers threatened by the present impotency of that assembly?
>
> I mean not by any thing here said, to throw censure on the measures which have been pursued by congress. I am sensible that they could not have done otherwise. The public interest, the necessity of the case, imposed upon them the task of overleaping their constitutional limits. But is not the fact an alarming proof of the danger resulting from a government, which does not possess regular powers commensurate to its objects? A dissolution, or usurpation, is the dreadful dilemma to which it is continually exposed.
>
> PUBLIUS.
>
> ## NUMBER XXXIX.
>
> BY MR. MADISON.
>
> *The Conformity of the Plan to Republican Principles: An Objection in respect to the powers of the Convention, examined.*
>
> THE last paper having concluded the observations, which were meant to introduce a candid survey of the plan of government reported by the convention, we now proceed to the execution of that part of our undertaking.
>
> The first question that offers itself is, whether the general form and aspect of the government be strictly republican? It is evident that no other form would be reconcileable with the genius of the people of America; with the fundamental principles of the revolution; or with that honourable determination, which animates every votary of freedom, to rest all our political experiments, on the capacity of mankind for self-government. If

In Federalist No. 39, James discussed the importance of governments building upon the other, working together to be most effective for the people.

liberty," Madison reminded the people of their sacred obligation to guard themselves from government overreach. "The people who are the authors of this blessing, must also be its guardians. Their eyes must be ever ready to mark, their voice to pronounce, and their arm to repel or repair aggressions on the authority of their constitutions. . . ," he stated with simplicity and sincerity.

"Spirit of Governments"

"Governments," Madison explained, may be "properly divided, according to their predominant spirit and principles into three species. . . ." Understanding Madison's taxonomy of governments will assist modern Americans in vigilantly ensuring that their own governments are of the sort best suited to sustaining liberty.

The first of the three types of government is one "operating by a permanent military force, which at once maintains the government, and is maintained by it; which is at once the cause of burdens on the people, and of submission in the people to their burdens." The second sort of government described by Madison in this essay is one to which he implores America to "never descend." He described it thus:

> A government operating by corrupt influence; substituting the motive of private interest in place of public duty; converting its pecuniary dispensations into bounties to favorites, or bribes to opponents; accommodating its measures to the avidity of a part of the nation instead of the benefit of the whole: in a word, enlisting an army of interested partizans, whose tongues, whose pens, whose intrigues, and whose active combinations, by supplying the terror of the sword, may support a real domination of the few, under an apparent liberty of the many. Such a government, wherever to be found, is an imposter.

His words could not be more timely or more terrifying. He went on to say while describing that last type of government that "It will be both happy and honorable for the United States, if they never descend to mimic the costly pageantry of its form, nor betray themselves into the venal spirit of its administration." The critical inquiry for modern Americans, then, is this: Have we descended to a place where we accept this sort of spirit in our governing councils? Fortunately, we have Madison's words to warn us and make us aware of the serious damage done by such despotic regimes.

The final type of government is a government "deriving its energy from the will of the society, and operating by the reason of its measures, on the understanding and interest of the society." James Madison proclaimed proudly that such governments are "the republican governments which it is the glory of America to have invented, and her unrivalled happiness to possess." The message here is that Americans will continue to be happy as long as they continue to support the republican form of government, government founded firmly on the consent of the governed.

"Property"

The final essay written anonymously by Madison and published in the *National Gazette* that will be discussed in this book is the one titled "Property." In his treatment of this subject, he portrayed it as one which "embraces every thing to which a man may attach a value and have a right; and *which leaves to every one else the like advantage*." (Emphasis in original.)

Property, Madison explained in finer detail, includes "a man's land, or merchandize, or money," as well as "his opinions and the free communication of them." That is a very expansive definition of property, and it shines a bright light not only on the Founders' profound desire to protect property, but on exactly what they meant when they said "property."

He proceeded in this vein to enumerate the various forms of property that a man may be said to possess:

> He has a property of peculiar value in his religious opinions, and in the profession and practice dictated by them. He has a property very dear to him in the safety and liberty of his person. He has an equal property in the free use of his faculties and free choice of the objects on which to employ them. In a word, as a man is said to have a right to his property, he may be equally said to have a property in his rights.

With this conception of property provided by James Madison, one more fully appreciates the protections afforded by the Bill of Rights. When the Founders explicitly protected "life, liberty, [and] property" in the Fifth Amendment, the last of those words did not simply refer to the physical terrain a man might possess or plow. They were speaking of the full spectrum of rights a man possesses, as well as his unfettered right to use them as he may see fit, provided he does not thereby infringe on those same rights possessed by another man. To Madison and the men of the Founding Generation, a man's freedom, then, was no less his property than his farm.

As for how the government of the United States should treat the property rights of its citizens, Madison declared that the government would be unjust if it permitted property to be "violated by arbitrary seizures of one class of citizens for the service of the rest." In other words, that government is unjust which establishes a system wherein the laws are manipulated to redistribute wealth from those who work to those who do not.

Another symptom of a system of government suffering from the disease of despotism is one "where arbitrary restrictions, exemptions, and monopolies deny to part of its citizens that free use of their faculties, and free choice of their occupations, which not only constitute their property in the general sense of the word; but are the means of acquiring property strictly so called." So, not only is the redistribution of wealth unjust, but the prevention of a man from keeping the fruits of his labor is also a type of tyranny. Any laws or regulations aimed at depriving Americans (or any man) from the full enjoyment of the full panoply of his rights of property are, Madison insists, "in violation of that sacred property, which Heaven, in decreeing man to earn his bread by the sweat of his brow, kindly reserved to him."

Regarding the propensity of governments throughout history to impose heavy taxes that burden one class and benefit another, Madison made his position very clear:

> A just security to property is not afforded by that government, under which unequal taxes oppress one species of property and reward another species: where arbitrary taxes invade the domestic sanctuaries of the rich, and excessive taxes grind the faces of the poor; where the keenness and competitions of want are deemed an insufficient spur to labor, and taxes are again applied, by an unfeeling policy....

Property rights are threatened, then, not only by a redistribution of property, but by an oppressive system of taxation wherein the poor are prevented from ever prospering and the homes of all people are ravaged by the regulations.

Finally, Madison declared that if the governments of the United States are to be praiseworthy:

> they will equally respect the rights of property, and the property in rights: they will rival the government that most sacredly guards the former; and by repelling its example in violating the latter, will make themselves a pattern to that and all other governments.

There you have it—James Madison clearly pointing the way for his posterity to enjoy the bounty and peace that are the products of establishing and maintaining a government devoted unwaveringly to the protection of the rights of property—in all its forms—and to the avoidance of any scheme of taxation wherein men are denied the benefits of the fruit of their labors so that another class may be preserved.

In light of the immense influence that Madison had on the formation of the United States—in the drafting of the Constitution, the co-authorship of *The Federalist*, and the sponsoring of the Bill of Rights in the first Congress—the essays examined above are included in this book because they are rarely taught today.

As for the reception of Madison's essays, the newspaper—the *National Gazette*—went from zero to 1,700 subscribers during the period in which the paper published them.

Alma mater, CC BY-SA 3.0, via Wikimedia Commons

James Madison, the pseudonymous proponent of peace, prosperity, and the rights of man to the enjoyment of all varieties of his property, would soon surrender his anonymity to step into the office of secretary of state, serving under his friend and fellow Republican Party leader, President Thomas Jefferson.

Chapter 14
Secretary of State

James Madison served as secretary of state under Thomas Jefferson for all eight years of the Jefferson administration. Jefferson, of course, knew he could trust Madison and, what's more, he knew that Madison's concept of constitutional construction mirrored his own.

Late in December 1800, Jefferson wrote to Madison asking him to hurry to Washington, D.C., so that he could inspire in the Republicans in Congress "confidence & joy unbounded" before they headed home for the holidays. Sadly, circumstances beyond his control would keep Madison at home in Montpelier longer than Jefferson would have liked, as he suffered a setback in his always fragile health and was unable to travel. A greater tragedy would follow on the heels of that misfortune, however.

"The Flame of Life Went Out":
The Death of James Madison, Sr.
On February 27, 1801, James Madison, Sr. passed away after suffering for some time from ill health. As the oldest son and executor of his will—written 13 years before his death—James had little time to mourn his father's passing; his filial and legal duties demanded he undertake the delicate and time-consuming task of settling his father's estate. The "melancholy" that descended upon James Madison, Jr. is understandable, particularly when one takes into account the decades of devotion to his father. The tenderness of that devotion was manifest in nearly every letter from son to father, letters always opening with the salutation "Honored Sir" and always ending with the title "Your dutiful son."

In a letter written to an anxious Thomas Jefferson, Madison expressed his heartache at losing his father:

> I had proposed to leave home in a few days, so as to be with you shortly after the 4th. of March. A melancholy occurrence has arrested this intention. My father's health for several weeks latterly seemed to revive, and we had hopes that the approach of milder seasons would still further contribute to keep him with us. A few days past however he became sensibly worse, and yesterday morning rather suddenly, tho' very gently the flame of life went out.

In his biography of Madison, Ralph Ketcham eloquently eulogized the filial relationship of James Madison, Jr. to "the old colonel," James Madison, Sr.:

> Thus ended for his [James Madison, Sr.'s] fifty-year-old son decades of trust, reliable support, and admired example. His letters to his father covering a span of over thirty years, and invariably opening with an "Honored sir" and closing with "Your dutiful son," never showed the slightest ill-will or irascibility, and scarcely ever even any misunderstanding. The father had made an immense contribution to the moral and practical education of his son, and deserves therefore an important share of the credit for the sensible, human qualities of the son's statesmanship.

As was consistent with his character, Madison settled his father's estate carefully and equitably, without the least record of sibling squabble. He made sure that all his surviving brothers and sisters, as well as the surviving children of his deceased siblings, were provided for amply by his father's many holdings, and kept Montpelier and the surrounding acreage for himself. With the larger, more complicated probate matters managed successfully, James handed over control of the residue of the estate to his brother William, and set out for Washington, D.C., and his new post as a member of the president's Cabinet.

James Madison, Sr. was a beaming example to James, and was always a supportive and nurturing father.

"The Political Lien to Which I Have Subjected Myself": Madison Devotes His Time to Faithfully Executing His Duties

Madison arrived in Washington, D.C., on May 1, 1801. On May 2, he was administered the oath of office, officially assuming the office of the secretary of state of the United States. For nearly three weeks, James and Dolley were guests at the White House, then called the "President's House." The house was as yet unfinished, so it would have likely seemed cramped quarters to men used to the ample accommodations of Monticello and Montpelier.

James Madison began work right away, a particular benefit to Thomas Jefferson, who had been effectively serving as his own secretary of state while Madison was home in Virginia. Madison set about to "devote the whole of [his] time and pen to public duties."

He always took very seriously his service to his country, and considered it an obligation of sorts to do all he could to perpetuate the liberty won on the battlefields of the War of Independence. He would not—and could not—forget the "lives, fortunes, and sacred honor" sacrificed by so many of his contemporaries. This memory spurred him to carry out his duties with exactness and excellence.

The new secretary of state would face several constitutional challenges during his time holding that office, but he would never abandon his principles, no matter the motivation. The first and perhaps historically most notable of these challenges was the negotiation of the Louisiana Purchase in 1803.

"A Truly Noble Acquisition": The Louisiana Purchase

Within two years of President Jefferson's inauguration, his secretary of state was handling one of the world's most historic transfers of land. Robert R. Livingston was the ambassador of the United States to France, and Jefferson appointed James Monroe to be a special assistant to Livingston in Paris. Those men, along with Charles Pinckney, the minister to Spain, which claimed part of Louisiana, were under orders from Madison (under whose jurisdiction foreign relations fell) to never forget the "value applied to the distinct Territories in question [Louisiana Territory]," and that as such they "deserve[d] particular attention."

Monroe arrived in France on April 10, 1803, and within 24 hours, the French Minister of Foreign Affairs, Charles Talleyrand, made an offer to Monroe that Madison and Jefferson couldn't refuse: Would the United States like to buy the whole of the Louisiana Territory?

After many late-night negotiations between Monroe and Livingston for the Americans and the French liaisons working for Napoleon, Livingston began to believe that the price for this prize would be too good to pass up, and he wrote a letter telling just that to Secretary of State James Madison. From its opening lines, one can sense the surprise and urgency in Livingston's letter: "I have just come from the Minister of the Treasury our conversation was so important that I think it necessary to write it while the impressions

In 1803, Robert R. Livingston negotiated the Louisiana Purchase.

are strong upon my mind," Livingston wrote, no doubt feverishly. "[And] the rather as I fear that I shall not have time to copy & send this letter if I differ it till morning."

After chronicling the nearly hour-by-hour details of the intricate diplomatic intrigues, Livingston seemingly giddily writes to Madison, "We shall do all we can to *cheapen the purchase but my present sentiment is that we shall buy.*" (Emphasis in original.)

And buy it they did! On April 30, 1803, Livingston and Monroe signed a preliminary agreement transferring "the whole of Louisiana" to the United States in consideration of the payment of $11,250,000 in cash and the cancellation of about $3,750,000 in French debt, adding up to a grand total of $15 million paid for over 820,000 square miles of territory that would now belong to the United States.

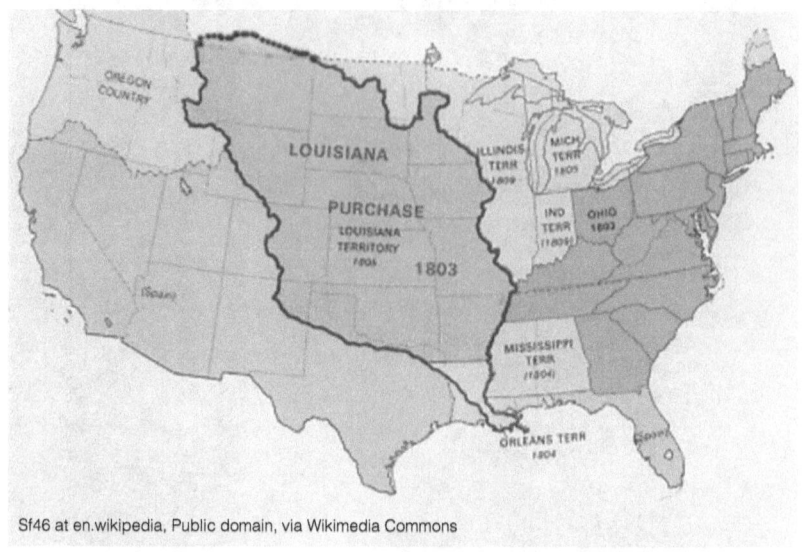

Sf46 at en.wikipedia, Public domain, via Wikimedia Commons

Madison counseled the president to maintain a position of integrity in acquiring Louisiana through a treaty.

Now, there were those who protested President Jefferson and Secretary Madison's agreement to purchase land in the name of the United States. Some, such as Senator John Quincy Adams, argued that as the Constitution was silent on the issue, an amendment would need to be added before the deal with France could be finalized. Even some members of Jefferson and Madison's own party criticized the agreement, claiming the pair were abandoning their "strict constructionist" roots. The president and his secretary of state denied this accusation, pointed to provisions of the Constitution that authorized the acquisition, and explained how the purchase of the Louisiana territory would actually advance key principles of American liberty.

First, Jefferson and Madison met at Monticello to deliberate over precisely how to address the charges of constitutional violations coming from those within their own party. They knew that simply saying that

Chapter Fourteen: Secretary of State

the purchase was the right thing to do would be insufficient to quell the criticism. Next, in the meeting, Madison noted that the purchase of Louisiana would be the result of a treaty signed between the United States and France, therefore, Article II, Section 2 of the Constitution granted President Jefferson the authority to make the deal.

Article II, Section 2 reads, in relevant part: "He [the president] shall have power, by and with the advice and consent of the Senate, to make treaties, provided two thirds of the Senators present concur. . . ." Madison insisted that, provided that two-thirds of the Senate ratified the treaty (which they did by a vote of 24-7 on October 20), then neither the Constitution's separation of powers nor its enumeration would be trespassed.

Furthermore, Madison—in cooperation with Albert Gallatin, secretary of the Treasury—reassured President Jefferson that if the states had not intended for territory to be added to the United States by treaty, they would have expressly placed the power elsewhere, with another branch of the federal government, as such an act was certainly a general and not a local concern.

Finally, Madison reminded Jefferson that even though the purchase would be achieved by treaty, the money to close the deal would have to be approved by the House of Representatives as mandated by Article I, Section 7 of the Constitution, which reads in relevant part: "All bills for raising revenue shall originate in the House of Representatives. . . ." This, Madison said, would provide yet another constitutional check on the agreement. If the Senate failed to ratify the treaty or the House of Representatives failed to allocate funds to pay the cost agreed upon by Monroe, Livingston, and Talleyrand, then the purchase would not be made, there would be no cause for criticism, and, most importantly, the relevant clauses of the Constitution would have been strictly enforced.

President Jefferson listened to the wise counsel given him by James Madison, believing that there was nothing that could compel his friend and secretary of state to violate the very document he held so dear and had helped to craft in 1787. Jefferson trusted Madison's constitutional consistency and his personal integrity. In the end, that trust, more than anything, convinced Jefferson to give his "entire approbation" to the Louisiana Purchase.

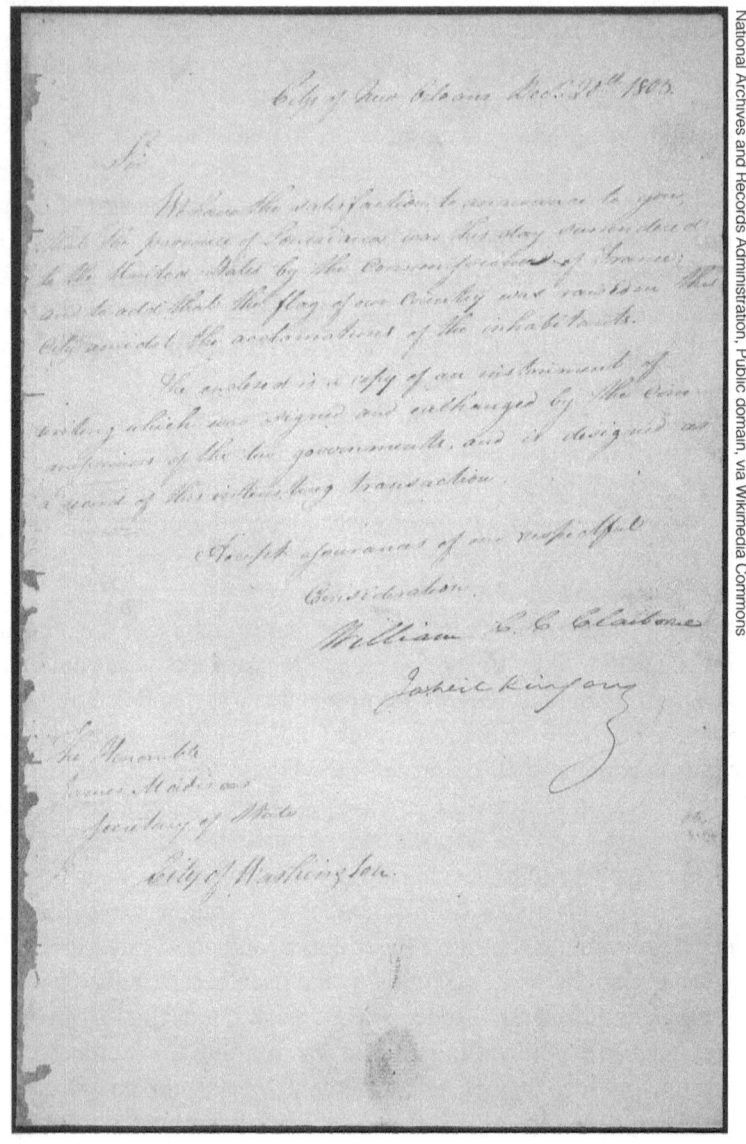

The letter from France written to James Madison that announced the surrender of Louisiana.

"The Security of Our Citizens and the Rights of Our Flag": Britain Begins Belligerent Behavior

As President Thomas Jefferson's second term of office began, so did Secretary of State James Madison's. Madison had developed a deftness in diplomacy, as well as a nearly indefatigable instinct to discern when the federal government or any of its agents were getting close to the constitutional boundaries of their power. This would serve him well as the exultation experienced after the Louisiana Purchase turned to trouble with our old foe: Great Britain.

As the war between France and Great Britain escalated, Britain ruled the seas nearly without challenge, and she pointed squadrons of her mighty navy westward toward the United States. In theory, this meant Great Britain would make sure that American trade was prevented from weakening His Majesty's subjects. In practice, however, the policy was one permitting impressment of American sailors, leaving them to choose between serving in the British navy or languishing for years in a foreign jail.

Considering this an effrontery to American sovereignty and neutrality, James Madison sent very direct diplomatic instructions to James Monroe (now serving in London) to confront the agents of the Crown and demand that such hostilities be ceased immediately. More than anything, Madison did not want war with Great Britain— or with any other power. It was a republican principle that war should be avoided and that no permanent military establishment should be created, lest the justifications for war be multiplied in proportion to the power of the military. Accordingly, he instructed Monroe that "it may be hoped that the way will be prepared for some permanent arrangement on this subject between the two nations, which will be conformable to equity, to reciprocity and to their mutual advantage."

Britain was not the only foreign power to vex the United States and threaten her peace, however. Spain, too, was behaving belligerently and demonstrating little if any regard for the remonstrances of Secretary of State Madison. For its part, Spain clung to its military posts on the Mississippi River, posts built on land now belonging the United States. The United States may have purchased the ground upon which the Spanish outposts were built, but the government of Spain knew that President Jefferson lacked the military might to physically occupy or control it. France, to whom the United States looked for backing in their border dispute with Spain, chose to remain aloof, preferring to leave the settlement of boundaries in Louisiana to Spain and the United States.

So outrageous and unbending was Spain's adamant refusal to abandon its forts that some in America cried for war, war that would once and for all determine the metes and bounds of the territory of the United States. In a letter to Jefferson, Madison reported that all the efforts toward peaceful resolution by U.S. ministers in Madrid regarding the irksome Spanish forts had met with "a refusal of all our overtures in a haughty tone, without any offer of other terms. . . ."

This was the Madisonian way: Adhere strictly to tried and true principles of liberty, never stray outside the boundaries of the Constitution, and pursue diplomatic solutions to all problems with foreign powers, thus avoiding the allure of "entanglements" that were so loathsome to George Washington and Thomas Jefferson.

Diplomacy was proving futile, however, because in addition to the uneasiness of the bellicosity of the British, Madison could find no friend in Europe willing to assist the American cause. The Continent was embroiled in a war that consumed nearly all the money and martial might of France and Great Britain, and each commanded its particular theatre: Britain the seas and Napoleon the land.

"A Logic Not to Be Controverted": American Interests Are Equal to Those of Every Other Nation

With her dominance of the Atlantic Ocean, Great Britain was committed to completely preventing America from trading in the West Indies and Europe. To justify its interference with American commercial shipping, the government of Great Britain, under the leadership of Prime Minister William Pitt (known as William Pitt, the Younger), relied upon an arcane provision of British maritime law called the Rule of 1756.

Basically, the Rule of 1756 was a policy enacted by Britain during the Seven Years' War (the American theater of which was called the French and Indian War) that prohibited ships from

Chapter Fourteen: Secretary of State

Under Prime Minister William Pitt's leadership, Great Britain prevented America from trading with the West Indies and Europe.

Thomas Gainsborough, Public domain, via Wikimedia Commons

neutral countries from carrying on any commercial trade during war which would have been prevented to them during peacetime. As the United States was neutral, Pitt invoked the rule, closed off ports in the West Indies to American trading vessels, and began seizing ships and impressing seamen.

In a letter to James Monroe dated April 12, 1805, James Madison eviscerated the rule, demonstrating through his careful yet passionate analysis that the rule was not law and was enacted and enforced by British courts simply as a means of perpetuating and protecting its maritime monopoly.

First, Madison insisted that the rule was invalid because it was "subservient to [Great Britain's] particular interest." In other words, it was not just, and laws were meant to promote the peace and justice of the people. Next, Madison argued that it was "manifestly contrary to the general interest of commercial nations, as well as to the law of nations settled by the most approved authorities." International maritime law placed "no restraints on the trade of nations not at war, with nations at war," with three recognized exceptions: transportation of military forces, the sale of military goods, and trading in blockaded ports.

Madison set out a list of reasons to reject application of the Rule of 1756. He then condemned British interference with American trade with French and Spanish colonies in the Caribbean as "violations of right" and informed Monroe that the government of Prime Minister Pitt and the British courts should begin to "repair the wrongs done in such cases. . . ." He ended his message to Monroe with a warning for William Pitt and the government of Great Britain:

> If Great Britain, disregarding the precepts of Justice, suffers herself to calculate the interest she has in spoliating or abridging our commerce by the value of it to the United States, she ought certainly not to forget that the United States must in that case, calculate by the same standard the measures which the stake will afford for counteracting her unjust and unfriendly policy.

The controversy of the Rule of 1756 and the disruption of American commercial shipping is rarely mentioned in biographies of Madison. This oversight leaves out the lessons learned from his attitude toward the British and the sovereignty of the United States of America: James Madison was a man committed to exalting the rule of law above the rule of men. He believed in studying not only the *what* of the law, but the *why*, as well.

During the British application of the Rule of 1756 and its disruption of American commerce, the property, lives, and livelihood of American citizens were being assaulted by Great Britain. It was not Madison's way to stand by idly and mutely witness such atrocities committed against his countrymen, and this was particularly so when he was in a position to right the wrong.

Accordingly, sometime in 1806, he wrote a book laying before the world the violations of international law on the part of Great

Britain, supplementing his arguments with references to the most admired and authoritative theorists on that subject. Madison quoted the leading lights on the matter, including Samuel Pufendorf, Hugo Grotius, and Emmerich de Vatel, among others. Additionally, and not surprisingly, he found it necessary to correct some of the translations present in these texts, and hired, according to Ketcham "a translator suggested by Duponceau for German books. . . ." Madison was in his element: reading, pondering, and synthesizing the works of the great thinkers, and committing the content of his mind on these matters to paper.

As for the result of his 204-page treatise refuting the Rule of 1756, in a letter written on February 11, 1806, President Jefferson told the Comte de Volney, a French historian and philosopher, that Madison's book "pulverized by a logic not to be controverted" the Rule of 1756. Regardless of how well Secretary Madison demolished the foundation and application of the Rule of 1756, he lamented that logic is not a weapon typically found in the arsenal of nations at war.

James Madison realized that whether it was Great Britain, France, Spain, or any other nation of the Old World, the United States was looked upon as a child playing in a man's game. This did not sit well with Madison, as he personally played an almost unparalleled role in the creation of the American Republic. Naturally, he was determined to see it afforded the same respect and regard as any other nation. Madison would see the strength and equal footing of the United States affirmed diplomatically, and, should the country be attacked, this position supported militarily.

"This Enormity Is not a Subject of Discussion": British Ship Fires on American Supply Ship

The strength of Madison's mettle regarding his affirmation of American strength and sovereignty would be tested once again in June 1807, when a British naval vessel, the HMS *Leopard*, fired on an American supply ship, the *Chesapeake*, just off the coast of Norfolk, Virginia, killing three of her crewmen and injuring 18 more. The commander of the *Leopard*, Captain Salusbury Pryce Humphreys, boarded the *Chesapeake*, demanding permission to

President Jefferson would not stand for the injustice Captain Humphreys inflicted upon the Americans on the Chesapeake.

John Christian Schetky, Public domain, via Wikimedia Commons

search for deserters. Commodore James Barron of the *Chesapeake* allowed the search, which proved fruitless. Humphreys returned to his ship, sounded a trumpet, and demanded that Barron surrender his ship. When Barron refused, Humphreys ordered gunners onboard the *Leopard* to fire a shot across the *Chesapeake*'s bow.

Following that symbolic volley, the *Leopard* fired all her guns into the side of the *Chesapeake*, disabling the frigate and killing or wounding nearly two dozen of the American crew serving on the ship. Barron was one of those killed in the unprovoked attack, but before he died, he struck his colors and surrendered the ship to Humphreys. Humphreys then boarded the *Chesapeake* once again, whereupon he found and arrested four men sailing on the *Chesapeake* that he charged with having deserted from the British navy. In the end, three of the four were proven to be American citizens; what's more, two of the three Americans were African-Americans.

As Ralph Ketcham so rightly records in his biography of Madison regarding the *Leopard*'s attack on the *Chesapeake*, "If Britain condoned this act, or if the United States suffered it, American honor and independence meant nothing." It certainly meant something to the president, who was also the author of the Declaration of Independence, and to his Secretary of State, who was the Father of the Constitution. Jefferson and Madison would not allow this injustice to go unavenged.

On July 2, 1807, President Jefferson called together his Cabinet, and they issued a proclamation the content and courage of which were almost completely from the mind of Madison. After rehearsing the "principles of peace" the United States had pursued with regard to its relations with the belligerent European powers, the statement made it clear why pacifism was no longer an option.

"At length a deed transcending all we have hitherto seen or suffered brings the public sensibility to a serious crisis and our forbearance to a necessary pause," the proclamation declared.

Madison, the man behind the prose, then drove a stake into the ground, marking the limits of American patience and her policy of peaceful avoidance of entanglements with Europe. "Hospitality under such circumstances ceases to be a duty," as the violence committed by the HMS *Leopard* had brought on "a rupture between the two nations," the government of the United States explained.

Even still, though, Madison was a republican and abhorred war. He would not suffer humiliation, but he would not allow himself to advocate for armed response, either. Therefore, the document signed in the name of President Thomas Jefferson and Secretary of State James Madison ordered all British ships out of American harbors, and ordered Americans to cease trading with or supplying British ships.

On his own, Madison, under his authority as secretary of state, sent a letter to the U.S. minister to the United Kingdom, James Monroe (written partially in code), informing him of the attack on the *Chesapeake* and the killing of her sailors:

> ... the spirit which has been roused ... pervades the whole community, is abolishing the distinctions of party; and, regarding only the indignity offered to the sovereignty and flag of the nation, and the blood of citizens so wantonly and wickedly shed, demands, in the loudest tone, an honorable reparation.

He then told Monroe that "the British Government is to be apprized of the importance of a full compliance with this expectation, to the thorough healing of the wound which has been made in the feelings of the American Nation." Madison concluded his letter by telling Monroe to assure the British that this pronouncement "is a measure not of reparation, but of precaution," and if the British government failed to conform to the American demands for redress, "the answer will be obvious."

Great Britain didn't flinch, however, and the relationship between the two nations disintegrated further. In an effort to avoid war at all cost, Madison supported an embargo of British goods. This privation however, served only to punish Americans who relied on the availability of British manufactured items. Once again, the United States was treated by Europe as nothing more than a pawn to be dealt with or ignored as the circumstance provided.

Within less than two years, though, James Madison would be president, and his courage and "ardent and determined patriotism" would spur him to change the game. Forever after, America would be a European pawn no more.

Chapter 15:
President James Madison

On Saturday, March 4, 1809, about 10,000 people stood outside in the unseasonably mild weather at the Hall of the House of Representatives (now the National Statuary Hall) to watch James Madison be sworn in by Chief Justice John Marshall as the fourth president of the United States. Madison benefited not only from the popularity of his predecessor, Thomas Jefferson (who stood among the throng of visitors to the event), but from the respect of his countrymen, who held him in high esteem for his many years of dedicated service to the cause of American liberty.

Despite his devotion to his country and his undeniable popularity, in 1808 Madison faced what we would call "primary challenges" from within his own party. John Taylor of Caroline, James Monroe, and George Clinton all sought the nomination of the Democratic-Republicans that year, but the leaders of the party quickly and nearly unanimously coalesced in their support of Madison, selecting him to represent them in the general election.

In the general election, Madison easily defeated his Federalist opponent, Charles Cotesworth Pinckney, receiving 122 electoral votes to Pinckney's 47. George Clinton of New York was the incumbent vice president, and he would continue in that position during the first Madison administration.

In his first inaugural address, a speech that lasted about 10 minutes, Madison began by paying homage to the extraordinary men who had occupied that office before him. "Unwilling to depart from examples of the most revered authority, I avail myself of the occasion now presented to express the profound impression made on me by the call of my country to the station to the duties of which

President Madison moved in to the White House after defeating Charles Cotesworth Pinckney in the election.

Benjamin Henry Latrobe, Public domain, via Wikimedia Commons

I am about to pledge myself by the most solemn of sanctions," he declared after taking the constitutionally mandated oath of office.

The new president then told the thousands gathered to hear him, "The present situation of the world is indeed without a parallel, and . . . our own country full of difficulties. . . ." He proceeded to strike a tone in his speech reminiscent of the recommendations made by George Washington and Thomas Jefferson in their own inaugural addresses. As did those great men, Madison proclaimed his commitment to keeping the United States free from foreign entanglements. "Indulging no passions which trespass on the rights or the repose of other nations, it has been the true glory of the United States to cultivate peace by observing justice, and to entitle themselves to the respect of the nations at war by fulfilling their neutral obligations with the most scrupulous impartiality," he reminded the audience. America has always been safer, stronger, and truer to her constitutional principles when she has refused to interfere in the affairs of other nations.

Within about a week of his inaugural address, James Madison and his family were finally able to move in to the White House. (It took Thomas Jefferson that long to move his personal belongings out.) Although they had no children together, James and Dolley had a houseful of what Madison called "connections," that is to say, close and distant relations. So many of these "connections," in fact, lived with the Madisons that James and Dolley lived in one part of the house and left the rest to their assorted relatives.

Richard and Anna Cutts (Dolley's youngest sister) and their children lived in the wing opposite James and Dolley. Dolley's son from her previous marriage, John Payne Todd, also lived in the White House when he was home from boarding school. (He was 17 years old when James became president.) Edward Coles was Dolley's cousin as well as President Madison's private secretary, and he too occasionally occupied a room at the White House.

In addition to the regular residents, the White House during James Madison's two terms as president was the temporary abode of any number of cousins, nieces, and nephews. As indicated above, even though the Madisons had no biological children, their house was never empty; they were always happy to host relatives and provide shelter for family members in need.

James Madison's presidency was marred by internecine feuds among the Republicans, as well as threats of war with Great Britain. Time spent with family—whether at the White House or Montpelier—would certainly have been a welcome respite from the duties of president, which one observer noted made Madison appear to be "bending under the weight and cares of office."

As he settled into the presidency, Madison wanted to surround himself with people whom he personally trusted, whom he could trust to act in the best interest of the United States, foregoing any selfish gain that could be made from political position. With the partisan pressures described above, he was increasingly worried that he would not be able to rely on the counsel of trusted friends and associates. His worries were well-founded, in fact, as a group of senators composed of Republicans disloyal to Madison and Jefferson, Federalists, and assorted other politicians feeling unfettered from the center of power combined to prevent President Madison from appointing his desired candidates to various Cabinet positions.

These obstructionists came to be known as the "Invisibles," and they worked tirelessly to thwart every attempt by Madison to surround himself with those he felt would be faithful and truthful. The conflict with the Invisibles proved less bellicose than they had perhaps wanted, as Madison was willing to compromise so that he could get some of his Cabinet appointments approved, thus having at least a small cadre of counselors upon whom he could rely for guidance and advice.

Madison would certainly need this advice, as war loomed on the horizon. Great Britain and France were at war. The United States planned to steer a neutral course, avoiding antagonizing either of the European powers, but this was difficult in the face of British attacks on American merchant vessels. During these attacks, American sailors were kidnapped and forced into the service of the British navy or imprisoned in England. The British felt justified in the apprehension and impressment of American commercial sailors, arguing that the boats were likely headed for French ports. They asserted that this was in violation of the Nonintercourse Act, signed into law just days before Madison took office in 1809.

As American resentment and desire for redress against their former foe continued its crescendo, President Madison received welcome news from London when the British government's representative in the United States, acting partially on his own and partially under orders from the British Foreign Secretary, offered a limited list of concessions. Among the British accommodations would be reparations for the attack by the HMS *Leopard* on the *Chesapeake* (including the return of the illegally impressed American seamen) and His Majesty's Navy would no longer harass American merchant vessels. The United States would be free to impose trade restrictions according to their own view of the best policy.

Particularly pleasing to President Madison—and to his countrymen desperate to resume trading with Great Britain—American ships would be welcome in British harbors. This provision of the negotiated agreement caused celebrations throughout the United States as merchants, farmers, sailors, and manufacturers rejoiced at the resumption of regular trade relations with Britain and the infusion of much-needed money that would follow.

In a letter to Granville Sharp, English scholar and abolitionist, written on June 20, 1809, Benjamin Rush described the domestic popularity of the accord, as recorded by Ketcham in his biography of Madison. "Our new president, Mr. Madison is very popular. Both the two great parties that have so long divided our country, have united in him. He possesses with uncommon talents & extensive knowledge, much of the prudence and common sense of General

Benjamin Rush spoke quite respectfully of the new president, crediting Madison with talent and knowledge.

Washington," Rush wrote with exuberance. There could be no higher praise of a president, of course, than to be compared favorably to the first of that number, George Washington. Such was the state of affairs in the days following the reopening of trade with Great Britain.

Unfortunately, David Montague Erskine, the British minister to the United States, was not authorized to make as many concessions as he did. Although trade resumed and the nation praised President Madison for his staunchness and sagacity, King George III and his foreign ministers were not willing to allow America—a country tottering on the brink of bankruptcy and completely unprepared to wage a war against the mighty British Empire—to recover her financial health with the help of English trade.

The government of Great Britain officially repudiated the agreement brokered by Erskine and reinstated its previously pronounced restrictions on the freedom of American ships to sail into European waters. James and Dolley were relaxing at home at Montpelier when the president received the disheartening news of the British rejection of the Erskine Agreement. He immediately returned to the capital and, after conferring with his Cabinet, issued an official proclamation renewing the suspension of trade with Great Britain.

Even in the days after the British about-face embarrassed President Madison, he remained true to his republican principles, making every diplomatic appeal to British members of Parliament to speak sense to the king and reject his anti-American policies. Madison refused to treat Great Britain with the same disdain and belligerence with which Great Britain treated the United States. He genuinely believed that good sense and the Golden Rule would win the day, and war would be avoided, trade would be restored, and peace would prevail.

He was, sadly, too optimistic. The American people were growing impatient and increasingly anxious for an Anglo-American showdown to settle these disputes once and for all.

Great Britain and Napoleon would continue using the United States as a weapon with which to injure one another. Promises made

Chapter Fifteen: President James Madison

James Madison—The fourth president of the United States, a political figure of integrity, and an intelligent man.

by both European powers were continually broken, and President Madison grew tired of seeing his country batted about by the belligerents for their own ends, as if it had no independent will. The United States would have to prove to England and France that they were a sovereign nation, possessed equally of all the powers of any other nation, European or otherwise. And this time, that confirmation would come at the cost of war, just as it had almost three decades earlier.

Chapter 16
The Second War of Independence: The War of 1812

For years, American merchant vessels had suffered from the deprivations brought about by the forced impressment of American sailors into the navies of Great Britain and, to a lesser degree, France. Each of these two European belligerents was determined to prevent the other from benefiting from the purchase of American raw materials and the sale of manufactured goods to America. Accordingly, war ships from each would harass American trading ships and kidnap the men aboard them, placing them against their will at the service of the Royal Navy or the navy of Emperor Napoleon. Despite efforts by Presidents John Adams and Thomas Jefferson to protect American ships, sailors, and trade from such moves by England and France, the attacks persisted into the administration of President Madison.

"Heaven Help You Through All Your Difficulties": Jefferson Wishes Madison Well

This was the wish expressed to President Madison by his friend and predecessor in office, Thomas Jefferson. Writing from Monticello just six months before war against Great Britain was declared by Congress (as requested by Madison), Jefferson lamented that only the death of George III would likely be enough to "keep up a hope of avoiding war." Well, that and Madison's "firm, rational, and dignified" approach to foreign policy.

> In response, Madison informed Jefferson on February 7, 1812 that "all that we see from [Great Britain] indicates an adherence to her mad policy towards the U.S." The "mad policy" Madison referred to included not only the forced impressment of American seamen, but a build-up of British forces on the Canadian border with the United States.

As war with Britain loomed, Madison knew that there would be a need to raise additional revenue beyond that which would regularly be required. In light of that, he requested that Congress approve a series of taxes and duties to generate the $11 million needed to ramp up the pre-war preparations.

While the raising of taxes to finance a war is nothing new or noteworthy, President Madison's proposal for raising that money is worthy of special note. The president's plan, as recorded in the Annals of Congress, called for additional duties on imports, the sale of goods at auction, the sale of stamps, and the sale of salt, and "a direct tax to be laid and apportioned among the several states."

The plan was so well-founded constitutionally and financially that it called for states that contributed their portion of the direct taxes before the apportionment was officially made to receive a 15-percent discount on the total amount due. States that contributed their proportional amount of the direct taxes before the statutory due date would receive a discount of seven-and-a-half percent.

As if the previous provisions weren't reasonable enough, President Madison's proposal included the instruction that the direct taxes and duties not be imposed until after a war "with a foreign European nation" had been declared or until letters of marque and reprisal (also constitutionally permissible) had been issued by Congress "against the subjects of such nation." Finally, the president's proposal mandated that the revenue-raising scheme be permitted to continue "one year after the conclusion of peace with such foreign nation and no longer."

Article I, Section 8, Clause 11 of the Constitution authorizes Congress to "grant Letters of Marque and Reprisal." In the 13th century, King Henry III of England began issuing what were then known as privateering commissions. According to Dutch jurist and natural-rights philosopher Hugo Grotius, letters of marque and reprisal were similar to a declaration of a "private war." By issuing such a letter, the sovereign of one nation commissioned a private individual or individuals to enter territory governed by a foreign prince and exact retribution against a person or persons believed to have committed a great wrong against the subjects of the authorizing monarch.

The American concept of letters of marque and reprisal was substantially informed by the *Commentaries on the Laws of England*, published in 1765 by English jurist William Blackstone. In Section I, page 249 of this influential work, Blackstone wrote:

> These letters are grantable by the law of nations, whenever the subjects of one state are oppressed and injured by those of another; and justice is denied by that state to which the oppressor belongs. In this case letters of marque and reprisal (words in themselves synonymous and signifying a taking in return) may be obtained, in order to seize the bodies or goods of the subjects of the offending state, until satisfaction be made, wherever they happen to be found. Indeed this custom of reprisals seems dictated by nature herself; and accordingly we find in the most ancient times very notable instances of it.

Forgotten Founding Father and legal practitioner St. George Tucker summarized Blackstone, writing that letters of marque and reprisal were justified "where individuals of one nation are oppressed or injured by those of another, and justice is denied by the state to which the author of such oppression or injury belongs."

In April 1781, during the War of Independence, the Confederation Congress passed a resolution giving to "captains or commanders of private armed vessels commissioned by letters of marque or general reprisals" the following instructions and guidelines:

St. George Tucker was a lawyer whom James Madison appointed as the United States District Court judge for Virginia.

You may by force of arms attack, subdue, and seize all ships, vessels and goods, belonging to the King or Crown of Great Britain, or to his subjects, or others inhabiting within any of the territories or possessions of the aforesaid King of Great Britain, on the high seas, or between high-water and low-water marks. And you may also annoy the enemy by all means in your power, by land as well as by water, taking care not to infringe or violate the laws of nations, or laws of neutrality.

By providing for letters of marque and reprisal, then, President Madison's proposal was yet another brick in the high, sturdy wall of constitutional fidelity he had built over many decades of public service.

"To Make Ready for It": War With Britain Looms

On April 5, 1812, Madison informed Jefferson that the British were continuing on their way toward war with the United States, and that "We have nothing left therefore, but to make ready for it." Although he was certainly resolved to resisting British assaults on American liberty, even at this late date (just two months before war would be declared) the president was determined to do nothing in relation to his dealings with Congress—in whose hands the declaration of war was placed by the Constitution—that would "add fuel to party discontent, and interested clamor." Furthermore, he was committed to pursuing any "rational and provident measure" that would avoid war and domestic discontent.

Despite his genuine efforts to avoid partisan reproaches, Madison faced opposition to his pre-war preparations not only from the Federalists (who almost universally opposed a declaration of war against Great Britain), but from within his own party, as well. The Federalists accused him of preferring France, as all his proposals thus far had focused on responses to British malfeasance, while Republicans (particularly the group known as the "Tertium Quids," led by John Taylor of Caroline and John Randolph of Roanoke) believed Madison was betraying his principles by prosecuting a war that they deemed unnecessary.

As with any leader, though, ultimately President Madison needed to be guided by his own conscience, not by the chorus of complainers. He was aware that France had committed her own unacceptable acts against the United States, and that the government of France refused to support the Madison administration in its policy of pushing back against British belligerence. He understood that should he undertake what he called a "triangular war"—war among the United States, Great Britain, and France—the effects would be devastating and would likely ruin the American economy by cutting off all access to the ports of Europe.

"Spectacle of Injuries and Indignities": Madison Asks Congress to Declare War on Great Britain

In the end, on June 1, 1812, President James Madison, unaided by France and unmoved by critics, sent a message to Congress asking legislators to declare war on Great Britain. The text of that letter reveals much about the real James Madison and his attitude toward war and toward the Constitution.

"[T]he conduct of [Great Britain's] government presents a series of acts hostile to the United States as an independent and neutral nation," the communiqué to Congress began. Madison went on to rehearse centuries-old international norms and laws that Britain was in "the continued practice of violating." These "severities of their discipline" prompted American "remonstrances and expostulations," all of which had been in vain.

For paragraphs, the president presented a catalog of British atrocities and arrogance, alongside a "crying enormity" of hostile and violent treatment of American ships, acts committed by the Crown so that Britain could develop a "monopoly which she covets for her own commerce and navigation." He then presented to Congress a "spectacle of injuries and indignities which have been heaped upon our country" that American "forbearance and conciliatory efforts have been able to avert." He reminded the gathered legislators that, according to all acceptable laws of nations, Great Britain had been in "a state of war against the United States" while the United States was following a path of "peace toward Great Britain."

Lamenting the depth of depravity to which the government of Great Britain had descended in its open, hostile, and violent treatment of American ships and its disdainful dismissal of American attempts at peaceful reconciliation, Madison recognized that there was now only one just and reasonable response. He declared:

> Whether the United States shall continue passive under these progressive usurpations and these accumulating wrongs, or, opposing force to force in defense of their national rights, shall commit a just cause into the hands of the Almighty Disposer of Events, avoiding all connections which might entangle it in the contest or views of other powers, and preserving a constant readiness to concur in an honorable reestablishment of peace and friendship, is a solemn question which the Constitution wisely confides to the legislative department of the government.

This discourse is perfectly in line with the essays Madison wrote (as Helvidius) nearly a decade earlier, as well as his speeches on the subject delivered at the Constitutional Convention of 1787. It is with the Congress, not with the executive branch, that the power to declare war is placed in the Constitution. Again, he hewed rigidly, even in the face of war, to the constitutional separations of and limits on power.

No matter the magnitude of the threat, Madison was a rock-ribbed republican and was steadfastly fixed on not conducting a war that would become a prolonged burden to the country. As Albert Gallatin, Madison's secretary of war, wrote to Thomas Jefferson in March 1812:

> With respect to the war, it is my wish . . . that the evils inseparable from it should, as far as practicable, be limited to its duration, and that at its end the United States may be burdened with the smallest possible quantity of debt, perpetual taxation, military establishments, and other corrupting or anti-republican habits or institutions.

Gallatin's views were in complete concert with those of his boss, President James Madison. Madison and his men believed that even if war was necessary and just, it must not be prosecuted with the customary concomitant increase in debt and centralization of unconstitutional powers in the hands of the president.

Accordingly, Madison sent a letter to Congress reminding them of all the British atrocities and acts of belligerence toward the United States. The letter did not, however, ask Congress to declare war.

Four days after their receipt of the president's letter, the House of Representatives and the Senate voted to declare war on Great Britain. One day later, on June 18, 1812, Madison signed Congress's declaration, officially beginning the War of 1812.

"It Shall Never Fall Into the Hands of the Enemy": Dolley Madison and the British Army's Attack on the White House

Perhaps the most famous act of courage chronicled in the War of 1812 was not performed by a soldier or sailor, but by Dolley Madison.

Although most of the battles of the War of 1812 were fought at sea, the British were determined to demolish the American capital, destroy her people's resolve, and thus conquer the colonies they had lost in the War of Independence. To that end, 5,000 British troops landed in the United States and began their march toward Washington, D.C., their ultimate prize. A messenger was sent to the White House informing the president that there were at least 50 British ships clogging the Potomac and that the troops were within striking distance. President Madison knew he needed to call out the militia and alert them to the imminent threat to the capital. Accordingly, he asked the states to send the citizen-soldiers to the defense of their country and their families. Even here, however, he held to his republican principles, reminding states to be frugal and wise, always "exerting all our vigilance on discovering the particular views of the enemy, and, by not prematurely or erroneously applying our means of defense, be more able to use them with effect where and when they become necessary."

Dolley became an unlikely hero in the War of 1812, when she courageously took with her a portrait of George Washington and the Declaration of Independence when she fled the White House, at risk of being caught by the British.

Mrs. Madison knew of the "views of the enemy" because she could practically see them! In a letter to Hannah Gallatin, she reported that British soldiers were "within 20 miles of the City [Washington, D.C.]. . . ." After midnight, a rider came to the White House, roused the Madisons, and informed the president that "The enemy are in full march for Washington." Though they didn't know it at the time, this was the last night the Madisons would spend in the White House.

President Madison rushed off to confer with his Cabinet and the military leaders, but not before asking his beloved wife, "Have you the courage to stay here till I come back, to-morrow or next day?" With courage, conviction, and palpable love for her husband and her country, Dolley responded, "I am not afraid of anything, if only you are not harmed and our army triumphs."

With that, Madison rode to a nearby hill to watch and command as the American militia fought bravely against the overwhelming British regulars. What the president saw gave him little hope of an American victory—and even less of preserving the White House—thus he quickly wrote a note to Dolley and sent it by a military messenger. The note said simply, "Enemy stronger than we heard at first. They may reach the city and destroy it. Be ready to leave at a moment's warning."

Later that afternoon, an American soldier galloped up to the White House, shouting, "Fly, fly! The house will be burned over your head!" Dolley secured a wagon from a friend and filled it with valuables. As she, some friends, and some servants were loading the silver and other goods onto the wagon, one of her friends reminded her that the British admiral of the fleet anchored in the Potomac threatened to take her and President Madison prisoner when the British occupied Washington, D.C. With that reminder ringing in her ears, Dolley was helped up into the wagon. Almost. Suddenly, she remembered that there were a couple of things more valuable than all the silver and finery already secured in the wagon. She jumped down and ran back inside the White House.

The rest of the story is eloquently told by Grace Humphrey in her book *Women in American History*. As she jumped down from the wagon, Dolley declared:

"Not yet—the portrait of Washington—it shall never fall into the hands of the enemy. That must be taken away before I leave the house."

The famous painting by Gilbert Stuart was in a heavy frame, screwed to the wall in the state dining-room, but in that frantic hurry there were no tools at hand to remove it.

"Get an axe and break the frame," commanded Dolly Madison. She watched the canvas taken from the stretcher, saw it rolled up carefully, and sent to a place of safety. Later it was returned to her, and to-day hangs over the mantel in the red room of the White House.

One more delay—the Declaration of Independence was kept in a glass case, separate from the other state papers. Notwithstanding all the protests of her friends, Dolly Madison ran back into the house, broke the glass, secured the Declaration with the autographs of the signers, got into her carriage and drove rapidly away to [a] house beyond Georgetown.

None too soon did she leave. The sound of approaching troops was heard. The British were upon the city. They broke into the executive mansion, ransacked it, had dinner there in the state dining-room, stole what they could carry, and then set fire to the building.

In her care for the priceless portrait of Washington and the historic Declaration of Independence, Dolley Madison, at the risk of being captured by British soldiers, proved herself a heroine of the War of 1812.

While English soldiers and sailors continued to destroy American cities, the Americans, under the command of Andrew Jackson of Tennessee, began pushing back, winning battle after battle in the South, and pushing Parliament closer to accepting American offers of peace being made by negotiators in Belgium.

Finally, the parties reached an accord and the United States was free. Or, in the words of a poem written by Francis Scott Key as he witnessed the British bombardment of Fort McHenry in Maryland:

> Then conquer we must, for our cause it is just.
>
> And this be our motto—"In God is our trust;"
>
> And the star-spangled banner in triumph shall wave
>
> O'er the land of the free, and the home of the brave.

The American flag still waved, and the sovereignty and peace of the United States were finally secure.

"Without the Sacrifice of Civil or Political Liberty": James Madison Conducts War Constitutionally

The War of 1812 lasted for two years and eight months, officially ending with the ratification by the U.S. Senate of the Treaty of Ghent on February 18, 1815. The two governments simply agreed to a cessation of hostilities, leaving the issues that incited the conflict in the first place unresolved. No matter. Throughout the ordeal, President Madison remained faithful to his oath to the Constitution. The executive branch emerged from its first major war intact and restrained. This, if nothing else, raises James Madison above many others who have acted as wartime executives. Most took full advantage of the opportunity to permanently consolidate the immense and irrevocable powers that were granted provisionally.

In his award-winning treatment of the Founding Generation in his book *Revolutionary Characters: What Made the Founders Different*, renowned historian Gordon Wood presents a similar assessment of President Madison's successful—constitutionally speaking—execution of the War of 1812, writing, "So even though the war settled nothing, it actually settled everything. It vindicated the grand revolutionary experiment in limited republican government."

On March 4, 1815, the citizens of Washington, D.C., delivered a

Chapter Sixteen: The Second War of Independence: The War of 1812

In June of 1812, Congress declared war on Great Britain.

Clockwise, from top: George Munger, John David Kelly, Anton Otto Fischer, William Emmons, Edward Percy Moran, Public domain, via Wikimedia Commons

proclamation to President Madison praising him for his constitutional circumspection and rejection of any consolidation of power into the hands of the presidency. This message is of particular importance given the destruction and deprivations the buildings and residents of the capital city had suffered at the hands of British invaders. In other words, even a city so ravaged by and still recuperating from the savagery of war was grateful to the man who was the commander-in-chief of the army for his constitutional fidelity and circumspection during the years of belligerent brutality. The city's citizens declared:

> Power and national glory, Sir, have often before, been acquired by the sword; but rarely without the sacrifice of civil or political liberty. It is here, preeminently, that the righteous triumph of the one, under the smiles of Heaven, secures the other. When we reflect that this sword was drawn under Your guidance, we cannot resist offering you our own, as well as a nations thanks, for the vigilance with which you have restrained it within its proper limits, the energy with which you have directed it to its proper objects, and the safety with which you have wielded an armed force of fifty thousand men, aided by an annual disbursement of many millions, without infringing a political, civil, or religious right.

Wood adds yet another voice to the chorus praising Madison's execution of the office of executive during the War of 1812, that of John Adams. James Madison, Adams wrote to Thomas Jefferson on February 2, 1817, "has acquired more glory, and established more Union, than all his three predecessors Washington, Adams, and Jefferson put together."

In his review of the era published in his book *The Democratic Republic: 1801-1815*, historian Marshall Smelser also recognizes the remarkable financial frugality and constitutional fidelity of Madison during the War of 1812. "[T]he Father of the Constitution was following his conviction that policy must rise from the people through their branch of government," Smelser states. "It is hardly a mark of weakness to take a firm view of the nature of the Constitution and to operate from it as a principle," he adds.

As a coda to the constitutional allegiance demonstrated by President James Madison during and after the War of 1812, when peace was restored and it was time to pay off the generous gifts paid by citizens to finance the war, Madison set in motion the legislative measures that would see the war debt—and the entire national debt—paid off within 20 years of the Treaty of Ghent.

The last word on James Madison's motivation to defend the liberty of his country and preserve the union he had helped create, even at the point of a sword, was eloquently and inspirationally expressed by Madison himself on December 7, 1813, in his annual message to Congress:

> It would be improper to close this communication without expressing a thankfulness, in which all ought to unite, for the numerous blessings with which our beloved country, continues to be favored; for the abundance which overspreads our land, and the prevailing health of its inhabitants; for the preservation of our internal tranquility, and the stability of our free institutions; and above all for the light of divine truth, and the protection of every man's conscience, in the enjoyment of it. And although among our blessings we cannot number an exemption from the evils of war; yet these will never be regarded as the greatest of evils, by the friends of liberty, and of the rights of nations. Our country has before preferred them to the degraded condition which was the alternative, when the sword was drawn in the cause, which gave birth to our national Independence; and none who contemplate the magnitude, and feel the value of that glorious event, will shrink from a struggle to maintain the high and happy ground, on which it placed the American people.

Madison's service as president would continue through another term, one marked by war and congressional attacks on the Constitution. All of these struggles would prove illustrative of the real James Madison.

Chapter 17
Madison's Second Term

As Madison's second term of office began, the country was still engaged in a war with Great Britain. Until then, most of the fighting had been at sea, with little to no effect visible on the landscape of the eastern shore of the United States. That soon changed with the burning and looting of the Capitol and the White House (then called the Executive Mansion) and the accompanying fearful flight of many of Washington D.C.'s residents, including as related above, President and Mrs. Madison.

On the day he was sworn into office for the second time, March 4, 1813, James Madison acknowledged the approaching storm and spoke in a manner intended to calm and inspire his fellow Americans. He began by assuring his countrymen that "the war with a powerful nation, which forms so prominent a feature in our situation, is stamped with that justice which invites the smiles of Heaven on the means of conducting it to a successful termination."

Next, he reminded the gathered throng that this present conflict was no war of aggression, no peremptory strike; it was a defensive struggle, a struggle to restore liberty and peace. This war, he said:

> was not declared on the part of the United States until it had been long made on them, in reality though not in name; until arguments and postulations had been exhausted; until a positive declaration had been received that the wrongs provoking it would not be discontinued; nor until this last appeal could no longer be delayed without breaking down the spirit of the nation, destroying all confidence in itself and in its political institutions, and either perpetuating a

From Last Rites to Bill of Rights: The Miraculous Life and Legacy of James Madison

James Madison served a second term as the president of the United States, trying harder than ever to increase the unity and strength of the United States.

state of disgraceful suffering or regaining by more costly sacrifices and more severe struggles our lost rank and respect among independent powers.

Regarding the prosecution of this unwanted war, the recently re-elected president declared that on the part of the armed forces of the United States, there was "no usage of civilized nations, no precept of courtesy or humanity... infringed. The war [had] been waged on our part with scrupulous regard to all these obligations."

Again, the humanity, the virtue, and the valor of James Madison percolate to the top of every speech, regardless of circumstance or conflict. Finally, he reminded the people that the best assurances of concluding the war quickly were "the patriotism, the good sense, and the manly spirit of our fellow-citizens."

Upon the successful cessation of hostilities with Great Britain, Madison set his face toward the formidable task of cementing timeless principles of constitutional republicanism within the framework of the federal government. In his seventh presidential report to the Senate and the House of Representatives, on December 5, 1815 (a speech we would call the State of the Union address), he enunciated not only his principles, but his proposals for strengthening the union, always a matter of utmost importance to him.

After reciting to the convened congressmen and senators the successes and failures experienced in the war with Great Britain, Madison reminded his audience that, unless the United States wanted to be forever vulnerable to attack by this or that foreign foe, "whether to prevent or repel danger, we ought not to be unprepared for it." Accordingly, he asked Congress (again, not presuming to carry out any of his proposals through the issuance of an unconstitutional executive order) for a "liberal provision for the immediate extension and gradual completion of the works of defense...."

"The Splendid Achievements of the Militia": State Militias Prove Why They Are Necessary to Preserve Liberty

With regard to the able defense of the United States, as manifest in the peaceful resolution of the War of 1812 and the preservation of

American territory, Madison specifically commended the "splendid achievements of the militia and the value of this resource for the public defense." It is for that purpose, the public defense, that the maintenance of a well-regulated militia is mandated by the Second Amendment to the Constitution. ("A well regulated Militia, being necessary to the security of a free State. . . ." it reads.)

This was not some new right or controversial establishment of a standing army; no, this was the codifying of a responsibility that had existed for over 400 years. A strong, well-ordered militia was an Anglo-American legal tradition that explicitly recognized the presence of an armed populace as a reliable deterrent to mayhem. In the Statute of Northampton, enacted in 1328, for example, an exemption to restrictions on the carrying of weapons in the presence of the king or his ministers was carved out for situations where there was "a cry made for arms to keep the peace, and the same in such places where such acts happen."

As for the need for state militias and their role in the protection of liberty, the Founding Fathers could not have been more clear. On August 23, 1787, at the Constitutional Convention in Philadelphia, Madison rose to speak on the subject of the militia, which was being debated by his fellow delegates. He declared:

> The discipline of the militia is evidently a national concern and ought to be provided for by a national constitution. . . . As the greatest danger is that of disunion of the states, it is necessary to guard against it by sufficient powers to the common government; and as the greatest danger to liberty is from large standing armies, it is best to prevent them, by an effectual provision for a good militia.

About a year later, in *Federalist* No. 46, Madison wrote that should the unthinkable (to him) happen and the federal government overrun the high fences placed by the states around its constitutional powers, the men of every state, serving in their states' militias, would stand as sentinels of liberty, preventing the abolition of constitutional limits on the general government. Specifically, he wrote that should the federal government somehow deceive the states and the people into aiding its accumulation of all power, the people, through the states, would recover their senses and "repel the danger" through a militia mustered and "fighting for their common liberties." These citizen-soldiers would form a popular armed force that Madison believed "could never be conquered."

Heedless of Madison's counsel, most states have failed to maintain an armed and disciplined militia capable of ably defending our country, as they so splendidly did in the War of 1812.

After the Militia Act of 1903, most states dissolved their militias, choosing rather to have—"state defense forces" that serve to support the National Guard and reserves.

Today, there remain only 23 state defense forces. (This does not include units of the National Guard and reserves which are under the command of the president and are effectively just reserves of the federal armed forces.) Even these state-run forces are not militias in the sense that Madison and the Founders recommended.

In its decision in the 1990 case of *Perpich v. Department of Defense* 496 U.S. 334 (1990), the Supreme Court effectively federalized even state defense forces. The ruling, although explicitly claiming not to be a ruling on the status of state defense forces, referenced a few federal statutes that seem to support federalization of state militias. The Court held:

> It is true that the state defense forces "may not be called, ordered, or drafted into the armed forces." 32 U.S.C. 109(c). It is nonetheless possible that they are subject to call under 10 U.S.C. 331-333, which distinguish the "militia" from the "armed forces," and which appear to subject all portions of the "militia"—organized or not—to call if needed for the purposes specified in the Militia Clauses.

Fortunately for us, during the war that secured our independence and the war that reinforced it (the War of 1812), our Founding Fathers could count on the citizen-soldiers, the militias, to be ready in a minute to mount up or march forth and make an armed defense against those who would conquer our country or abolish our liberty.

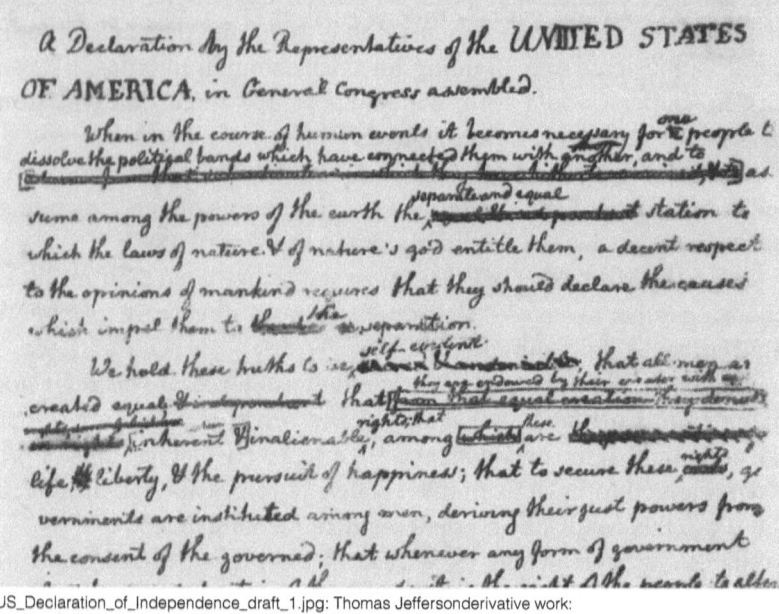

A draft of the Declaration of Independence. It is easily one of the most important documents in American history

"A Nursery of Enlightened Preceptors": Madison Proposes National University

Next, after making an appeal to Congress to follow the example of the states in the building of "new roads . . . navigable canals . . . and streams susceptible of navigation," wherever such projects would not exceed the powers granted to Congress in the Constitution, President Madison proposed and endorsed the establishment of a "national seminary of learning" for the purpose of training young Americans to learn to "enjoy" and "preserve" the principles of liberty upon which their nation was founded.

He suggested that a school be built in Washington, D.C., that would welcome "youth and genius from every part of [the] country. . . ." It was important that the school be established in the capital city so that it would be constitutional, as it would in no way infringe on the domestic affairs of the states. Even in this proposal, one about which he was so passionate and so particular, Madison refused to see it set in motion through either the exercise of any unconstitutional usurpation of authority on his part (or the part of the Congress) or an encroachment on the sovereign power of states to legislate within their own borders.

The curriculum of the school would focus on "the advancement of knowledge, without which the blessings of liberty can not be fully enjoyed or long preserved." Then, having been instilled with an understanding and appreciation of these lessons, the youth of America would become "examples of those national feelings, those liberal sentiments, and those congenial manners which contribute cement to our Union and strength to the great political fabric of which that is the foundation."

Madison, of course, knew how a good education—particularly one focused on learning the lessons of history—could prepare a person to play a key role in the establishment and support of a free government. Only a few years after delivering his second annual address to Congress, in a letter to W.T. Barry, Madison restated and reinforced his idea regarding the critical role of education in a republic:

> A popular Government, without popular information, or the means of acquiring it, is but a Prologue to a Farce or a Tragedy; or, perhaps both. Knowledge will forever govern ignorance: And a people who mean to be their own Governors, must arm themselves with the power which knowledge gives.

He continued with similar counsel later in that same letter, pointing particularly to the obligation Americans have as a model of freedom and education to the world:

> The American people owe it to themselves, and to the cause of free Government, to prove by their establishments for the advancement and diffusion of Knowledge, that their political Institutions, which are attracting observation

from every quarter, and are respected as Models, by the new-born States in our own Hemisphere, are as favorable to the intellectual and moral improvement of Man as they are conformable to his individual & social Rights. What spectacle can be more edifying or more seasonable, than that of Liberty and Learning, each leaning on the other for their mutual and surest support?

Finally, with gratitude to the "goodness of a superintending Providence, to which we are indebted for" our happiness as a nation, President Madison closed his address with advice that sounded very similar to that given by his predecessors regarding how Congress could take care to keep our country safe and happy:

It remains for the guardians of the public welfare to persevere in that justice and good will toward other nations which invite a return of these sentiments toward the United States; to cherish institutions which guarantee their safety and their liberties, civil and religious; and to combine with a liberal system of foreign commerce an improvement of the national advantages and a protection and extension of the independent resources of our highly favored and happy country.

"Constrained by the Insuperable Difficulty": Madison Refuses to Violate the Constitution

In 1817, Congress passed a bill known as the Bonus Bill of 1817. The measure was authored by John C. Calhoun of South Carolina and was aimed at taking the "bonus" (what we would call the surplus) from the revenue deposited in the newly re-chartered Bank of the United States (the Second Bank of the United States, officially) and spending it on various infrastructure building projects, namely, "roads and canals and improving the navigation of watercourses."

Although President Madison supported such strengthening of American "internal improvements" (as was highlighted above in his address to Congress in 1815), he vetoed the bill. The statement he wrote and sent to Congress explaining his rejection of the proposal became renowned for its concise and clear recitation of republican values and particularly strict adherence to the Constitution as ratified. This is a doctrine known as "strict constructionism" and James Madison was one of its staunchest and ablest advocates.

In his veto message to the House of Representatives, dated March 3, 1817, he declared: "I am constrained by the insuperable difficulty I feel in reconciling the bill with the Constitution of the United States." He then delineated the specific sections and provisions of the Constitution that he believed he would violate were he to sign the act into law. He firmly and confidently informed Congress:

> The legislative powers vested in Congress are specified and enumerated in the eighth section of the first article of the Constitution, and it does not appear that the power proposed to be exercised by the bill is among the enumerated powers, or that it falls by any just interpretation within the power to make laws necessary and proper for carrying into execution those or other powers vested by the Constitution in the Government of the United States.

He looked for but could not find an enumerated power granted by the states to the federal government in the Constitution to allow the spending. Therefore, he had no choice but to veto the bill when it arrived on his desk. The president then tailored his reasoning even more narrowly by defining the clauses in the Constitution relied upon by the bill's supporters to justify its constitutional conformity. First, Madison addressed the use of the Commerce Clause:

> "The power to regulate commerce among the several States" can not include a power to construct roads and canals, and to improve the navigation of water courses in order to facilitate, promote, and secure such commerce without a latitude of construction departing from the ordinary import of the terms strengthened by the known inconveniences which doubtless led to the grant of this remedial power to Congress.

Next up on Madison's chopping block (or under his veto pen): the General Welfare Clause:

> To refer the power in question to the clause "to provide for common defense and general welfare" would be contrary to the established and consistent rules of interpretation, as rendering the special and careful enumeration of powers which follow the clause nugatory and improper. Such a view of the Constitution would have the effect of giving to Congress a general power of legislation instead of the defined and limited one hitherto understood to belong to them, the terms "common defense and general welfare" embracing every object and act within the purview of a legislative trust.

And what would be the effect on federalism and the correct constitutional role of the federal and state governments? Madison had an answer for that, too:

> It would have the effect of subjecting both the Constitution and laws of the several States in all cases not specifically exempted to be superseded by laws of Congress, it being expressly declared "that the Constitution of the United States and laws made in pursuance thereof shall be the supreme law of the land, and the judges of every state shall be bound thereby, anything in the constitution or laws of any State to the contrary notwithstanding."

In other words, the Constitution and the laws of the states would be reduced to relics and would be effectively nullified any time Congress wanted to spend treasure on some new project, program, or policy.

The final paragraph of President Madison's veto is worthy of repeating every day in the halls of Congress and in the Oval Office:

> I am not unaware of the great importance of roads and canals and the improved navigation of water courses, and that a power in the National Legislature to provide for them

might be exercised with signal advantage to the general prosperity. But seeing that such a power is not expressly given by the Constitution, and believing that it can not be deduced from any part of it without an inadmissible latitude of construction and reliance on insufficient precedents; believing also that the permanent success of the Constitution depends on a definite partition of powers between the General and the State Governments, and that no adequate landmarks would be left by the constructive extension of the powers of Congress as proposed in the bill, I have no option but to withhold my signature from it. . . .

Just how persuasive was President Madison's steadfast stand against Congress's violation of the limits of its enumerated powers? An article by Burton W. Folsom, published in 2008 by the Foundation for Economic Education, relates the story of a couple of subsequent stances by later presidents that mirrored that of Mr. Madison. Folsom writes:

> Madison's principled veto of the Bonus Bill of 1817 set a precedent that lasted for generations. The Erie Canal, for example, never received federal funds. In 1830, however, Congress tested the resolve of President Andrew Jackson with the Maysville Road Bill, which would have used federal funds to build a turnpike in Kentucky.
>
> Jackson scrupulously followed Madison's lead and vetoed the bill. Sure, the proposed turnpike might be economically sound, Jackson conceded, but if the country used federal funds to build a turnpike in Kentucky, "there can be no local interest that may not with equal propriety be denominated national." He echoed Madison by adding, "A disregard of this distinction would of necessity lead to the subversion of the federal system."

Madison and Jackson were also following George Washington's advice in his Farewell Address. "[Avoid] the accumulation of debt," Washington admonished, "not only by shunning occasions of expense, but by vigorous exertions in time of peace to discharge the debts which unavoidable wars have occasioned, not ungenerously throwing upon posterity the burthen which we ourselves ought to bear."

It is worth mentioning at this point that, by following the advice given by George Washington in his famous Farewell Address, James Madison was actually heeding his own wise counsel.

Although not widely known—either today or at the time of its publication—George Washington's Farewell Address was the product of the minds of three men: George Washington, Alexander Hamilton, and James Madison.

As befitting his hubris, Hamilton later claimed that Washington's Farewell Address was "my own work." However, the correspondence among the three men makes it clear that in 1792, when Washington began pondering the writing of a farewell address, the man he turned to to write the first draft of such a seminal document was none other than James Madison.

And finally on the subject of Madison's literary fingerprints on George Washington's addresses, in 1789, Washington delivered his First Inaugural Address. Though Washington initially penned a 73-page draft, James Madison played a crucial role in refining the final iteration of the speech. During a stop at Mount Vernon on his way to New York, Madison crafted a concise four-page version for Washington to edit, and the two men continued to work on the speech together once they arrived in New York.

Following the address, the House of Representatives requested that Madison compose their formal response. Subsequently, Washington turned to Madison once again, asking him to draft his replies to the responses from both the House and the Senate. Through this process of drafting and redrafting, Madison became an indispensable voice behind Washington's written communication. In fact, in the case of

Andrew Jackson became the fifth United States president.

Public domain, via Wikimedia Commons

the First Inaugural Address, the Congressional response, and the presidential response to the congressional response, it surely must have seemed to Madison almost as if he were listening to himself speak!

With President Madison's example of steadfast fidelity to the Constitution lingering in Congress and the entire capital city, he and Mrs. Madison began the long journey back to their beloved home, Montpelier.

Chapter 18
Retirement to Montpelier

"I Anticipate Many Enjoyments":
James and Dolley Finally Head Home

James Madison spent his entire adult life in the service of his country, and what a fruitful life it was! Few people had been as instrumental to the establishment and strengthening of the American union. His was the mind behind the Virginia Plan, the list of provisions that became the agenda for the delegates to the Constitutional Convention of 1787, and he was the man who spoke the most at the convention. Writing as "Publius," he collaborated with Alexander Hamilton and John Jay in penning *The Federalist*, the clearest, most convincing, and most cogent explication of American constitutional principles ever written. Then, as a member of the House of Representatives, Madison shepherded the Bill of Rights through the Congress, fulfilling promises he made to political opponents during the ratification process. About a decade after the ratification of the Constitution in 1789, as co-founder of the Democratic-Republican Party, he authored the influential Virginia Resolutions, marking the boundaries of federal and state authority as set out in the Constitution. During Thomas Jefferson's first presidential administration, Madison served as the secretary of state who oversaw the acquisition of the Louisiana Purchase, adding territory totaling roughly 828,000 square miles and nearly doubling the size of the United States. And in the War of 1812, during his own first term as president of the United States, James Madison defeated Great Britain, preserving the independence of the United States, earned only 30 years earlier.

From Last Rites to Bill of Rights: The Miraculous Life and Legacy of James Madison

Albert Gallatin kindly recognized the good James did for the country.

In a letter written on July 17, 1817, Madison's friend Albert Gallatin described the boon to his country that James Madison's public service had been. Gallatin, then living in Paris, wrote:

> Most sincerely do I congratulate you on the happy & honorable termination of your political labours. Few indeed have the good fortune, after such career as yours, to carry in their retirement, the entire approbation of their fellow citizens with that of their own conscience. Never was a country left in a more flourishing situation than the United States at the end of your administration; and they are more united at home and respected abroad than at any period since the war of the independence.

James and Dolley were happy to be headed back to Montpelier, their bucolic Blue Ridge estate. What began as a modest home when construction first began in James' childhood was an impressive mansion by the time the recently retired James and the trendsetting former first lady arrived home for the last time in 1817.

In a letter sent to Gallatin sometime near the end of March of that year, James expressed his joy at leaving behind a legacy as a Founding Father and embarking on a new adventure as the owner and permanent occupant of Orange County's finest farm, Montpelier. "I am in the midst of preparations to get to my farm, where I shall make myself a fixture; and where I anticipate many enjoyments, which if not fully realized, will be a welcome exchange for the labors and solicitudes of public life," he wrote.

Ralph Ketcham, the author of arguably the finest single-volume biography of James Madison, described the look and layout of the Montpelier that greeted Dolley and James when they arrived from Washington, D.C., in 1817. "To the four-columned portico, the limestone plaster put on over the brick exterior, and other remodeling of 1800 had been added in 1809 the one-story wings on each side designed by Thornton and Latrobe," he wrote. As was typical of the times and the man, James Madison's Montpelier began as a modest home and was expanded slowly over the years, evolving into the impressive estate that is visited by thousands today.

Perhaps even more compelling than Ketcham's record of the improvements made to the mansion in the Madisons' absence is the account given by Dolley's niece, Mary Cutts (who lived briefly with the Madisons), of life at Montpelier after the Madisons returned home to the routines of a country gentleman and his wife:

> [Mr. Madison's] house was the resort of the distinguished men of the time; foreigners, tourists, artists and writers failed not to visit himself and Mr. Jefferson. . . . Mrs. Madison soon fell in with the Country customs. Barbecues were then at their height of popularity. To see the sumptuous board spread under the forest oaks, the growth of centuries, animals roasted whole, everything that a luxurious country could produce, wines, and the well filled punch bowl, to say nothing of the invigorating mountain air, was enough to fill the heart . . . with joy! . . . At these feasts the woods were alive with guests, carriages, horses, servants and children—for all went—often more than an hundred guests. All happy at the prospect of a meeting, which was a scene of pleasure and hilarity. The laugh with hearty good will, the jest, after the crops, "farmer's topics" and politics had been discussed. If not too late, these meetings were terminated by a dance.

A similarly pastoral and personable scene is described by George Ticknor of Boston, Massachusetts. Ticknor served as a fellow of the American Academy of Arts and Sciences and was renowned throughout the country for his erudition and his large personal library of rare books, bought in Europe. In December 1824, Ticknor was traveling from Washington, D.C., through Virginia with the eminent orator and congressman Daniel Webster, and the pair called on Dolley and James at Montpelier. In a letter to William H. Prescott written at Monticello (Thomas Jefferson's home), Ticknor recorded his memories of Montpelier and of Mr. and Mrs. Madison:

> On Saturday morning we reached Mr. Madison's, at Montpellier, on the west side of what is called the

Southwest Mountain; a very fine, commanding situation, with the magnificent range of the Blue Ridge stretching along the whole horizon in front, at the distance of from twenty to thirty miles. . . . We were received with a good deal of dignity and much cordiality, by Mr. Madison and Mrs. Madison, in the portico, and immediately placed at ease; for they were apprised of our coming an hour or two before we arrived, and were therefore all in order, to show a little of that ceremony in which Mrs. Madison still delights. Mr. Madison is a younger-looking man—he is now seventy-four—than he was when I saw him ten years ago, with an unsuccessful war grinding him to the earth; and he is one of the most pleasant men I have met, both from the variety and vivacity of his conversation. He lives, apparently, with great regularity. We breakfasted at nine, dined about four, drank tea at seven, and went to bed at ten; that is, we went to our rooms, where we were furnished with everything we wanted, and where Mrs. Madison sent us a nice supper every night and a nice luncheon every forenoon. From ten o'clock in the morning till three we rode, walked, or remained in our rooms, Mr. Madison and Mrs. Madison being then occupied. The table is very ample and elegant, and somewhat luxurious; it is evidently a serious item in the account of Mr. M[adison]'s happiness, and it seems to be his habit to pass about an hour, after the cloth is removed, with a variety of wines of no mean quality. (*The Life, Letters and Journals of George Ticknor*, ed. George Hillard)

"His Peaceful Dwelling": The Marquis de Lafayette Comes to Montpelier

Perhaps one of the most celebrated guests ever to visit the Madisons at Montpelier was none other than Marie-Joseph-Paul-Yves-Roch-Gilbert de Motier, also known as the Marquis de Lafayette.

After returning to France following his service in the Continental

Army during the American War of Independence, Lafayette tried entering the arena of public service in his homeland, but found the political climate less than agreeable. So hostile was this, that the Marquis was actually imprisoned for over five years, finally relying on his American citizenship and concerted efforts by the American embassy to persuade Napoleon to release Lafayette and his family.

Upon his release from prison, Napoleon offered the Marquis a position in his government, but Lafayette demurred, preferring to retire from public life altogether.

After years of searching for some employment that would provide him with some sort of professional and personal satisfaction, of the type he had found in his adopted home of America, Lafayette longed for the company of his old friends and fellow soldiers. Consequently, he planned to take a lengthy tour of the country he had called home for so many years, the country he helped free from British tyranny: les États-Unis d'Amérique, known to its natives as the United States of America.

The Marquis, accompanied by his son Georges Washington (named in memory of his mentor and hero, the late President George Washington) and his secretary, Auguste Levasseur, arrived in New York City on August 15, 1824.

Upon disembarking, the Marquis de Lafayette was warmly greeted by throngs of cheering Americans grateful for the selfless service rendered by him in the War of Independence, service that included the shedding of his own blood at the Battle of Brandywine.

After spending time with many luminaries, including John Adams and Andrew Jackson, Lafayette and his company visited his old friend, Thomas Jefferson, at Monticello.

After a delightful stay of nearly two weeks with Jefferson and other guests at Monticello, the Marquis de Lafayette, his son, and his secretary set off for Montpelier for a four-day visit with James and Dolley Madison, from November 15-19, 1824. The following account of the time Lafayette spent in the company of Mr. and Mrs. Madison and their Orange County neighbors is taken from the Marquis' journal of his American tour, published in 1829:

Mr. Madison at the time of our visit was seventy-four years of age, but his well preserved frame contained a youthful soul full of sensibility, which he did not hesitate to show, when he expressed to general Lafayette the pleasure he felt at having him in his house. Although the habit of reflection and application, give to his countenance an aspect of severity, all the impressions of his heart are rapidly depicted in his features, and his conversation is usually animated with a gentle gaiety. Mrs. Madison also contributes much by the graces of her mind, and the amenity of her character to exalt the excellence of that frank hospitality with which strangers are received at Montpelier.

The four days passed with Mr. Madison were agreeably employed in promenades over his beautiful estate, and still more agreeably by our evening conversations, particularly concerning all the great American interests, which are so dear to general Lafayette. The society which at this time habitually assembled at Montpelier, was almost entirely composed of the neighbouring planters, who for the most part appeared as well versed in all great political questions as in agriculture.

In a conversation with his host and the other Virginia planters and slaveowners, the Marquis brought up the delicate question of slavery, hoping not to offend Mr. Madison and rather counting on his frankness and foresight.

"[The institution of slavery] was approached and discussed by them frankly, and in a manner to confirm me in the opinion I had previously formed concerning the noble sentiments of the majority of Virginians upon this deplorable circumstance. It appears to me, that slavery cannot exist a long time in Virginia, because all enlightened men condemn the principle of it, and when public opinion condemns a principle, its consequences cannot long continue to subsist," the Marquis' secretary recorded.

On the evening of November 19, 1824, the Marquis and his retinue ate dinner with the Madisons and their household and then departed from Montpelier, planning to head to Fredericksburg. Lafayette's record of his four-day sojourn with Mr. and Mrs. Madison closed with a comment on the health and hospitality of his hosts.

Levasseur wrote, "After the dinner, we parted from Mr. Madison, who, notwithstanding his seventy-four years, mounted his horse with activity, and set out through the woods for his peaceful dwelling."

After a few more stops, the Marquis de Lafayette and his traveling companions returned to New York. On September 7, 1825, after a stay of 16 months during which they visited each of the 24 states, they boarded a ship christened the USS *Brandywine* in his honor and headed back to France.

In light of so many terrific testimonies of the delight taken by James in his retirement at Montpelier, it is little wonder that he never again left. In fact, Madison was determined to stay out of politics. (George Ticknor reported that Madison "seems determined not to be again involved in them.") He would be, of course, involved with his pen and his opinions, but he loved Montpelier, he loved Dolley, and, most of all, he loved the life the two of them shared during their dotage at Montpelier.

"A Magnificent Institute":
James Madison and The University of Virginia

As previously noted, James Madison was an ardent supporter of education. He believed that "learned institutions . . . throw light over the public mind which is the best security against crafty and dangerous encroachments on the public liberty." When in 1822 he received a letter from the lieutenant governor of Kentucky, William T. Barry, regarding a proposal to establish a popularly supported university, Madison praised the idea and provided Barry with a bit of wisdom and counsel for the battle he would face with those opposed to the plan:

> A popular Government, without popular information, or the means of acquiring it, is but a prologue to a Farce

or a Tragedy; or perhaps both. Knowledge will forever govern ignorance: and a people who mean to be their own Governors, must arm themselves with the power which knowledge gives.

Thomas Jefferson, of course, agreed with Madison and had written so on many occasions, including in his *Notes on the State of Virginia*. So, it is no surprise that Jefferson asked Madison to be on the inaugural Board of Directors of the University of Virginia. When asked by Jefferson to approve a list of books and documents Jefferson believed mandatory for students at that new institution (sadly, a copy of that list has not been found), Madison provided his opinion as well as some history on this vital subject. On February 5, 1825, he wrote:

The west lawn at the University of Virginia.

Rufus W. Holsinger (1866 - 1930), Public domain, via Wikimedia Commons

> It is certainly very material that the true doctrines of liberty, as exemplified in our Political System, should be inculcated on those who are to sustain and may administer it. It is, at the same time, not easy to find standard books that will be both guides & guards for the purpose. Sidney & Locke are admirably calculated to impress on young minds the right of Nations to establish their own Governments, and to inspire a love of free ones; but afford no aid in guarding our Republican Charters against constructive violations. The Declaration of Independence, tho' rich in fundamental principles, and saying every thing that could be said in the same number of words, falls nearly under a like observation. The "Federalist" may fairly enough be regarded as the most authentic exposition of the text of the federal Constitution, as understood by the Body which prepared & the Authority which accepted it.

Madison then added George Washington's Inaugural and Farewell Addresses to Jefferson's list. He closed his reply with the following "Sketch" of a political creed for the University of Virginia (and for America):

> And on the distinctive principles of the Government of our own State, and of that of the U. States, the best guides are to be found in—1. The Declaration of Independence, as the fundamental act of Union of these States. 2. the book known by the title of the "Federalist," being an Authority to which appeal is habitually made by all & rarely declined or denied by any, as evidence of the general opinion of those who framed & those who accepted the Constitution of the U. States on questions as to its genuine meaning. 3. the Resolutions of the General Assembly of Virga. in 1799, on the subject of the Alien & Sedition laws, which appeared to accord with the predominant sense of the people of the U.S. 4. The Inaugural Speech & Farewell Address of President Washington, as conveying political lessons of peculiar value; and that in the branch of the

School of law which is to treat on the subject of Govt., these shall be used as the text & documents of the School.

Madison's suggestions were accepted, and the following guidelines for students applying to the University of Virginia were published in February 1825:

> Whereas it is the duty of this board to the government under which we live, and especially to that of which this University is the immediate creation to pay especial attention to the principles of govmt which shall be inculcated therein, and to provide that none shall be inculcated which are incompatible with those on which the constitutions of this state and of the U.S. were genuinely based in the common opinion; and for this purpose it may be necessary to point out specifically where these principles are to be found legitimately developed;

> Resolved that it is the opinion of this board that as to the general principles of liberty and the rights of man, in nature, and in society, the doctrines of Locke in his "Essay concerning the true original, extent, & end of civil govmt," and of Sydney in his "Discourses on govmt," may be considered as those generally approved by our fellow citizens of this, and of the US. and that on the distinctive principles of the govmt of our own state, and of that of the US. as understood and assented to when brought into union 1. The book known by the title of the "Federalist," 2. The Resolns of the General assembly of Virga, in 1799 on the subject of the alien and sedition laws, and 3. The Declaration of Independence, ought to be considered as possessing the general approbation of our fellow-citizens. The 1st as an authority to which appeal is habitually made by all, and rarely declined or denied by any, as evidence of the general opinion of those who made and of those who accepted the constitn of the US. on questions as to

its genuine meaning. the 2d as sanctioned by the people of the US. as manifested in the exercise of their rights of suffrage immediately subsequent to that publication; and the 3d as the fundamental act of union of these states. And that in the branch of the school of Law which is to treat on the subject of government, these shall be used as the text and documents of the school; and no principles shall be inculcated which do not harmonise with them.

In light of the ringing endorsement by James Madison and Thomas Jefferson of these authors, it is worth wondering why these men and the books that were so influential on the founding of our country are now unknown to most Americans, even those who study history.

Beyond their recommendations for a curriculum, Madison and Jefferson co-authored the "Report of the Board of Commissioners" of the University of Virginia on August 4, 1818. In this document, Madison further discusses his views on the proper mode of education and the most beneficial scholarly culture. The report's highlights include the following: First, Madison and Jefferson recommend dormitories with rooms for two students, as they believed this arrangement would be most "advantageous to morals, to order, & to uninterrupted study." Next, the pair laid out the "purposes" of the university's instruction. Their list would serve as an exemplary mission statement for any institution aiming at educating youth. Madison and Jefferson proposed:

> To expound the principles & structure of government, the laws which regulate the intercourse of nations, those formed municipally for our own government, and a sound spirit of legislation, which banishing all arbitrary & unnecessary restraint on individual action shall leave us free to do whatever does not violate the equal rights of another.

> To harmonize & promote the interests of agriculture, manufactures & commerce and by well informed views

of political economy to give a free scope to the public industry.

To develop the reasoning faculties of our youth, enlarge their minds cultivate their morals, & instil into them the precepts of virtue & order.

To enlighten them with mathematical and physical sciences which advance the arts & administer to the health, the subsistence & comforts of human life.

And generally to form them to habits of reflection, and correct action, rendering them examples of virtue to others & of happiness within themselves.

Law, history, agriculture, math, science, morality, and "habits of reflection and correct action" are the subjects that should be taught in America's schools, according to two of our country's most well-educated, well-rounded, and well-respected statesmen.

Later in the minutes of the meeting, Madison and Jefferson reminded readers of the myriad benefits one may, if he cares to, derive from taking his education seriously. On that subject, they stated that the Board of Directors of the University of Virginia are:

sensible that the advantages of well directed education, moral, political & economical are truly above all estimate. Education generates habits of application, order and the love of virtue; and controls, by the force of habit, any innate obliquities in our moral organization.

Furthermore, "Education," they insisted, "improves what in [one's] nature was vicious & perverse, into qualities of virtue and social worth."

Their report ended with an additional benefit that may be obtained through a sound education after the manner they propose:

> Nor must we omit to mention, among the benefits of education, the incalculable advantage of training up able counsellors to administer the affairs of our Country in all its departments, Legislative, Executive, and Judiciary, and to bear their proper share in the councils of Our National Government; nothing, more than education, adorning the prosperity, the power and the happiness of a nation.

Jefferson served as the first rector (what we might call a "dean" or "president") of the University of Virginia from 1819 until his death in 1826. Then, at 75 years old, James Madison filled that position until his own death a decade later.

In the story of the founding of the University of Virginia, much is learned of the mind and methods of James Madison, particularly as pertains to education, a lifelong endeavor that he believed was critical to the preservation of liberty.

"Closely Connected With the Tranquility of the State": James Madison Attends The Virginia State Constitutional Convention of 1829-1830

James Madison's final act of public service was a familiar one: helping craft a constitution. He had served at Virginia's first post-Colonial Constitutional Convention in 1776, he was the leading delegate at the Constitutional Convention of 1787, and he was a vocal proponent of the product of that convention at Virginia's Ratification Convention of 1788.

In 1829, He was compelled, in spite of his increasingly flagging physical condition, to serve as a representative of Orange County at a convention called to write a new constitution for the Old Dominion. The account of how Madison became involved in this historic event was given in his own words as part of his very short autobiography, written in the winter of 1830-1831. Here is Madison's recounting of the story, written in his own words, albeit in third person:

> In 1829, he was prevailed on, notwithstanding his age & very feeble health being but convalescent from a spell of sickness to serve as a member of the convention which revised the Const[itutio]n of the States.

Madison then noted that his primary purpose in attending the convention was:

> to promote a compromise of ideas between parties fixed in their pol[itical] opinion, by their local interests, & threatening an abortive result to an experiment closely connected with the tranquility of the State, & the capacity of man for self-gov[ernmen]t.

James Madison was the last surviving member of the Constitutional Convention of 1787, and as such was treated as a celebrity, a "mythic figure," and a "demigod" at the Virginia Constitutional Convention of 1829-1830. Although there were many leading lights of Virginia's political class (James Monroe and John Marshall, for example), no one

James and Dolley retired and returned to Montpelier, though James continued to serve the public.

Carole J. Buckwalter, CC BY-SA 4.0, via Wikimedia Commons

approached the status of statesman that James Madison had earned. As such, any time he spoke, the record of the convention reports, "the members rushed from their seats and crowded around him."

As he had done at a similar gathering in Philadelphia over 40 years earlier, Madison attended every session of the Virginia Constitutional Convention. While there, he was faced with many familiar constitutional controversies: the rights of the minority, the principle of representative government, and the sovereignty of the people. On December 2, 1829, the feeble yet abundantly able James Madison rose to make "a few observations" on these key issues.

In his biography of Madison, Ketcham quotes a contemporary account of Madison's appearance at the convention, published in the *Richmond Enquirer*: "His voice was low and weak, but his sentences were rounding and complete; and his enunciation, though tremulous and full of feeling, was distinct to those who heard him," the paper reported.

Madison, dressed in formal clothes and in a powdered wig, began his discourse by focusing on the relationship of property and government:

> It is sufficiently obvious, that Persons and Property, are the two great subjects on which Governments are to act: and that the rights of persons, and the rights of property are the objects for the protection of which Government was instituted. These rights cannot well be separated. The personal right to acquire property, which is a natural right, gives to property when acquired a right to protection as a social right.

He was just hitting his stride, as he then moved to a full-throated declaration of the nature of government. "The essence of Government is power; and power lodged as it must be, in human hands, will ever be liable to abuse," he professed. Then, he compared the three classical forms of government: monarchy, aristocracy, and republic, and explained that in a republic, "the great danger is that the majority may not sufficiently respect the rights of the Minority."

In his autobiographical commentary on this moment at the

Virginia Constitutional Convention, Madison made special mention of this principle of power and precisely what steps a tyrant would take in overthrowing the liberty of a republic, particularly the United States of America. His pronouncement is somewhat prescient. "A republic . . . could not be safe with a numerical and physical force against, without a standing army, an enslaved press, and a disarmed populace," he warned.

In his speech at the convention, Madison then weighed in on the importance of the consideration of character in the election of representatives in a republic. "Character," he said, is "too often overruled by other motives." He continued, lamenting, "When numbers of men act in a body, respect for character is often lost, just in proportion as it is necessary to control what is not right." In other words, the ability of a man to resist the temptation to do "what is not right"—to usurp power over his fellow man—is reduced in proportion to the availability of such power to that man.

In this and the following statements, Madison echoed Jefferson's warning, written in 1798: "In questions of power, then, let no more be heard of confidence in man, but bind him down from mischief by the chains of the Constitution." At this, his final constitutional convention, Madison expressed the same sentiment in other words. "Those favorable attributes of the human character are all valuable, as auxiliaries; but they will not serve as a substitute for the coercive provisions belonging to government and law," he told his fellow delegates.

Madison was aware that while his renown was unchallenged, his political opinions were not. Appreciating this, he concluded his address of December 2, 1829 by calling for "the spirit of compromise." Then, with noticeable pride, he praised the United States for what he called the "miracle" of the Constitution and the hope it gives the states of remaining united and weathering any storm through which such a people must pass:

> Other Nations are surprised at nothing so much as our having been able to form Constitutions in the manner which has been exemplified in this Country. Even the Union of so many States is in the eyes of the world a wonder: the

James worked hard to keep Americans on the right path at the Virginia Constitutional Convention.

George Catlin, Public domain, via Wikimedia Commons

harmonious establishment of a common Government over them all, a miracle. I cannot but flatter myself, that, without a miracle, we shall be able to arrange all our difficulties. I never have despaired. Notwithstanding all the threatening appearances we have passed through. I have now more than a hope, a consoling confidence that we shall at last find that our labours have not been in vain.

Madison considered his efforts at the Virginia Constitutional Convention of 1829-1830 to have been in vain, however, as partisanship held sway over the opinions of the delegates. That reality, he wrote, was "most pregnant with danger. . . ."

Chapter 19
The Death of James Madison

Ralph Ketcham writes that through 1835 and 1836, "the candle of the old man of Montpelier sputtered toward its socket." James Madison, at 85 years old, had outlived all of his fellow Founding Fathers. Jefferson, his friend and collaborator for over 50 years, had passed away 10 years earlier. Madison was quite literally the last of a dying breed.

As is well known, John Adams died on the same day as Jefferson, the 50th anniversary of the Declaration of Independence. James Monroe, Madison's sometime political rival and perpetual friend, died in 1831, five years before Madison. George Washington, the "Father of His Country," preceded them all in death, having been gone some 37 years by the time Madison passed away.

Despite advancing toward the end of his life, visitors to Montpelier reported, Madison was always "eager for conversation" and would stay awake reading and talking from "nine in the morning until ten at night." One of the last people to record their recollections of time spent with Madison during the last days of his life was Congressman Charles Ingersoll of Pennsylvania. Ingersoll and his eldest daughter journeyed to Montpelier on May 2, 1836, and Ingersoll spoke at length with his old acquaintance just over a month before Madison breathed his last.

Ingersoll published the events of that meeting in the *Daily Washington Globe*, a newspaper published in the capital city. "A purer, brighter, juster spirit has seldom existed," Ingersoll said of Madison in his report. Of the former president's health, Ingersoll wrote that Mr. Madison was frail of body, but his mind was clear and sharp. Madison's mind, it seems, from his first days on earth until his last, was clear and sharp. He was a man undeniably gifted with a keenness of intellect and a sincerity of expression that outpaced similar gifts in all but a few of his contemporaries.

One bit of evidence of the character of the man is the fact that as he was literally running out of hours on earth, he was found reading over a biography of his friend, Thomas Jefferson, written by St. George Tucker, a jurist and commentator on law. Tucker, according to Ketcham, reported that Madison signed off on the manuscript of the Jefferson biography "about thirteen hours before his decease."

In a letter to Lucy Todd, written sometime in May 1836, Dolley Madison described her husband's physical condition in his final days. "I am grieved to tell you that my dear Husband has been unusually sick for some days, and is at present unable to write, or even to exert his thoughts, without oppressive fatigue," she reported with noticeable anguish.

Despite such suffering, James Madison refused to take tonics prescribed by doctors for the purpose of preserving his life until the anniversary of the Declaration of Independence on July 4, 1836. The physicians, apparently, thought it appropriate to attempt to prolong the life of the former president so that he might die on the same day as his lifelong companion, Thomas Jefferson, albeit 10 years later. Madison would have none of it. He would die when it was time, neither before nor after, at "the appointed hour," as Ketcham calls it.

As for how he spent his last few earthbound hours, the story is best related by a man who knew him better than most: Paul Jennings. Paul Jennings was James Madison's personal servant and spent every day with the former president for 16 years. There will be more on Jennings and his opinion of Madison below, but here is his firsthand account of the moment Madison passed away:

> I was always with Mr. Madison till he died, and shaved him every other day for sixteen years. For six months before his death, he was unable to walk, and spent most of his time reclined on a couch; but his mind was bright, and with his numerous visitors he talked with as much

Chapter Nineteen: The Death of James Madison

animation and strength of voice as I ever heard him in his best days.

I was present when he died. That morning Sukey [a household servant] brought him his breakfast, as usual. He could not swallow. His niece, Mrs. Willis, said, "What is the matter, Uncle James?"

"Nothing more than a change of mind, my dear."

His head instantly dropped, and he ceased breathing as quietly as the snuff of a candle goes out.

Paul Jennings wrote a beautiful account describing James' last days. It captured the strong character such a small man possessed, even to his last day.

Memorials and Eulogies:
Farewell to the Last of the Founding Fathers

The day after he passed away, four of Madison's neighbors served their friend one last time. Acting as pallbearers, they carried his body to his family's graveyard about a half a mile down the hill from Montpelier.

In the procession to the grave site, Dolley led, followed by scores of friends and neighbors from all over Orange County. The service was performed according to the rites of the Episcopal Church, with almost absolute silence observed throughout, being disrupted only at the end by the sobbing of many mourners.

As one would expect given James Madison's monumental role in the establishment of the United States, as word of his passing spread throughout the country, nearly every newspaper printed a eulogy praising him for his patriotism and personal virtue.

One of the most poetic obituaries was printed in the pages of the *Daily National Intelligencer*, the most-read newspaper in Washington, D.C. The paper reported, as recounted in Ketcham's biography, that "the last of the great lights of the Revolution . . . has sunk below the horizon . . . [and] left a radiance in the firmament."

Perhaps the most moving tribute was that penned by the English author Harriet Martineau who visited the Madisons at Montpelier in February 1835, a little more than a year before President Madison passed away.

Martineau's eulogy was published in a book she wrote chronicling her visit with James and Dolley Madison, as well as other notable American statesmen. She wrote of James:

> There is no need to add another to the many eulogies of Madison; I will only mention that the finest of his characteristics appeared to me to be his inexhaustible faith; faith that a well-founded commonwealth may, as our motto declares, be immortal; not only because the people, its constituency never die, but because the principles of justice in which such a commonwealth originates, never die out in the people's heart and mind. This faith

shone brightly through the whole of Mr. Madison's conversations.

Naturally, many notable Americans eulogized Madison at memorials held throughout the country. At the service conducted at Boston, Massachusetts, on September 27, 1836, John Quincy Adams delivered an address that reportedly lasted over two hours. In his eulogy, he rehearsed a bit of ancient history, as well as the important events of the War of Independence and Mr. Madison's contribution to the Constitution.

There is one paragraph of Adams' address that bears duplicating here. He declared:

> Let us look back then for consolation from the thought of the shortness of human life, as urged upon us by the recent decease of James Madison, one of the pillars and ornaments of his country and of his age. His time on earth was short, yet he died full of years and of glory—less, far less than one hundred years have elapsed since the day of his birth—yet has he fulfilled, nobly fulfilled, his destinies as a man and a Christian. He has improved his own condition by improving that of his country and his kind.

He concluded his remarks by calling upon all Americans to listen to

> the voice that stills the raging of the waves and the tumults of the people—that spoke the words of peace—of harmony—of union. And for that voice, may you and your children's children "to the last syllable of recorded time," fix your eyes upon the memory, and listen with your ears to the life of James Madison.

Undoubtedly, it would have pleased Madison that Adams mentioned peace and union as two hallmarks of the former's time in the service of the country he helped create.

The "last of the Founding Fathers" had now passed on to his reward and into the pages of history. James Madison outlived all of the remarkable men of his remarkable generation, and exceeded them in more ways than just the number of his days on earth. Not only did he surpass his contemporaries in the length of his life, but, with a very few exceptions, he surpassed them in the length of the shadow of his influence, as well.

"No Atom of Ill Will":
Madison's Political Adversaries Praise His Character

Even among those few men who would have considered themselves foes of James Madison, there was scarcely ever a word that was written or spoken by them impugning the character of the man. They had their political differences with him to be sure, but of his integrity, there was seemingly no debate.

One of his political rivals was also one of his closest friends, James Monroe with whom he competed for a seat in the House of Representatives of the very first Congress in March 1789. Madison was opposed to campaigning, as he found it distasteful and un-republican to ask for votes.

Patrick Henry wanted Monroe rather than Madison to represent his district in Virginia (no doubt a lingering result of the latter's victory at the Virginia Ratifying Convention the previous year) and exerted his immense influence toward that end. Madison and Monroe were friends, though, and would not be manipulated into ruining their relationship by the pettiness of partisan politics.

Madison's feelings regarding the electoral challenge made by Monroe is evident in a letter he wrote to Thomas Jefferson on March 29, 1789, after he had won the contested seat:

> It was my misfortune to be thrown into a contest with our friend, Col. Monroe. The occasion produced considerable efforts among our respective friends. Between ourselves, I have no reason to doubt that the distinction was duly kept in mind between political and personal views, and that it has saved our friendship from the smallest diminution.

For his part, just before his death, Monroe said of Madison, "I regret that I should leave this world without again beholding him."

It is likely for his approach to the "distinction . . . between political and personal views" that James Madison was so highly regarded, even by his rivals. George Washington, with whom Madison would have several political rows, manifested his respect for Madison by asking him to write several speeches for him, including the very first inaugural address, delivered on April 30, 1789. Washington's admiration for Madison was evident in nearly every letter he wrote to him. On March 2, 1788, upon hearing that Madison would allow himself to be put forward as a delegate to Virginia's Ratifying Convention, Washington wrote him, thanking him for his decision to serve:

> The determination you have come to, will give pleasure to your friends. From those in your own county you will learn with more certainty than from me, the expediency of your attending the Election in it.

There was no one, perhaps, who was a more frequent and fiery political foe of James Madison than his one-time *Federalist* collaborator, Alexander Hamilton. Hamilton's financial plans, his views on a standing army, and his support of the Alien and Sedition Acts all placed him in opposition to Madison. And, as was discussed earlier in regards to the Pacificus-Helvidius debates, Madison was not one to back away from the awesome presence that was Alexander Hamilton. In spite of their political schism, though, Hamilton, in a conversation with George Beckwith in March 1789, said of Madison, "That he is uncorrupted and incorruptible, I have no doubt."

Finally, one of the most eloquent yet simple sketches of James Madison's character was written by William Pierce of Georgia. Pierce was a fellow delegate with Madison at the Constitutional Convention in Philadelphia in 1787 and, like Madison, kept notes on the speeches and debates heard in that historic council. As part of the journal kept by Pierce of his time at the convention, perhaps the most interesting and unique is the section of his notes he called "Characters in the convention of the states held at Philadelphia, May, 1787." In this section, Pierce penned a brief biographical sketch of each of his fellow attendees. Here is the description he gave of James Madison, as reprinted in Max Farrand's *The Records of the Federal Convention of 1787*, Volume 3, Appendix A:

Mr. Maddison is a character who has long been in public life; and what is very remarkable every Person seems to acknowledge his greatness. He blends together the profound politician, with the Scholar. In the management of every great question he evidently took the lead in the Convention, and tho' he cannot be called an Orator, he is a most agreeable, eloquent, and convincing Speaker. From a spirit of industry and application which he possesses in a most eminent degree, he always comes forward the best informed Man of any point in debate. The affairs of the United States, he perhaps, has the most correct knowledge of, of any Man in the Union. He has been twice a Member of Congress, and was always thought one of the ablest Members that ever sat in that Council. Mr. Maddison is about 37 years of age, a Gentleman of great modesty, with a remarkable sweet temper. He is easy and unreserved among his acquaintance, and has a most agreable style of conversation.

"One of the Best Men That Ever Lived"

Finally, there is an old French maxim (attributed to various famous Frenchmen) that says "no man is a hero to his valet." The meaning behind this proverb is that a gentleman's personal servant would know the "real" man behind the public persona. He would not be as impressed with him as the people at large, for he would be familiar with the faults and folly of a man judged by others to be infallible.

Paul Jennings was James Madison's "body servant" until Madison's death. In a brief memoir published in 1865, Jennings recalled with great fondness and familiarity the "real" James Madison:

> Mr. Madison, I think, was one of the best men that ever lived. I never saw him in a passion, and never knew him to strike a slave, although he had over one hundred; neither would he allow an overseer to do it. Whenever any slaves were reported to him as stealing or "cutting up" badly, he would send for them and admonish them privately, and never mortify them by doing it before others. They generally

Chapter Nineteen: The Death of James Madison

After Madison's death, Daniel Webster purchased Paul Jennings' freedom and paid him a salary.

served him very faithfully. He was temperate in his habits. I don't think he drank a quart of brandy in his whole life. He ate light breakfasts and no suppers, but rather a hearty dinner, with which he took invariably but one glass of wine. When he had hard drinkers at his table, who had put away his choice Madeira pretty freely, in response to their numerous toasts, he would just touch the glass to his lips, or dilute it with water, as they pushed about the decanters. For the last fifteen years of his life he drank no wine at all.

Jennings was a slave, it is true, but his encomium of Madison was written years after his freedom was purchased, by none other than Daniel Webster. Webster purchased Jennings' freedom from Mrs. Madison for $120, and agreed to pay Jennings "eight dollars a month" as a salary to work as a free man. For many years after gaining his freedom and after the death of James Madison, Daniel Webster would send Paul Jennings down to Montpelier to take Mrs. Madison food, money, and the supplies that she needed. Such was the soul of Daniel Webster and Paul Jennings—and such was the devotion inspired in them and most other men by James Madison.

Chapter 20
"Madison's Memorial ... A Free Country Governed by the Rule of Law"

Despite being called the "Father of the Constitution," there is no monument to James Madison in Washington, D.C. In fairness, there is a small statue of him inside the Library of Congress annex, but it is dwarfed (as was the man himself) by the massive marble markers dedicated to his contemporaries George Washington and Thomas Jefferson. In 2001, on the 250th anniversary of Madison's birth, columnist George Will lamented the discrepancy:

> There is no monument to James Madison in Washington. There is a tall, austere monument to the tall (six foot two), austere man for whom the city is named, a man of Roman virtues and eloquent reticence. There is a Greek-revival memorial to Madison's boon companion, the tall (six foot two), elegant, eloquent Jefferson, who is to subsequent generations the most charismatic of the Founders. But there is no monument to the smallest (five foot four) but subtlest of the Founders, without whose mind Jefferson's Declaration and Washington's generalship could not have resulted in this republic.

In an article published in 2015, presidential historian Richard Brookhiser summed up the slight with a perfect metaphor. He writes:

The fourth US president is often ignored—he's not even on the currency anymore—but four new books remind us that tiny James Madison was a man to reckon with.

The Bible tells us that where our treasure is, there will our hearts be also. So where do we put the Founding Fathers on our money? George Washington occupies the quarter and, most important, the dollar bill. Over the years the Mint has rolled out dollar coins showing Ike, Susan B. Anthony, or Sacagawea, to no avail; Americans want the dollar to be scruffy paper with George on it. Thomas Jefferson holds the ubiquitous nickel and the elusive $2 bill. Alexander Hamilton gazes, buff and brash, from the tenner. And high rollers and drug dealers greet healthy, wealthy, and wise Benjamin Franklin on the C-note.

And where did we put James Madison? On the $5,000 bill. Which was discontinued in 1969.

No monument. No money. No matter.

To understand why this apparent slight wouldn't bother the diminutive Madison, take a visit to his grave on the grounds of his Orange County, Virginia home. One would instantly recognize the humility that was a hallmark of his life. The monument is an understated and seemingly unpolished stone obelisk etched with none of Madison's impressive achievements, but bearing the simple engraving:

MADISON

BORN MARCH 16TH, 1751

DIED JUNE 28TH, 1836

Chapter Twenty: Madison's Memorial... A Free Country Governed by the Rule of Law

President James Madison's gravestone was erected as a simple and humble memorial that could not possibly begin to represent the impact he had on history.

For a bit of contrast, make the short drive to the much more popular Monticello (Thomas Jefferson's estate). There, one can't miss the large obelisk signaling the final resting place of the third president.

Additionally, one sees Jefferson's résumé etched into the stone, just as he directed. This is from the Monticello website:

> Before his death, Thomas Jefferson left explicit instructions regarding the monument to be erected over his grave. In this document (undated), Jefferson supplied a sketch of the shape of the marker, and the epitaph with which he wanted it to be inscribed: ". . . on the faces of the Obelisk the following inscription, & not a word more: because by these," he explained, "as testimonials that I have lived, I wish most to be remembered."
>
> Here was buried
>
> Thomas Jefferson
>
> Author of the Declaration of American Independence
>
> of the Statute of Virginia for religious freedom
>
> & Father of the University of Virginia

Chief Justice John Roberts addressed the issue of a lack of memorial to James Madison when he spoke at the celebration of the completion of the restoration of Montpelier. Roberts said:

> Montpelier restored is certainly beautiful but is in no sense the most fitting memorial to James Madison. If you're looking for Madison's memorial, look around . . . look around at a free country governed by the rule of law.

That would certainly be memorial enough for Mr. Madison!

"Advice to My Country": Madison's Hopes for His Posterity

Sometime around 1834, James Madison penned a brief document entitled "Advice to My Country." It is valuable for many reasons, not the least of which is the fact that it is wisdom drawn like sweet water straight from the source, not downstream, and not filtered through the prejudices or presuppositions of a biographer or commentator. The statement's value is increased by its reference to the fear Madison had that the union that he had worked so long and hard to create, nurture, and maintain was soon to be dissolved. This was the counsel Madison bequeathed his countrymen:

> As this advice, if it ever see the light will not do it till I am no more it may be considered as issuing from the tomb where truth alone can be respected, and the happiness of man alone consulted. It will be entitled therefore to whatever weight can be derived from good intentions, and from the experience of one, who has served his Country in various stations through a period of forty years, who espoused in his youth and adhered through his life to the cause of its liberty, and who has borne a part in most of the great transactions which will constitute epochs of its destiny.
>
> The advice nearest to my heart and deepest in my convictions is that the Union of the States be cherished & perpetuated. Let the open enemy to it be regarded as a Pandora with her box opened; and the disguised one, as the Serpent creeping with his deadly wiles into Paradise.

All who knew him—even most of those who knew him and didn't agree with him—considered James Madison to be a gentleman in the truest sense of that word. He was a man who overcame and overlooked his own physical impediments. He was, as were most of the great men of his time, born before excuses were invented.

The last word in this biography will be appropriately given to

Madison himself. He was a man among men, a man of unwavering commitment to the Constitution, to the union it perfected, and to the cause of religious liberty. Despite being in the public eye for over half a century, his character remained unsullied, and despite serving in nearly every available political office, Madison's integrity was never sacrificed for self-aggrandizement or the unwarranted promotion of his friends and allies.

We close, then, with the words James Madison delivered in his annual message to Congress at the beginning of his second term as president of the United States. Notably, these poignant words were spoken in a time of war, a time of national unrest. Contemporary Americans can appreciate times such as those. For our benefit, then, we repeat and conclude with the comforting and clarion counsel of President James Madison:

> It would be improper to close this communication without expressing a thankfulness, in which all ought to unite, for the numerous blessings with which our beloved country, continues to be favored; for the abundance which overspreads our land, and the prevailing health of its inhabitants; for the preservation of our internal tranquility, and the stability of our free institutions; and above all for the light of divine truth, and the protection of every man's conscience, in the enjoyment of it. And although among our blessings we cannot number an exemption from the evils of war; yet these will never be regarded as the greatest of evils, by the friends of liberty, and of the rights of nations. Our country has before preferred them to the degraded condition which was the alternative, when the sword was drawn in the cause, which gave birth to our national Independence; and none who contemplate the magnitude, and feel the value of that glorious event, will shrink from a struggle to maintain the high and happy ground, on which it placed the American people.

[It is] the capacity and the destiny of the United States to be a great, a flourishing, and a powerful nation; worthy of the friendship which it is disposed to cultivate with all others; and authorized, by its own example, to require from all, an observance of the laws of justice and reciprocity. Beyond these, their claims have never extended; and in contending for these, we behold a subject for our congratulations, in the daily testimonies of increasing harmony throughout the nation, and may humbly repose our trust in the smiles of heaven, on so righteous a cause.

Hear, hear, Mr. Madison! Hear, hear!

Appendix 1:
James Madison's Autobiography

In 1831, the noted American author James Kirke Paulding wrote to James Madison asking him to write an outline autobiography, which Paulding planned to use in writing his own book of biographies of famous men of the Revolutionary War. According to historian Douglass Adair, Madison "had a high personal opinion of Paulding," so he decided to contribute to Paulding's book. By this time, Madison was 80 years old and unable to write a fresh autobiography, so he decided to use a brief sketch he'd written some years earlier.

He wrote to Paulding explaining the reason for not writing a new and longer autobiography. "It was my purpose to have enlarged some parts of it, and to have revised and probably blotted out others," Madison wrote. "But the crippled state of my health makes me shun the task and the uncertainty of the future induces me to commit the paper, crude as it is, to your friendly discretion," he adds.

In the end, Adair says, Paulding never wrote the biography of Madison, so Madison's failure to complete a fuller account of his extraordinary life did not affect that plan. Adair records that the following autobiography was written by Madison some time after the letter sent to Paulding, but was "modelled on the Paulding sketch." Madison wrote it in third person, and its value to us comes from its putting "into sharp focus the extent to which adherence to theory governed Madison's conduct as a practicing republican statesman." None of the spelling or punctuation of the original manuscript has been updated, corrected, or changed in any way.

J. M. was born on the 5th of Mar. (O. 5) 1751. His parents J. M. & N. (Conway) Madison, resided in the County of Orange in Virga. At the time of his birth they were on a visit to her mother, who resided on the Rappahannoc, at Port Conway in the County of King George.

At the age of about 12 years, he was placed by his father under the tuition of Donald Robertson, from Scotland, a man of extensive learning, and a distinguished Teacher, in the County of King & Queen. With him he studied the Latin & Greek Languages, was taught to read but not to speak French; and besides Arithmetic and Geography, made some progress in Algebra & Geometry. Miscellaneous literature was also embraced by the Plan of the School.

Having remained 3 or 4 years with Mr. Robertson, he prosecuted his Studies for a year or two under the Revd. Ths. Martin the Parish Minister of the Estabd. Church, (of England as then called) who lived with his father as a private Tutor.

One of the Earliest books which engaged his attention was the "Spectator," which, from his own experience, he inferred to be particularly adapted to inculcate in youthful minds, just sentiments an appetite for knowledge, and a taste for the improvement of the mind and manners.

*see letter to Rd. D. Cutts.

In the year 1769, by the advice of Mr. Martin, and his brother Alexander, both of whom had been educated at Nassau Hall in N. J., he was sent to that College, of which Docr. Witherspoon was then President in preference to William & Mary, the climate of which was unhealthy for persons going from a mountainous Region. He there went thro' the ordinary Course of Studies, and in the Autumn of 1771, recd. a diploma of B. of Arts. His health being at the time too infirm for a journey home, he passed the ensuing winter in Princeton, employing his time in miscellaneous Studies; but not without a reference to the profession of the Law; He availed himself of this opportunity of acquiring a slight knowledge of the Hebrew, which was not among the College Studies.

His very infirm health, had been occasioned not a little by a redoubled labour, in which he was joined by a fellow Student Jas. Ross, in accomplishing the studies of two years within one, having obtained from the faculty a promise that in case their preparation for t[he] usual degree, should be found unexceptionable, the honor should be conferred. The effect on his health, was increased also by an indiscreet experiment of the minimum of sleep & the maximum of application, which the Constitution would bear. The former was reduced for some weeks, to less than five hours in the 24.*

*He became satisfied that no real progress was gained by such a disproportionate extension of the hours of study, nor did he consider their success in performing the task of two years in one as any extraordinary atchievement. It could have been effected by others with little more than the ordinary exertion. The effect on his health proceeded from the extraordinary exertion made to justify the indulgence granted by the Faculty and to insure the attainment of his object. Hence it is probable they were better qualified in one year than they would have been in two by the ordinary application.

The extreme neglect of the French language at that day in the public Seminaries will appear from an incident soon after he had entered the College, then one of the most conspicuous in the Colonies. Docr. Witherspoon who spoke the language, had invited a visit from a French Gentleman, who could not speak a word of English. The Gentleman happened to arrive, when the Docr. happened to be absent, and not a single member of the family knew a word of French. In this embarrassment Mrs. Witherspoon, sent to the College for some one who cd relieve her from it. On application to the members of the faculty, it was found that not one of them knew any thing of French; and it was found also on successive applications to the Students, that all of them were equally ignorant, with the single exception of himself, who conscious of his incapacity for a conversation in the language, endeavored to decline the task. As nothing better, however could be done, it was insisted that he should meet the stranger. The meeting took place, with a salutation & questions on his part, wch. tho' they wd have been intelligible to the eye were perfectly otherwise gall to the ear, especially from the rapid utterances of the Speaker The Scene was as awkward as possible; but fortunately after abortive efforts sufficiently repeated, the Docr. arrived to the great relief of all the parties, and not a moment lost in the escape of the discomfited Interpreter.

On his return to Virga. he continued for several years in very feeble health but without neglecting a course of reading, which mingled miscellaneous subjects with the studies intended to qualify him for the Bar, for a practice at which however he never formed any absolute determination.

On the commencement of the dispute with G-B, he entered with the prevailing Zeal into the Amn cause; being under very early and strong impressions in favor of liberty both Civil & Religious. His devotion to the latter found a particular occasion for its exercise in the persecution instituted in his County as elsewhere agst the preachers belonging to the Sect of Baptists then beginning to spread thro' the Country. Notwithstandg—the enthusiasm which contributed to render them obnoxious to the sober public opinion as well as to the laws then in force, against Parishes descending from the Estabd. Religion, he spared no exertion to [save] them from imprisonment & to promote their release from it. This interposition, tho' a mere duty prescribed by his conscience, obtained for him a lasting place in the favor of that particular sect. Happily it was not long before the fruits of Independence and of the spirit & principles which led to it, included a compleat establishment of the Rights of Conscience without any distinction of Sects or individuals.

In 1775. He was elected a member of the Convn. for the County, living at the time with his father (who was Chairman of it) and had a part in the County proceedings belonging to the period. The spirit of the epoch may be seen in the address to P. H. on His expedition having for object the military Stores in Williamsburg, rifled by Govr. Dunmore.

He was restrained from entering into the military service by the unsettled state of his health and the discouraging feebleness of his Constitution of which he was fully admonished by his experience during the exercises and movements of a minute Company which he had joined.

In the Spring of 1776, he was initiated into the political career by a County election to the Convention which formed the original Constitution of the State with the Declaration of Rights prefixed to it; and which on the 16 day of May unanimously instructed the Deputies in Congs. to propose the final separation from G. B. as Declared by that Body on the 4th. of July following. Being young & in the midst of distinguished & experienced members of the Convention, he did not enter into its debates; tho he occasionally suggested amendments; the most material of which was a change of the terms in which the freedom of Conscience was expressed in the proposed Declaration of Rights. This important & meritorious Instrument was drawn by Geo: Mason, who had inadvertently adopted the word <u>toleration,</u> in the article on that subject. The change suggested and accepted, substituted a phraseology which—declared designated the freedom of Conscience to be a <u>nat. & absolute</u> right. See in the files of J. M. the <u>printed</u> report of the Committee, with the proposed change in the hand of J. M.

In the election of Delegates to the Legislature for the ensuing year (1777), he was an unsuccessful candidate. Previous to the Revolution the Election of the County representatives, was as in England, septennial, and it was as there, the usage, for the candidates to recommend themselves to the voters, not only by personal solicitation, but by the corrupting influence of spirituous liquors, and other treats, having a like tendency. Regarding these as equally inconsistent with the purity of moral & of republican principles; and anxious to promote, by his example, the proper reform, he trusted to the new views of the subject which he hoped would prevail with the people; whilst his competitors adhered to the old practice. The consequence was that the election went against him; his abstinence being represented as the effect of pride or parsimony.

In the course of the ensuing Session of the Legislature he was appointed by it a member of the Council of State, P. Henry being then Govr. of that Body he continued a member till late in the year 1779. Ths. Jefferson being then Govr; when he was appointed a Delegate to the Revolutionary Congs.

To prepare himself for this service, he employed an unavoidable detention from it, in making himself acquainted with the State of the Continental affairs, and particularly that of the finances which, owing to the depreciation of the paper currency, was truly deplorable. The view he was led to take of the evil and its causes, was put on a paper, now to be found in several periodical publications, particularly in Freneau's Natl. Gazette No.

He took his Seat in Congs. in March 1780, and was continued a member by annual re-elections till the expiration of the allowed term of three years, computed from the definitive ratification of the Articles of Confederation in 1781. On his arrival, &c at Philada. he found that Congs. had, after prolonged discussions just adopted the new Scheme of a Currency, by which forty of the paper dollars in circulation, were to be replaced by a single one.

For the proceedings of Congress during the above period & his participation in them see their journals; secret & public, his correspondence from the Spot, with Jos: Jones. Edm. Randolph, Ths. Jefferson, & others on his files; and the debates which he took down commencing Novr. 1782, and continued to the end of his term in the year following; see particularly, in a Communication in Niles Register for a correction of an erroneous Statement of an important transaction relating to the Mississippi, which first appeared in Ramsay's History of the Revolution, and has been followed in other publications; Pitkin's history among them. The right of the U. S., to the navigation of that River, was maintained by him, in every situation & on every occasion, which made it proper. One proof of his solicitude & exertions in its behalf, may be seen in the Instructions of Congress drawn by him given to Mr. Jay on the day of 1780. See also his Letter of to Lafayette, on his files.

On his return to private life he resumed his Law studies, to which the forenoon was chiefly dedicated. In the afternoon he indulged in miscellaneous reading; which embraced among other works of philosophical cast, those of Buffon whose views of nature, however fanciful & even absurd in some instances, were highly attractive in others, & especially by the fascinating eloquence wch. distinguishes them. Whilst engaged on the zoological volumes, he availed himself of the means occasionally falling into his hands, of making minute comparisons of sundry of our quadrupeds, with those bearing the name, or having the resemblance of them in Europe. Among his papers are notes of the details, which might save in a small degree the labour of more scientific & systematic observers.

He was soon however called from this disposal of his time, by the wish of his Countrymen, that he should be one of their representatives in the Legislature of the State; a service to which he yielded with the less reluctance, as it wd. give him an opportunity of placing in a favorable position, the cause of reform in our federal System, then in the paroxism of its infirmities, and filling every well informed patriot with the most acute anxieties.

He was accordingly elected in the Spring of 1784, & reelected for the two successive years. For the Legislative proceedings of Virga. during that interesting period embracing the Convention at Annapolis, proposed grants of power to Congs, & its recommendation of that at Phila; the project of a Religious Estabt. & the separation of Kentucky from Virga., the effort for paper money, the revised Code of laws prepared by J. W. & P., the case of British debts, the offered & declined donations to Genl. W. the attempted one to Ths. Paine &c. see his correspondence with Genl. W. E. R. and particularly the copious one, with Mr. J__n during the period.

see also the Memorial & Remonstrance agst. the Religs. Establ. and an explanatory letter to Geo: Mason of Green Spring, notes of the proceedings at Annapolis, and an explanatory Correspondence with Noah Webster, as to the origin of the Convention there. In the Statement prefixed to the Laws of U. S. edited by Rush & Colvin, there is an error in ascribing the Resolns. of Virga. in 1785 i e those cited to J. M. They were the Report of a Come. on his advice it varied them from a longer duration to that of years. This circumstance contributed to abandonment of them.

The Convention at Annapolis having recommended another with enlarged powers to be held at Phila. the year following, He brought forward the Act of compliance on the part of Virga. assembly which availing itself of the early period of [ ] set the first example of deciding on the measure, tho' it is believed that the legisl, of N. J. was the first in taking the measure into consideration. See the act of Virga; also his correspondence with Genl. Washington, & Mr. Jefferson.

After his appt. as a deputy to that Convention, he turned his attention and researches to the sources ancient & modern, of information and guidance as to its object. Of the result of these he had the use both in the Convention and afterwards in the "Federalist." For the first shoots in his thoughts, of a plan of Fedl. Govt. see his letter to Ths Jeff 19. March E. R. of 8 Feby 1787. and to Genl. W. of the same year.

Of the proceedings of the Convention & his part in them, see the debates taken by him at great length; and with great care: and which will fill 3 vols. 8[0.] or more. The notes of Judge Yates full of errors, some of them very gross. see his letter to Jon: Elliott, & others, particularly N. P. Trist—

During this period & until the expiration of the Old Congress he continued a member of that Body. Of its proceedings previous to & subsequent to the Convention of 1787, see the debates taken by him, and his correspondence with E. R. Mr. Jos. Jones, Mr. Pendleton & Mr. Jefferson. His main object in returning to a service in that Body; was to bring abt. if possible, the cancelling, of the project of Mr. Jay for shutting the Mississippi wch. threatened an alienation of Kentucky then a part of Virga. from any increase of Fedl. power, with such an evidence in view [of] a disposition in those possessing it to make that sacrifice.

It was in this interval between the close of the Fedl. Convention, and the meeting of the State Conventions, that the "Federalist"—was written. For his share in it see Gideons Edition

The papers first meant for the important & doubtful State of N. Y. and signed "A Citizen of N. Y. afterwards meant for all the States—under—Publius—In the early Stage, the papers shewn by the writers each to another before going to the press. This inconvenient as Nos being required for a week & committing too much each for the other, that was dropped.*

*The numbers subsequent to the last written by him were first seen by him, in print, after his return to Virginia which was hastened by the approaching election.

In the month of April 1788, he was elected by the County of Orange a delegate to the State Convention which was to decide on the Constitution proposed by the Fedl. Convention a part of the session absent from confinement with bilious fever. For his part in it see the published debates, which tho' impartially are defectively taken, and in his case sometimes erroneously, sometimes unintelligibly; see his correspondence during the Session with Alexr. Hamilton & Rufus King.

In Feby. 1789, he was elected a Representative from the district in wch. he lived, to the first Congs. under the new Constn. and was continued a member by re-elections till Mar. 1797, when he declined being longer a Candidate. He had become wearied with pub. life, and longed for a return to a State in which he cd. Endulge his relish for the intellectual pleasures of the Closet, and the pursuits of rural life, the only resources of his future support. He had also in the year 1794. entered the married State, with a partner who favored these views; and added every happiness to his life which femal[e] merit could impart. In retiring from the pub. service at that juncture he had the example of Gen. W. and his testimony of the prosperous condition of the Country.

For the preference he had felt in the outset of the New Govt. of a seat in the House of Reps. to one in the Senate; for the particular means used to prevent his election to the latter, and the party arrang[emen]t. of the [H. of R] districts with a view to prevent his election to the former, see the letters of E. R. Edmd. Carrington, F. C. & Geo. Lee Turberville.—See also a letter of J. M. to. E. Randolph Mar. 4. 1789.

For the acct. of inaugural address of Genl. W. 1789 see papers of Genl. W. in hands of Mr. Sparks & correspondence of J M with Gen W.

On the question of giving a <u>title</u> to the P. see Journals of 2 Houses particularly the entry on that of Senate; See letters of J. M. to E. R. &—

For the answer to the address drawn by J. M. as chairman of the Committee & place of delivering it, [ ] in a Come Room See his letters to .

[printer's fist] Observ[atio]n. J. M. was detained by sickness on the road from the Commencement of the 2d. session, and found on his arrival at N. Y. that the answers of both Houses had been delivered by the Speakers heading the members, at the dwelling of the P.

For the etiquette of the first Levee, see the printed letter of Mr. J—n on the subject. (J. M. was present on the occasion)

For his course* whilst a member of the H. of Reps. in relation to amendts. to the Constn.—to the trade with G. B. & particularly her W. I. Colonies.—to the tariff—to the power of Removal—to the funding System*—to the [t dagger] Bank—to the Carriage tax—to the resolutions, called the Virga. Resols—for an alternative impost on imports from Nats. not in treaty with the U. S. or to Giles Resoln. agst. Secy of Treasy. to Jays treaty*—&c. &c. <u>see</u> Debates in Congs. (Freneaus Nat: Gazette) the pamphlets "Pol Observations (by J. M. & Helvidius). the correspondence wth. E. R. Jos. Jones. Mr. Jefferson et al.—particularly letters of J. M. to E. R. apl. 12. May 30 & 31, June 15. & 17. 24. July 15. augt. 21. 1789. Mar. 14. 21. 30. May 6. 10. 1790. see also [thorn sign]e. draft of Objectn. to Bank at the request of Genl. W. (on his files, for the use of Genl—in the event of his negativing [thorn sign]e. Bill *see letter of J. M. to H. Wheaton Feby. 26. 1827

For an explanation of the mystery enveloping the case that produced Giles Resolns—see letter of E. R.—1811. as stated in a paper on the files of J M.

Note, Mr. Dalton a Senator communicated to Mr. Jones, that Genl. W observed to him, that he wd. not have sanctioned the Bill putting the commerce of Engd. on the same footing with Nations in Treaty; but that he was given to understand that the Senate had in view another mode of operating on her monopolizing policy.

In relation to the Valedy. Address of Genl. W—see correspondence with Gen. W. and Notes of Conversations with him on the subject of his retiring at the end of his first term.

In 1799, being not disinclined, as urged by his friends (particularly Col J. Taylor & W. C. Nicholas (see their letters)), to be a Candidate for the Legisl: which wd. have before it the Alien & Sedn. laws; he was elected a delegate from the County for that year. He was the more bound to co-operate on the occasion, as he had drawn the Resolns, of the preceding Session, a vindication of which was called for by the animadversions on them, by other States. See the Resoln. of 98.– & the Report of the Come. thereon, in 99. also the Explanation of them in his letter to Mr. Everett in the N. A. Review in 1830. & in papers on his files

[printer's fist] X He forbore to follow the example, to wch he believes he was the sole exception, of receiving at the public expence the Articles of Stationery provided for the members, wch. he thought he was no more entitled, than to the Supply of other wants incident to his station. To this resolution he adhered throughout, tho' witht. attracting any notice to it that might lead to a reflection on others. On his first entering pub. life he had laid down strict rules for himself, in pecuniary matters. One, invariably observed was never to deal in pub. property, lands, debts contracts & money, whilst a member of the Body, whose proceedings might influence these transactions. He highly disapproved of pub. Bodies raising the wages of themselves, and declined receiving the addition made by the Leg. of Virga. to the wages of members whilst he was one. In this he was not singular. He was much surprized & disappd. at the incompleting of the Ratificn of the prohibitory Article proposed to the Constn. of the U. S. in 1798, which he had included in the proposed amendts & in 1790-1 and had much at heart.

He disapproved also of Chaplains to Congress pd. out of the pub. Treasy. as a violation of principles He thought the only legitimate & becoming mode would be that of voluntary contribution from the members. See remarks on the subject in his manuscript papers on file.

[dagger] for the ground on wch. he changed his opinion as to its Constitutionality of bank—see his message to Congs.—his letter to Mr. Haynes of Georgia—and the paper on his files, in favor of precedents of a given character See also his letter to Jos. Cabell. & to C: J Ingersoll

[crossed dagger] his opinion in favor of dividing the payment of the public debt between the original holders, and the purchasers, grew out of the enormous gain of the latter particularly out of Soldiers Certificates and the sacrifice of those to whom the public faith had not been fulfilled. Whilst the case of this class of Creditors was less in view he had opposed any discrimination; as in the Congress of 1782 prior to the final settlement with the Army. In the address drawn by him recommending the plan providing for the debt, til indeed the subject came close into view & the sacrifice of the Soldiers was brought home to reflection, he had not sufficiently scanned and felt the magnitude of the evil. Hence in a hasty answer to a letter from the Secretary of the Treasury, wch followed him after the adjournments he did not suggest the idea of discrimination, as one of the ingredients in a funding System. It grew rapidly on him on his return to Congs. as the subject unfolded itself; and the outrageous speculations on the floating paper pressed on the attention Such was the spirit which was stimulated by the prospect of converting the depreciated paper into par value, that it seized members of Congs who did not shrink from the practice, of purchasing thro' Brokers, the certificates at little price, and contributing by their votes at the same moment; to transmute them into the value of the precious metals.

In 1800 he was appointed one of the Virga. Electors who voted for Th. J. & A. B. to be President & V. P. of the U. S. It was with much difficulty that a unanimous vote cd. be obtained in the Va. college of Electors for both, lest an equality might throw the choice into the H. of Reps. or otherwise endanger the known object of the people. J. M. had recd. assurances from a Confidl. friend of Burr that in a certain quarter votes would be thrown from B. with a view to secure a majority for J–n. This authy. alone with the persuasive language of the other Electors, overcame the anxiety of Mr. Wythe, whose devoted regard for Mr. J–n made him nearly inflexible. The event proved that he did not overrate the danger: the votes in the pledged quarter, being all given to B as well as to J–n, which produced the scene at the final choice by Congs See letter of D. G. to J. M. Virga. was at that time extremely averse to the institution of Genl. Tickets for District elections & yielded only to the necessity of being on an equal footing with other States, by following their examples, and securing a unanimity in the voice of the State.

In 1801. He was appd. Secy. of State and remained such till 1809, when he was elected to the Presidy. In 1812 he was re-elected for another term ending in 1817.

For his agency as Secretary of State see files of the Dept & State papers in print: his private correspondence with the Presidt. when one or the other or both were absent from Washington, and with foreign ministers—see the pamphlet on the B. Doctrine as to neutral trade with the Cols. of her Enemies—For the origin of the Embargo misrepresented by Mr. Pickering & others, see a letter to Henry Wheaton July 11 & 21 1824 see his correspondence with Mr. J-n. particularly the letter of Mr. J-n in his printed works. See a note among his papers of the opinion of Mr. Story & Mr. Bacon, & the alarm from Massts. producing it. The Embargo, if enforced wd. have been effectual, & could have been enforced, if instead of relying on a fidelity to the law, violations of it had been guarded agst. by Arming Coasting Cruisers, & authorizing the carriage of captured Smugglers into ports where the Courts wd. have condemned them: See in the publ. Archives the offer of service by the Seamen of Marblehead; who alone would have sufficed & at an expence greatly inferior to the object.

For his career in the Executive Magistracy, see State papers—his correspondence with Heads of Depts including Instructions to them—his private Correspondence with our Ministers abroad, see particularly with Barlow, and his account of Bonaparte's [slight?] of my letter to Barlow—his correspondence with Mr. Jefferson, Mr. Pendleton & others on his files see statement of what passed with Rob. Smith, Eustis, Hamilton & Armstrong on their separation from their respective Departmts—see also a publication of Armstrong in the Literary & Scientific Repository, and an exposure on file of its deceptive representation of the appt. of Genl. Jackson to a Command in the Regular army. see also the ground on which he recomended, in compliance with multiplied applications, the proclamation of a day for Religious Service; the ground being a <u>voluntary</u> concurrence of those who approved a general union, on such an occasion, for which the mere intimation of a day would be sufficient. See the danger of mingling political & even party views, with such proclamation, in the Remarks of Hamilton on the Proclamn. drafted for Genl W. by Edmd. Randolph. The files of the Dept of State contain the original draft with the notes referred to. A copy from the office of State is among the papers of J. M.

For the origin of the War, & its [preparations? proportions?] & early operations, see letter to H. Wheaton Feby 26— 1827.

After the close of his pub. life under the U. S. he devoted himself to his farm & his books; with much avocation however from both, by an extensive & often laborious correspondence (as his files shew) which seems to be entailed on Ex-Presidts. especially when they have passd. a like prolonged & diversified career in the pub. service. See his letters on pol: and Constl. subjects: particularly to J. Adams, S. Roane, J. G. Jackson, Jefferson, Hayne, Hurlbut M. L.

Everett, Haynes—Trist—C. J. Ingersoll—Rush—Walsh—Defense of Mr. J-n agst. sons of Mr. Bayard, Nichs. Biddle, S. H. Smith, J. Robertson Jas. Hillhouse See also sundry letters & papers on Constl. and other subjects never printed on his files

A small part of his time has also been given to the Agricl. Socy of albemarle, of which he was appd. President & of course obliged to make an address which see also a paper drawn up with a view to a professorship of Agriculture.

A longer portion of his time given, as first a Visitor, then the Rector of the University. see his Obituary tribute on the Journal to Mr. J-n and correspondence with visitors & Professors.

In 1829, he was prevailed on, notwithstanding his age & very feeble health being but convalescent from a spell of sickness to serve as a member of the convention which revised the Constn. of the States. See the letter of the Come. inviting him & his answer. The printed Debates shew the small part he had in them. His main object was to promote a compromise of ideas between parties fixed in their pol: opinion, by their local interests, & threatening an abortive result to an experiment closely connected with the tranquility of the State, & the capacity of man for self-govt. His personal opinion on the rule of suffrage and apportionment of Reps. on the mode of chusing the Govr. & the functions to be assigned him, were either Controuled by the known will & <u>meditated</u> instruction of his Consts. or by the necessity of securing an effective & tranquil result, by indulging the party, whose defeat would have been most pregnant with danger to it. His preference wd. have been the White basis for one branch, and the mixed or federal basis for the other; in the appt. of Govr., he wd. have preferred the people to the Legisl: allowing the Govr a qualified veto on the laws, and a nominating power to the Senate as in the Govt. of U. S. & some of the individual States. Tho' aware of the danger of universal suffrage, in a future state of Socy. such as the present State in Europe; he wd. have extended it so far as to secure in every event & change in the state of Society a majy. of the people on the side of power; a Govt. resting on a minority, is an aristocracy not a Repubc. and cd. not be safe, with a [ ]& physical force agst it, witht a standing army, an enslaved press, and a disarmed population. He thought also the ratio of apportionment, as well as the right of suffrage, being both fundamental principles, in free Govt. ought to be prescribed by the Constn. and unalterable by the Legisle: which otherwise might so narrow the latter & new model the former, as to transform the Repub. into an Aristocracy: When it had been found impossible to obtain a fixed ratio apportioning the Represents. and it being obvious, that inequalities wd. occur, that wd. make a re-appt. necessary, he proposed that the Legisl: sd. make [thorn sign]n an abuse of such a power being guarded agst. by requiring for the purpose 2/3 of each House. It was found that those most likely to suffer by the omission of some remedial provision preferred that omission, to the proposed supply of it. The explanation is that they wished for an impossibility of redress without a new Convention, as the ground of a struggle for a new Convention: For his views of a form of Govt. for Repub: at different epochs of his life & of his pol: experience, see letters to J. Brown of Kentucky correspondence with Mr. J-n. (Mr. J-n would have acquiesced in a Constn. for Virga. wth. a freehold suffrage for one Branch of Legis: as was found in a Conversation of J. M. wth. him, in the year 1823 or 24)

It has been remarked that the biography of an Author must be a history of his writings. So must that of one whose life has in a manner been a public life, be gathered from his official transactions, and his manuscript papers on public subjects including letters to as well as from him This last fund of materials in the case of J. M. is so voluminous, as doubtless in many other cases, as to make it a forbidding task to consult the whole & not a little difficult to abridge [thorn sign]e task by select & special references, separating the relevant from the redundant or irrelative. This with the little time that could be devoted to the attempt, will account for the imperfect manner, in which the references to his files has been executed. A proper execution wd. have required not only a review of every thing penned by himself, but a great mass of letters from his correspondents; a labour, irreconcilable, at his age, with other indispensable demands on his time.

Appendix 2:
"Vices of the Political System of the United States," April 1787

Spelling and punctuation of Madison's original manuscript retained.

Apr. 1787

1. Failure of the States to comply with the Constitutional requisitions.

This evil has been so fully experienced both during the war and since the peace, results so naturally from the number and independent authority of the States and has been so uniformly examplified in every similar Confederacy, that it may be considered as not less radically and permanently inherent in, than it is fatal to the object of, the present System.

2. Encroachments by the States on the federal authority.

Examples of this are numerous and repetitions may be foreseen in almost every case where any favorite object of a State shall present a temptation. Among these examples are the wars and Treaties of Georgia with the Indians—The unlicensed compacts between Virginia and Maryland, and between Pena. & N. Jersey—the troops raised and to be kept up by Massts.

3. Violations of the law of nations and of treaties.

From the number of Legislatures, the sphere of life from which most of their members are taken, and the circumstances under which their legislative business is carried on, irregularities of this kind must frequently happen. Accordingly not a year has passed without instances of them in some one or other of the States. The Treaty of peace—the treaty with France—the treaty with Holland have each been violated. The causes of these irregularities must necessarily produce frequent violations of the law of nations in other respects.

As yet foreign powers have not been rigorous in animadverting on us. This moderation however cannot be mistaken for a permanent partiality to our faults, or a permanent security agst. those disputes with other nations, which being among the greatest of public calamities, it ought to be least in the power of any part of the Community to bring on the whole.

4. Trespasses of the States on the rights of each other.

These are alarming symptoms, and may be daily apprehended as we are admonished by daily experience. See the law of Virginia restricting foreign vessels to certain ports—of Maryland in favor of vessels belonging to her own citizens—of N. York in favor of the same.

Paper money, instalments of debts, occlusion of Courts, making property a legal tender, may likewise be deemed aggressions on the rights of other States. As the Citizens of every State aggregately taken stand more or less in the relation of Creditors or debtors, to the Citizens of every other States, Acts of the debtor State in favor of debtors, affect the Creditor State, in the same manner, as they do its own citizens who are relatively creditors towards other citizens. This remark may be extended to foreign nations. If the exclusive regulation of the value and alloy of coin was properly delegated to the federal authority, the policy of it equally requires a controul on the States in the cases above mentioned. It must have been meant 1. to preserve uniformity in the circulating medium throughout the nation. 2. to prevent those frauds on the citizens of other States, and the subjects of foreign powers, which might disturb the tranquility at home, or involve the Union in foreign contests.

The practice of many States in restricting the commercial intercourse with other States, and putting their productions and manufactures on the same footing with those of foreign nations, though not contrary to the federal articles, is certainly adverse to the spirit of the Union, and tends to beget retaliating regulations, not less expensive & vexatious in themselves, than they are destructive of the general harmony.

5. want of concert in matters where common interest requires it.

This defect is strongly illustrated in the state of our commercial affairs. How much has the national dignity, interest, and revenue suffered from this cause? Instances of inferior moment are the want of uniformity in the laws concerning naturalization & literary property; of provision for national seminaries, for grants of incorporation for national purposes, for canals and other works of general utility, wch. may at present be defeated by the perverseness of particular States whose concurrence is necessary.

6. want of guaranty to the States of their Constitutions & laws against internal violence.

The confederation is silent on this point and therefore by the second article the hands of the federal authority are tied. According to Republican Theory, Right and power being both vested in the majority, are held to be synonimous. According to fact and experience a minority may in an appeal to force, be an overmatch for the majority. 1. If the minority happen to include all such as possess the skill and habits of military life, & such as possess the great pecuniary resources, one third only may conquer the remaining two thirds. 2. One third of those who participate in the choice of the rulers, may be rendered a majority by the accession of those whose poverty excludes them from a right of suffrage, and who for obvious reasons will be more likely to join the standard of sedition than that of the established Government. 3. Where slavery exists the republican Theory becomes still more fallacious.

7. want of sanction to the laws, and of coercion in the Government of the Confederacy.

A sanction is essential to the idea of law, as coercion is to that of Government. The federal system being destitute of both, wants the great vital principles of a Political Cons[ti]tution. Under the form of such a Constitution, it is in fact nothing more than a treaty of amity of commerce and of alliance, between so many independent and Sovereign States. From what cause could so fatal an omission have happened in the articles of Confederation? from a mistaken confidence that the justice, the good faith, the honor, the sound policy, of the several legislative assemblies would render superfluous any appeal to the ordinary motives by which the laws secure the obedience of individuals: a confidence which does honor to the enthusiastic virtue of the compilers, as much as the inexperience of the crisis apologizes for their errors. The time which has since elapsed has had the double effect, of increasing the light, and tempering the warmth, with which the arduous work may be revised. It is no longer doubted that a unanimous and punctual obedience of 13 independent bodies, to the acts of the federal Government, ought not be calculated on. Even during the war, when external danger supplied in some degree the defect of legal & coercive sanctions, how imperfectly did the States fulfil their obligations to the Union? In time of peace, we see already what is to be expected. How indeed could it be otherwise? In the first place, Every general act of the Union must necessarily bear unequally hard on some particular member or members of it. Secondly the partiality of the members to their own interests and rights, a partiality which will be fostered by the Courtiers of popularity, will naturally exaggerate the inequality where it exists, and even suspect it where it has no existence. Thirdly a distrust of the voluntary compliance of each other may prevent the compliance of any, although it should be the latent disposition of all. Here are causes & pretexts which will never fail to render federal measures abortive. If the laws of the States, were merely recommendatory to their citizens, or if they were to be rejudged by County authorities, what security, what probability would exist, that they would be carried into execution? Is the security or probability greater in favor of the acts of Congs. which depending for their execution on the will of the state legislatures, wch. are tho' nominally authoritative, in fact recommendatory only.

8. Want of ratification by the people of the articles of Confederation.

In some of the States the Confederation is recognized by, and forms a part of the constitution. In others however it has received no other sanction than that of the Legislative authority. From this defect two evils result: 1. Whenever a law of a State happens to be repugnant to an act of Congress, particularly when the latter is of posterior date to the former, it will be at least questionable whether the latter must not prevail; and as the question must be decided by the Tribunals of the State, they will be most likely to lean on the side of the State. 2. As far as the Union of the States is to be regarded as a league of sovereign powers, and not as a political Constitution by virtue of which they are become one sovereign power, so far it seems to follow from the doctrine of compacts, that a breach of any of the articles of the confederation by any of the parties to it, absolves the other parties from their respective obligations, and gives them a right if they chuse to exert it, of dissolving the Union altogether.

9. Multiplicity of laws in the several States.

In developing the evils which viciate the political system of the U. S. it is proper to include those which are found within the States individually, as well as those which directly affect the States collectively, since the former class have an indirect influence on the general malady and must not be overlooked in forming a compleat remedy. Among the evils then of our situation may well be ranked the multiplicity of laws from which no State is exempt. As far as laws are necessary, to mark with precision the duties of those who are to obey them, and to take from those who are to administer them a discretion, which might be abused, their number is the price of liberty. As far as the laws exceed this limit, they are a nusance: a nusance of the most pestilent kind. Try the Codes of the several States by this test, and what a luxuriancy of legislation do they present. The short period of independency has filled as many pages as the century which preceded it. Every year, almost every session, adds a new volume. This may be the effect in part, but it can only be in part, of the situation in which the revolution has placed us.

A review of the several codes will shew that every necessary and useful part of the least voluminous of them might be compressed into one tenth of the compass, and at the same time be rendered tenfold as perspicuous.

10. mutability of the laws of the States.

This evil is intimately connected with the former yet deserves a distinct notice as it emphatically denotes a vicious legislation. We daily see laws repealed or superseded, before any trial can have been made of their merits: and even before a knowledge of them can have reached the remoter districts within which they were to operate. In the regulations of trade this instability becomes a snare not only to our citizens but to foreigners also.

11. Injustice of the laws of States.

If the multiplicity and mutability of laws prove a want of wisdom, their injustice betrays a defect still more alarming: more alarming not merely because it is a greater evil in itself, but because it brings more into question the fundamental principle of republican Government, that the majority who rule in such Governments, are the safest Guardians both of public Good and of private rights. To what causes is this evil to be ascribed?

These causes lie 1. in the Representative bodies.

2. in the people themselves.

1. Representative appointments are sought from 3 motives. 1. ambition 2. personal interest. 3. public good. Unhappily the two first are proved by experience to be most prevalent. Hence the candidates who feel them, particularly, the second, are most industrious, and most successful in pursuing their object: and forming often a majority in the legislative Councils, with interested views, contrary to the interest, and views, of their Constituents, join in a perfidious sacrifice of the latter to the former. A succeeding election it might be supposed, would displace the offenders, and repair the mischief.

But how easily are base and selfish measures, masked by pretexts of public good and apparent expediency? How frequently will a repetition of the same arts and industry which succeeded in the first instance, again prevail on the unwary to misplace their confidence?

How frequently too will the honest but unenlightened representative be the dupe of a favorite leader, veiling his selfish views under the professions of public good, and varnishing his sophistical arguments with the glowing colours of popular eloquence?

2. A still more fatal if not more frequent cause lies among the people themselves. All civilized societies are divided into different interests and factions, as they happen to be creditors or debtors—Rich or poor—husbandmen, merchants or manufacturers—members of different religious sects—followers of different political leaders—inhabitants of different districts—owners of different kinds of property &c &c. In republican Government the majority however composed, ultimately give the law. Whenever therefore an apparent interest or common passion unites a majority what is to restrain them from unjust violations of the rights and interests of the minority, or of individuals? Three motives only 1. a prudent regard to their own good as involved in the general and permanent good of the Community. This consideration although of decisive weight in itself, is found by experience to be too often unheeded. It is too often forgotten, by nations as well as by individuals that honesty is the best policy. 2dly. respect for character. However strong this motive may be in individuals, it is considered as very insufficient to restrain them from injustice. In a multitude its efficacy is diminished in proportion to the number which is to share the praise or the blame. Besides, as it has reference to public opinion, which within a particular Society, is the opinion of the majority, the standard is fixed by those whose conduct is to be measured by it. The public opinion without the Society, will be little respected by the people at large of any Country. Individuals of extended views, and of national pride, may bring the public proceedings to this standard, but the example will never be followed by the multitude. Is it to be imagined that an ordinary citizen or even an assemblyman of R. Island in estimating

the policy of paper money, ever considered or cared in what light the measure would be viewed in France or Holland; or even in Massts or Connect.? It was a sufficient temptation to both that it was for their interest: it was a sufficient sanction to the latter that it was popular in the State; to the former that it was so in the neighbourhood. 3dly. will Religion the only remaining motive be a sufficient restraint? It is not pretended to be such on men individually considered. Will its effect be greater on them considered in an aggregate view? quite the reverse. The conduct of every popular assembly acting on oath, the strongest of religious Ties, proves that individuals join without remorse in acts, against which their consciences would revolt if proposed to them under the like sanction, separately in their closets. When indeed Religion is kindled into enthusiasm, its force like that of other passions, is increased by the sympathy of a multitude. But enthusiasm is only a temporary state of religion, and while it lasts will hardly be seen with pleasure at the helm of Government. Besides as religion in its coolest state, is not infallible, it may become a motive to oppression as well as a restraint from injustice. Place three individuals in a situation wherein the interest of each depends on the voice of the others, and give to two of them an interest opposed to the rights of the third? Will the latter be secure? The prudence of every man would shun the danger. The rules & forms of justice suppose & guard against it. Will two thousand in a like situation be less likely to encroach on the rights of one thousand? The contrary is witnessed by the notorious factions & oppressions which take place in corporate towns limited as the opportunities are, and in little republics when uncontrouled by apprehensions of external danger. If an enlargement of the sphere is found to lessen the insecurity of private rights, it is not because the impulse of a common interest or passion is less predominant in this case with the majority; but because a common interest or passion is less apt to be felt and the requisite combinations less easy to be formed by a great than by a small number. The Society becomes broken into a greater variety of interests, of pursuits, of passions, which check each other, whilst those who may feel a common sentiment have less opportunity of communication and concert. It may be inferred that the inconveniences of popular States contrary to the prevailing Theory, are in proportion not to the extent, but to the narrowness of their limits.

The great desideratum in Government is such a modification of the Sovereignty as will render it sufficiently neutral between the different interests and factions, to controul one part of the Society from invading the rights of another, and at the same time sufficiently controuled itself, from setting up an interest adverse to that of the whole Society. In absolute Monarchies, the prince is sufficiently, neutral towards his subjects, but frequently sacrifices their happiness to his ambition or his avarice. In small Republics, the sovereign will is sufficiently controuled from such a Sacrifice of the entire Society, but is not sufficiently neutral towards the parts composing it. As a limited Monarchy tempers the evils of an absolute one; so an extensive Republic meliorates the administration of a small Republic.

An auxiliary desideratum for the melioration of the Republican form is such a process of elections as will most certainly extract from the mass of the Society the purest and noblest characters which it contains; such as will at once feel most strongly the proper motives to pursue the end of their appointment, and be most capable to devise the proper means of attaining it.

12. Impotence of the laws of the States

Appendix 3:
"Political Observations"

An essay covering several subjects relating to government and politics. All spelling and punctuation from Madison's original manuscript are retained.

April 20, 1795

A variety of publications, in pamphlets and other forms, have appeared in different parts of the union, since the session of Congress which ended in June, 1794; endeavoring, by discoloured representations of our public affairs, and particularly of certain occurrences of that session, to turn the tide of public opinion into a party channel. The immediate object of the writers, was either avowedly or evidently to operate on the approaching elections of Federal Representatives. As that crisis will have entirely elapsed, before the following observations will appear; they will, at least, be free from a charge of the same views; and will, consequently, have the stronger claim to that deliberate attention and reflection to which they are submitted.

The publications alluded to, have passed slightly over the transactions of the First and Second Congress; and so far, their example will here be followed.

Whether, indeed, the funding system was modelled, either on the principles of substantial justice, or on the demands of public faith? Whether it did not contain ingredients friendly to the duration of the public debt, and implying that it was regarded as a public good? Whether the assumption of the state debts was not enforced by overcharged representations; and Whether, if the burdens had been equalized only, instead of being assumed in the gross, the states could not have discharged their respective proportions, by their local resources, sooner and more conveniently, than the general government will be able to discharge the whole debts, by general resources? Whether the excise system, be congenial with the spirit, and conducive to the happiness of our country; or can even justify itself as a productive source of Revenue? Whether again the bank was not established without authority from the constitution? Whether it did not throw unnecessary and unreasonable advantages into the hands of men; previously enriched beyond reason or necessity? And whether it can be allowed the praise of a salutary operation, until its effects shall have been more accurately traced, and its hidden transactions shall be fully unveiled to the public eye: These and others are questions, which, though of great importance, it is not intended here to examine. Most of them have been finally decided by the competent authority; and the rest have, no doubt, already impressed themselves on the public attention.

Passing on then to the session of Congress preceding the last, we are met in the first place, by the most serious charges against the southern members of Congress in general, and particularly against the representatives of Virginia. They are charged with having supported a policy which would inevitably have involved the United States in the war of Europe, have reduced us from the rank of a free people, to that of French colonies, and possibly have landed us in disunion, anarchy, and misery; and the policy, from which these tremendous calamities was to flow, is referred to certain commercial resolutions moved by a member from Virginia, in the house of Representatives.

To place in its true light, the fallacy which infers such consequences from such a cause, it will be proper to review the circumstances which preceded and attended the resoluti(ons).

It is well known, that at the peace between the United States and Great Britain, it became a question with the latter, whether she should endeavor to regain the lost commerce of America, by liberal and reciprocal arrangements; or trust to a relapse of it, into its former channels, without the price of such arrangements on her part. Whilst she was fearful that our commerce would be conducted into new and rival channels, she leaned to the first side of the alternative, and a bill was actually carried in the House of Commons, by the present Prime Minister corresponding with that sentiment. She soon, however, began to discover (or to hope) that the weakness of our Federal Government, and the want of concurrence among the state governments, would secure her against the danger at first apprehended. From that moment all ideas of conciliation and concession vanished. She determined to enjoy at once the full benefit of the freedom allowed by our regulations, and of the monopolies, established by her own.

In this state of things, the pride, as well as the interest of America were every where aroused. The mercantile world in particular, was all on fire; complaints flew from one end of the continent to the other; projects of retaliation and redress, engrossed the public attention. At one time, the states endeavored by separate efforts, to counteract the unequal laws of Great Britain. At another, correspondencies were opened for uniting their efforts. An attempt was also made, to vest in the former Congress, a limited power for a limited time, in order to give effect to the general will.

All these experiments, instead of answering the purpose in view, served only to confirm Great Britain in her first belief, that her restrictive plans, were in no danger of retaliation.

It was at length determined by the Legislature of Virginia to go to work in a new way. It was proposed, and most of the states agreed, to send commissioners to digest some change in our general system, that might prove an effectual remedy. The Commissioners met; but finding their powers too circumscribed for the great object, which expanded itself before them, they proposed a convention on a more enlarged plan, for a general revision of the Federal Government.

From this convention proceeded the present Federal Constitution, which gives to the general will, the means of providing in the several necessary cases, for the general welfare; and particularly in the case of regulating our commerce in such manner as may be required by the regulations of other countries.

It was natural to expect, that one of the first objects of deliberation under the new constitution, would be that which had been first, and most contemplated in forming it. Accordingly it was, at the first session, proposed that something should be done analagous to the wishes of the several states, and expressive of the efficiency of the new government. A discrimination between nations in treaty, and those not in treaty, the mode most generally embraced by the states, was agreed to in several forms, and adhered to in repeated votes, by a very great majority of the house of Representatives. The Senate, however, did not concur with the house of representatives, and our commercial arrangements were made up without any provision on the subject.

From that date to the session of Congress ending in June, 1794, the interval passed without any effective appeal to the interest of Great Britain. A silent reliance was placed on her voluntary justice, or her enlightened interest.

The long and patient reliance being ascribed (as was foretold) to other causes, than a generous forbearance on the part of the United States, had, at the commencement of the third Congress, left us with respect to a reciprocity of commercial regulations between the two countries, precisely where the commencement of the first Congress had found us. This was not all; the western posts, which entailed an expensive Indian war on us, continued to be withheld; although all pretext for it had been removed on our part. Depredations, as derogatory to our rights, as grievous to our interests, had been licenced by the British Government against our lawful commerce on the high seas. And it was believed, on the most probable grounds, that the measure by which the Algerine Pirates were let loose on the Atlantic, had not taken place without the participation of the same unfriendly counsels. In a word, to say nothing of the American victims to savages and barbarians, it was estimated that our annual damages from Great Britain, were not less than three or four millions of dollars.

This distressing situation spoke the more loudly to the patriotism of the Representatives of the people, as the nature and manner of the communications from the President, seemed to make a formal and affecting appeal on the subject, to their co-operation. The necessity of some effort was palpable. The only room for different opinions seemed to lie in the different modes of redress proposed. On one side nothing was proposed, beyond the eventual measures of defence, in which all concurred, except the building of six frigates, for the purpose of enforcing our rights against Algiers. The other side considering this measure, as pointed at one only of our evils, and as inadequate even to that, thought it best to seek for some safe, but powerful remedy, that might be applied to the root of them; and with this view the Commercial Propositions were introduced.

They were at first opposed on the ground, that Great-Britain was amicably disposed towards the United States; and that we ought to await the event of the depending negociation. To this it was replied, that more than four years of appeal to that disposition, had been tried in vain, by the new government; that the negociation had been abortive, and was no longer depending; that the late letters from Mr. Pinckney, the minister at London, had not only cut off all remaining hope from that source, but had expressly pointed Commercial Regulations as the most eligible redress to be pursued.

Another ground of opposition, was, that the United States were more dependant on the trade of Great Britain, than Great Britain was on the trade of the United States. This will appear scarcely credible to those who understand the commerce between the two countries, who recollect, that it supplies us chiefly with superfluities; whilst in return it employs the industry of one part of her people, sends to another part the very bread which keeps them from starving, and remits moreover, an annual balance in specie of ten or twelve millions of dollars. It is true, nevertheless, as the debate shews, that this was the language, however strange, of some who combated the propositions.

Nay, what is still more extraordinary, it was maintained that the United States, had, on the whole, little or no reason to complain of the footing of their commerce with Great Britain; although such complaints had prevailed in every state, among every class of citizens, ever since the year 1783; and although the Federal Constitution had originated in those complaints, and had been established with the known view of redressing them.

As such objections could have little effect in convincing the judgement of the House of Representatives, and still less that of the public at large; a new mode of assailing the propositions has been substituted. The American People love peace; and the cry of war might alarm when no hope remained of convincing them. The cry of war has accordingly been echoed through the continent, with a loudness proportioned to the emptiness of the pretext; and to this cry has been added, another still more absurd, that the propositions would in the end, enslave the United States to their allies, and plunge them into anarchy and misery.

It is truly mortifying to be obliged to tax the patience of the reader, with an examination of such gross absurdities; but it may be of use to expose, where there may be no necessity to refute them.

What were the Commercial Propositions? They discriminated between nations in treaty, and nations not in treaty, by an additional duty on the manufactures and trade of the latter; and they reciprocated the navigation laws of all nations, who excluded the vessels of the United States, from a common right of being used in the trade between the United States, and such nations.

Is there any thing here that could afford a cause, or a pretext for war, to Great Britain or any other nation? If we hold at present the rank of a free people; if we are no longer colonies of Great Britain; if we have not already relapsed into some dependence on that nation, we have the self-evident right, to regulate our trade according to our own will, and our own interest, not according to her will or her interest. This right can be denied to no independent nation. It has not been, and will not be denied to ourselves, by any opponent of the propositions.

If the propositions could give no right to Great Britain to make war, would they have given any color to her for such an outrage on us? No American Citizen will affirm it. No British subject, who is a man of candor, will pretend it; because he must know, that the commercial regulations of Great Britain herself have discriminated among foreign nations, whenever it was thought convenient. They have discriminated against particular nations by name; they have discriminated, with respect to particular articles by name, by the nations producing them, and by the places exporting them. And as to the navigation articles proposed, they were not only common to the other countries along with Great Britain; but reciprocal between Great Britain and the United States: Nay, it is notorious, that they fell short of an immediate and exact reciprocity of her own Navigation Laws.

Would any nation be so barefaced as to quarrel with another, for doing the same thing which she herself has done; for doing less than she herself has done, towards that particular nation? It is impossible that Great Britain would ever expose herself by so absurd, as well as arrogant a proceeding. If she really meant to quarrel with this country, common prudence, and common decency, would prescribe some other less odious pretext for her hostility.

It is the more astonishing that such a charge against the propositions should have been hazarded, when the opinion, and the proceedings, of America, on the subject of our commercial policy is reviewed.

Whilst the power over trade, remained with the several States, there were few of them that did not exercise it, on the principle, if not in the mode, of the commercial propositions. The eastern States generally passed laws, either discriminating between some foreign nations and others, or levelled against Great Britain by name. Maryland

and Virginia did the same, so did two, if not the three, of the more southern States. Was it ever, during that period, pretended at home or abroad, that a cause or pretext for quarrel, was given to Great Britain or any other nation? or were our rights better understood at that time, than at this, or more likely then, than now, to command the respect due to them.

Let it not be said, Great Britain was then at peace, she is now at war. If she would not wantonly attempt to controul the exercise of our sovereign rights, when she had no other enemy on her hands, will she be mad enough to make the attempt, when her hands are fully employed with the war already on them? Would not those who say now, postpone the measures until Great Britain shall be at peace, be more ready, and have more reason to say in time of peace, postpone them until she shall be at war; there will then be no danger of her throwing new enemies into the scale against her.

Nor let it be said, that the combined powers, would aid and stimulate Great Britain, to wage an unjust war on the United States. They also are too fully occupied with their present enemy, to wish for another on their hands; not to add, that two of those powers, being in treaty with the United States, are favored by the propositions; and that all of them are well known to entertain an habitual jealousy of the monopolizing character and maritime ascendency of that nation.

One thing ought to be regarded as certain and conclusive on this head; whilst the war against France remains unsuccessful, the United States are in no danger, from any of the powers engaged in it. In the event of a complete overthrow of that Republic, it is impossible to say, what might follow. But if the hostile views of the combination, should be turned towards this continent, it would clearly not be, to vindicate the commercial interests of Great Britain against the commercial rights of the United States. The object would be, to root out Liberty from the face of the earth. No pretext would be wanted, or a better would be contrived than anything to be found in the commercial propositions.

Appendix 3: "Political Observations"

On whatever other side we view the clamor against these propositions as inevitably productive of war, it presents neither evidence to justify it nor argument to colour it.

The allegation necessarily supposes either that the friends of the plan could discover no probability, where its opponents could see a certainty, or that the former were less averse to war than the latter.

The first supposition will not be discussed. A few observations on the other may throw new lights on the whole subject.

The members, in general, who espoused these propositions have been constantly in that part of the Congress who have professed with most zeal, and pursued with most scruple, the characteristics of republican government. They have adhered to these characteristics in defining the meaning of the Constitution, in adjusting the ceremonial of public proceedings, and in marking out the course of the Administration. They have manifested, particularly, a deep conviction of the danger to liberty and the Constitution, from a gradual assumption or extension of discretionary powers in the executive departments; from successive augmentations of a standing army; and from the perpetuity and progression of public debts and taxes. They have been sometimes reprehended in debate for an excess of caution and jealousy on these points. And the newspapers of a certain stamp, by distorting and discolouring this part of their conduct, have painted it in all the deformity which the most industrious calumny could devise.

Those best acquainted with the individuals who more particularly supported the propositions will be foremost to testify, that such are the principles which not only govern them in public life, but which are invariably maintained by them in every other situation. And it cannot be believed nor suspected, that with such principles they could view war as less an evil than it appeared to their opponents.

Of all the enemies to public liberty war is, perhaps, the most to be dreaded, because it comprises and develops the germ of every other. War is the parent of armies; from these proceed debts and taxes; and armies, and debts, and taxes are the known instruments for bringing the many under the domination of the few. In war, too, the discretionary power of the Executive is extended; its influence in dealing out offices, honors, and emoluments is multiplied; and all the means of seducing the minds, are added to those of subduing the force, of the people. The same malignant aspect in republicanism may be traced in the inequality of fortunes, and the opportunities of fraud, growing out of a state of war, and in the degeneracy of manners and of morals, engendered by both. No nation could preserve its freedom in the midst of continual warfare.

Those truths are well established. They are read in every page which records the progression from a less arbitrary to a more arbitrary government, or the transition from a popular government to an aristocracy or a monarchy.

It must be evident, then, that in the same degree as the friends of the propositions were jealous of armies, and debts, and prerogative, as dangerous to a republican Constitution, they must have been averse to war, as favourable to armies and debts, and prerogative.

The fact accordingly appears to be, that they were particularly averse to war. They not only considered the propositions as having no tendency to war, but preferred them, as the most likely means of obtaining our objects without war. They thought, and thought truly, that Great Britain was more vulnerable in her commerce than in her fleets and armies; that she valued our necessaries for her markets, and our markets for her superfluities, more than she feared our frigates or our militia; and that she would, consequently, be more ready to make proper concessions under the influence of the former, than of the latter motive.

Great Britain is a commercial nation. Her power, as well as her wealth, is derived from commerce. The American commerce is the most valuable branch she enjoys. It is the more valuable, not only as being of vital importance to her in some respects, but of growing importance beyond estimate in its general character. She will not easily part with such a resource. She will not rashly hazard it. She would be particularly aware of forcing a perpetuity of regulations, which not merely diminish her share; but may favour the rivalship of other nations. If anything, therefore, in the power of the United States could overcome her pride, her avidity, and her repugnancy to this country, it was justly concluded to be, not the fear of our arms, which, though invincible in defence, are little formidable in a war of offence, but the fear of suffering in the most fruitful branch of her trade, and of seeing it distributed among her rivals.

If any doubt on this subject could exist, it would vanish on a recollection of the conduct of the British ministry at the close of the war in 1783. It is a fact which has been already touched, and it is as notorious as it is instructive, that during the apprehension of finding her commerce with the United States abridged or endangered by the consequences of the revolution, Great-Britain was ready to purchase it, even at the expence of her West-Indies monopoly. It was not until after she began to perceive the weakness of the federal government, the discord in the counteracting plans of the state governments, and the interest she would be able to establish here, that she ventured on that system to which she has since inflexibly adhered. Had the present federal government, on its first establishment, done what it ought to have done, what it was instituted and expected to do, and what was actually proposed and intended it should do; had it revived and confirmed the belief in Great-Britain, that our trade and navigation would not be free to her, without an equal and reciprocal freedom to us, in her trade and navigation, we have her own authority for saying, that she would long since have met us on proper ground; because the same motives which produced the bill brought into the British parliament by Mr. Pitt, in order to prevent the evil apprehended, would have produced the same concession at least, in order to obtain a recall of the evil, after it had taken place.

The aversion to war in the friends of the propositions, may be traced through the whole proceedings and debates of the session. After the depredations in the West-Indies, which seemed to fill up the measure of British aggressions, they adhered to their original policy of pursuing redress, rather by commercial, than by hostile operations; and with this view unanimously concurred in the bill for suspending importations from British ports; a bill that was carried through the house by a vote of fifty-eight against thirty-four. The friends of the propositions appeared, indeed, never to have admitted, that Great-Britain could seriously mean to force a war with the United States, unless in the event of prostrating the French Republic; and they did not believe that such an event was to be apprehended.

Confiding in this opinion, to which Time has given its full sanction, they could not accede to those extraordinary measures, which nothing short of the most obvious and imperious necessity could plead for. They were as ready as any, to fortify our harbours, and fill our magazines and arsenals; these were safe and requisite provisions for our permanent defence. They were ready and anxious for arming and preparing our militia; that was the true republican bulwark of our security. They joined also in the addition of a regiment of artillery to the military establishment, in order to complete the defensive arrangement on our eastern frontier. These facts are on record, and are the proper answer to those shameless calumnies which have asserted, that the friends of the commercial propositions were enemies to every proposition for the national security.

But it was their opponents, not they, who continually maintained, that on a failure of negotiation, it would be more eligible to seek redress by war, than by commercial regulations; who talked of raising armies, that might threaten the neighbouring possessions of foreign powers; who contended for delegating to the executive the prerogatives of deciding whether the country was at war or not, and of levying, organizing, and calling into the field, a regular army of ten, fifteen, nay, of twenty-five thousand men.

It is of some importance that this part of the history of the session, which has found no place in the late reviews of it, should be well understood. They who are curious to learn the particulars, must examine the debates and the votes. A full narrative would exceed the limits which are here prescribed. It must suffice to remark, that the efforts were varied and repeated until the last moment of the session, even after the departure of a number of members; forbade new propositions, much more a renewal of rejected ones; and that the powers proposed to be surrendered to the executive, were those which the constitution has most jealously appropriated to the legislature.

The reader shall judge on this subject for himself.

The constitution expressly and exclusively vests in the legislature the power of declaring a state of war: it was proposed, that the executive might, in the recess of the legislature, declare the United States to be in a state of war.

The constitution expressly and exclusively vests in the legislature the power of raising armies: it was proposed, that in the recess of the legislature, the executive might, at its pleasure, raise or not raise an army of ten, fifteen, or twenty-five thousand men.

The constitution expressly and exclusively vests in the legislature the power of creating offices: it was proposed, that the executive, in the recess of the legislature, might create offices, as well as appoint officers for an army of ten, fifteen, or twenty-five thousand men.

A delegation of such powers would have struck, not only at the fabric of our constitution, but at the foundation of all well organized and well checked governments.

The separation of the power of declaring war, from that of conducting it, is wisely contrived, to exclude the danger of its being declared for the sake of its being conducted.

The separation of the power of raising armies, from the power of commanding them, is intended to prevent the raising of armies for the sake of commanding them.

The separation of the power of creating offices, from that of filling them, is an essential guard against the temptation to create offices, for the sake of gratifying favorites, or multiplying dependants.

Where would be the difference between the blending of these incompatible powers, by surrendering the legislative part of them into the hands of the executive, and by assuming the executive part of them into the hands of the legislature? In either case the principle would be equally destroyed, and the consequences equally dangerous.

An attempt to answer these observations, by appealing to the virtues of the present chief magistrate, and to the confidence justly placed in them, will be little calculated, either for his genuine patriotism, or for the sound judgment of the American public.

The people of the United States would not merit the praise universally allowed to their intelligence, if they did not distinguish between the respect due to the man, and the functions belonging to the office. In expressing the former, there is no limit or guide, but the feelings of their grateful hearts. In deciding the latter, they will consult the constitution; they will consider human nature, and, looking beyond the character of the existing magistrate, fix their eyes on the precedent which must descend to his successors.

Will it be more than truth to say, that this great and venerable name is too often assumed for what cannot recommend itself, and for what there is neither proof nor probability, that its sanction can be claimed? Do arguments fail? Is the public mind to be encountered? There are not a few ever ready to invoke the name of Washington; to garnish their heretical doctrines with his virtues, and season their unpallatable measures with his populari⟨ty⟩. Those who take this liberty, will not, however, be mistaken; his truest friends will be the last to sport with his influence, above all, for electioneering purposes. And it is but a fair suspicion, that they who draw most largely on that fund, are hastening fastest to bankruptcy in their own.

As vain would be the attempt to explain away such alarming attacks on the constitution, by pleading the difficulty, in some cases, of drawing a line between the different departments of power; or by recurring to the little precedents which may have crept in, at urgent or unguarded moments.

Appendix 3: "Political Observations"

It cannot be denied, that there may, in certain cases, be a difficulty in distinguishing the exact boundary between legislative and executive powers; but the real friend of the constitution, and of liberty, by his endeavors to lessen or avoid the difficulty, will easily be known from him who labours to encrease the obscurity, in order to remove the constitutional land-marks without notice.

Nor will it be denied, that precedents may be found, where the line of separation between these powers has not been sufficiently regarded; where an improper latitude of discretion, particularly, has been given, or allowed, to the executive departments. But what does this prove? That the line ought to be considered as imaginary; that constitutional organizations of power ought to lose their effect? No—It proves with how much deliberation precedents ought to be established, and with how much caution arguments from them should be admitted. It may furnish another criterion, also, between the real and ostensible friend of constitutional liberty. The first will be as vigilant in resisting, as the last will be in promoting, the growth of inconsiderate or insidious precedents, into established encroachments.

The next charge to be examined, is the tendency of the propositions to degrade the United States into French colonies.

As it is difficult to argue against suppositions made and multiplied at will, so it is happily impossible to impose on the good sense of this country, by arguments which rest on suppositions only. In the present question it is first supposed, that the exercise of the self-evident and sovereign right of regulating trade, after the example of all independent nations, and that of the example of Great-Britain towards the United States, would inevitably involve the United States in a war with Great Britain. It is then supposed, that the other combined powers, though some of them be favored by the regulations proposed, and all of them be jealous of the maritime predominance of Great Britain, would support the wrongs of Great Britain against the rights of the United States. It is lastly supposed, that our allies (the French) in the event of success in establishing their own liberties, which they owe to our example, would be willing, as well as able, to rob us of ours, which they assisted us in obtaining; and that so malignant is their disposition on this head, that we should not be spared, even if embarked in a war against her own enemy. To finish the picture, it is intimated, that in the character of allies, we are the more exposed to this danger, from the secret and hostile ambition of France.

It will not be expected, that any formal refutation should be wasted on absurdities which answer themselves. None but those who have surrendered their reasoning faculties to the violence of their prejudices, will listen to suggestions implying, that the freest nation in Europe is the basest people on the face of the earth; that instead of the friendly and festive sympathy indulged by the people of the United States, they ought to go into mourning at every triumph of the French arms; that instead of regarding the French revolution as a blessing to mankind, and a bulwark to their own, they ought to anticipate its success as of all events the most formidable to their liberty and sovereignty; and that, calculating on the political connection with that nation, as the source of additional danger from its enmity and its usurpation, the first favorable moment ought to be seized for putting an end to it.

It is not easy to dismiss this subject, however, without reflecting, with grief and surprize, on the readiness with which many launch into speculations unfriendly to the struggles of France, and regardless of the interesting relations in which that country stands to this. They seem to be more struck with every circumstance that can be made a topic of reproach, or of chimerical apprehensions, than with all the splendid objects which are visible through the gloom of a revolution. But if there be an American who can see, without benevolent joy, the progress of that liberty to which he owes his own happiness, interest, at least, ought to find a place in his calculations: And if he cannot enlarge his views to the influence of the successes and friendship of France, or our safety as a nation, and particularly as a republic, how can he be insensible to the benefits presented to the United States in her commerce? The French markets consume more of our best productions, than are consumed by any other nation. If a balance in specie be as favorable as is usually supposed, the sum which supplies the immense drains of our specie, is derived also from the same source, more than from any other. And in the great and precious article of navigation, the share of American tonnage employed in the trade with the French dominions, gives to that trade a distinguished value; as well to that part of the union which most depends on ships and seamen for its prosperity, as to that which most requires them for its protection.

Whenever these considerations shall have that full weight, which a calm review will not fail to allow them, none will wonder more than the mercantile class of citizens themselves, that whilst they so anxiously wait stipulations from Great Britain, which are always within our command, so much indifference should be felt to those more important privileges in the trade of France, which, if not secured by a seasonable improvement of the commercial treaty with her, may possibly be forever lost to us.

Among the aspersions propagated against the friends, and the merits arrogated by the opponents, of the commercial propositions, much use has been made of the envoy-ship extraordinary to Great Britain. It has been affirmed, that the former was averse to the measure, on account of its pacific tendency; and that it was embraced by the latter, as the proper substitute for all commercial operations on the policy of Great Britain. It is to be remembered, however,

1. That this measure originated wholly with the executive.
2. That the opposition to it in the senate (as far as the public have any knowledge of it) was made, not to the measure of appointing an envoy extraordinary, but to the appointment of the chief justice of the United States for that service.
3. That the house of representatives never gave any opinion on the occasion, and that no opinion appears to have been expressed in debate by any individual of that house, which can be tortured into a disapprobation of the

measure, on account of its pacific tendency.
4. That the measure did not take place until the commercial propositions had received all the opposition that could be given to them.
5. That there is no spark of evidence, that if the envoyship had never taken place, or been thought of, the opponents of the propositions would have concurred in any commercial measures whatever, even after the West-India spoliations had laid in their full claim to the public attention.

But it may be fairly asked of those who opposed first the Commercial Propositions, and then the Non-Importation bill, and who rest their justification on the appointment of an envoy extraordinary; wherein lay the inconsistency between these Legislative and Executive plans?

Was it thought best to appeal to the Voluntary Justice, or liberal policy of Great Britain, and to these only? This was not certainly the case with those, who opposed the Commercial Appeals to the interest and the apprehension of Great Britain; Because they were the most zealous for appealing to her fears, by military preparations and menaces. If these had any meaning, they avowed that Great Britain was not to be brought to reason, otherwise than by the danger of injury to herself. And such being her disposition, she would, of course, be most influenced by measures, of which the comparative operation would be most against her. Whether that would be apprehended from measures of the one, or the other kind will easily be decided. But in every view, if fear was a proper auxiliary to negociation, the appeal to it in the Commercial Measures proposed, could not be inconsistent with the Envoyship. The inconsistency belongs to the reasoning of those who would pronounce it proper and effectual to say to Great-Britain, do us justice, or we will seize on Canada, though the loss will be trifling to you, whilst the cost will be immense to us; and who pronounce it improper and ineffectual to say to Great-Britain, do us justice, or you will suffer a wound, where you will most of all feel it, in a branch of your commerce, which feeds one part of your dominions, and sends annually to the other, a balance in specie of more than ten millions of dollars.

The opponents of the commercial measures may be asked, in the next place, to what cause the issue of the envoy-ship, if successful, ought to be ascribed?

Will it have been the pure effect of a benevolent and conciliatory disposition in Great Britain towards the United States? This will hardly be pretended by her warmest admirers and advocates. It is disproved by the whole tenor of her conduct ever since we were an independent and republican nation. Had this cordial disposition, or even a disposition to do us justice, been really felt; the delay would not have been spun out to so late a day. The moment would rather have been chosen, when we were least in condition, to vindicate our interest, by united councils and persevering efforts. The motives then would have been strongest, and the merit most conspicuous. Instead of this honorable and prudent course, it has been the vigilant study of Great Britain, to take all possible advantage of our embarrassments; nor has the least inclination been shewn to relax her system, except at the crisis in 1783, already mentioned, when, not foreseeing these embarrassments, she was alarmed for her commerce with the United States.

Will the success be ascribeable to the respect paid to that country by the measure, or to the talents and address of the envoy.

Such an explanation of the fact, is absolutely precluded by a series of other facts.

Soon after the peace, Mr. Adams, the present Vice President of the United States, was appointed Minister Plenipotentiary to the British Court. The measure was the more respectful as no mutual arrangement had been premised between the two countries, nor any intimation received from Great Britain, that the civility should be returned; nor was the civility returned during the whole period of his residence. The manner in which he was treated, and the United States, through him, his protracted exertions, and the mortifying inefficacy of them, are too much in the public remembrance to need a rehearsal.

This first essay on the temper of Great Britain, towards the United

States, was prior to the establishment of the Federal Constitution. The important change produced in our situation by this event, led to another essay, which is not unknown to the public. Although in strictness, it might not unreasonably have been expected, after what had been done in the instance of Mr. Adams, that the advance towards a diplomatic accommodation should then have come from Great Britain, Mr. G. Morris was made an agent for feeling her pulse, and soothing her pride, a second time. The history of his operations is not particularly known. It is certain, however, that this repetition of the advance, produced no sensible change on her disposition towards us, much less any actual compliance with our just expectations and demands. The most that can be said is, that it was, after a considerable interval, followed by the mission of Mr. Hammond to the United States, who, as it is said, however, refused, notwithstanding the long residence of Mr. Adams at the court of London, without a return of the civility, to commit the dignity of his master, until the most explicit assurances were given, that Mr. Pinckney should immediately counterplace him.

The mission of this last respectable citizen, forms a third appeal to the justice and good will of the British Government, on the subjects between the two countries. His negociations on that side the Atlantic, as well as those through Mr. Hammond on this, having been laid before the Congress, and printed for general information, will speak for themselves. It will only be remarked, that they terminated here in the disclosure, that Mr. Hammond had no authority, either to adjust the differences connected with the Treaty of Peace, or to concur in any solid arrangements, for reciprocity in Commerce and Navigation; and that in Great Britain, they terminated in the conviction of Mr. Pinckney, that nothing was to be expected from the voluntary justice or policy of that country, and in his advice, before quoted, of Commercial Regulations, as the best means for obtaining a compliance with our just claims.

All who weigh these facts with candor, will join in concluding, that the success of the envoyship must be otherwise explained, than by the operation of diplomatic compliments, or of personal talents.

To what causes then will the United States be truly indebted, for any favorable result to the envoyship?

Every well-informed and unprejudiced mind, will answer, to the following:

1. The spirit of America, expressed by the vote of the House of Representatives, on the subject of the Commercial Propositions, by the large majority of that house (overruled by the casting voice in the Senate) in favor of the non-importation bill, and by the act laying an embargo. Although these proceedings would, doubtless, have been more efficacious, if the two former had obtained the sanction of laws, and if the last had not been so soon repealed; yet they must have had no little effect, as warnings to the British government; that if her obstinacy should take away the last pretext from the opponents of such measures, it might be impossible to divide or mislead our public councils with respect to them in future.

There is no room to pretend, that her relaxation in this case, if she should relax, will be the effect, not of those proceedings, but of the ultimate defeat of them. Former defeats of a like policy, had repeatedly taken place, and are known to have produced, instead of relaxation, a more confirmed perseverance on the part of Great-Britain. Under the old confederation, the United States had not the power over commerce: of that situation she took advantage. The new government which contained the power, did not evince the will to exert it; of that situation she still took the advantage. Should she yield then at the present juncture? The problem ought not to be solved, without presuming her to be satisfied by what has lately passed—that the United States have now, not only the power, but the will to exert it.

The reasoning is short and conclusive; in the year 1783, when Great Britain apprehended Commercial Restrictions from the United States, she was disposed to concede and to accommodate. From the year 1783 to the year 1794, when she apprehended no Commercial Restrictions, she shewed no disposition to concede or to accommodate. In the year 1794, when alarming evidence was given of the danger of Commercial Restrictions, she did concede and accommodate.

If any thing can have weakened the operation of the proceedings above referred to on the British government, it must be the laboured and vehement attempts of their opponents to show, that the United States had little to demand, and every thing to dread, from Great Britain; that the commerce between the two countries was more essential to us, than to her; that our citizens would be less willing than her subjects to bear, and our government less able than hers to enforce, restrictions or interruptions of it. In a word, that we were more dependent on her, than she was on us; and, therefore, ought to court her not to withdraw from us her supplies, though chiefly luxuries, instead of threatening to withdraw from her our supplies, though mostly necessaries.

It is difficult to say, whether the indiscretion or the fallacy of such arguments be the more remarkable feature in them. All that can be hoped is, that an antidote to their mischievous tendency in Great Britain may be found in the consciousness there, of the errors on which they are founded, and the contempt which they will be known to have excited in this country.

2. The other cause will be, the posture into which Europe has been thrown, by the war with France, and particularly by the campaign of 1794. The combined armies have every where felt the superior valour, discipline, and resources of their republican enemies. Prussia, after heavy and perfidious draughts on the British treasury, has retired from the common standard, to contend with new dangers peculiar to herself. Austria, worn out in unavailing resistance, her arms disgraced, her treasure exhausted, and her vassals discontented, seeks her last consolation in the same source of British subsidy. The Dutch, instead of continuing their proportion of aids for the war, have their whole faculties turned over to France. Spain, with all her wealth and all her pride, is palsied in every nerve, and forced to the last resorts of royalty, to a reduction of salaries and pensions, and to the hoards of

superstition. Great Britain herself has seen her military glory eclipsed, her projects confounded, her hopes blasted, her marine threatened, her resources overcharged, and her government in danger of losing its energy, by the despotic excesses into which it has been overstrained.

If, under such circumstances, she does not abandon herself to apathy and despair, it is because she finds her credit still alive, and in that credit sees some possibility of making terms with misfortune. But what is the basis of that credit? Her commerce. And what is the most valuable remnant of that resource? The commerce with the U. States. Will she risk this best part of her last resource, by persevering in her selfish and unjust treatment of the United States?

Time will give a final answer to this question. All that can be now pronounced is, that if, on the awful precipice to which G. Britain is driven, she will open neither her eyes to her danger, nor her heart to her duty, her character must be a greater contrast to the picture of it drawn by the opponents of the commercial measures, than could have easily been imagined. If, on the other hand, she should relent, and consult her reason, the change will be accounted for by her prospects on the other side of the atlantic, and the countenance exhibited on this; without supposing her character to vary, in a single feature, from the view of it entertained by the friends of such measures.

That the rising spirit of America, and the successes of France, will have been the real causes of any favorable terms obtained by the mission of Mr. Jay, cannot be controverted. Had the same forbearance, which was tried for ten years on the part of the United States, been continued; and had the combined powers proceeded in the victorious career which has signalized the French arms; under this reverse of circumstances, the most bigoted Englishman will be ashamed to say, that any relaxing change in the policy of his government, was to be hoped for by the United States.

Such are the reflections which occur on the supposition of a successful issue to the envoy-ship. Should it unhappily turn out, that neither the new countenance presented by America, nor the adverse fortunes of

Great Britain, can bend the latter to a reasonable accommodation, it may be worth while to enquire, what will probably be the evidence furnished by the friends and adversaries of commercial measures, with respect to their comparative attachments to peace?

If any regard be paid to consistency, those who opposed all such measures must be for an instant resort to arms. With them there was no alternative, but negociation or war. Their language was, let us try the former, but be prepared for the latter; if the olive branch fail, let the sword vindicate our rights, as it has vindicated the rights of other nations. A real war is both more honorable and more eligible than commercial regulations. In these G. B. is an overmatch for us.

On the other side, the friends of commercial measures, if consistent, will prefer these measures, as an intermediate experiment between negociation and war. They will persist in their language, that Great-Britain is more dependent on us, than we are on her; that this has ever been the American sentiment, and is the true basis of American policy; that war should not be resorted to, till every thing short of war has been tried; that if Great-Britain be invulnerable to our attacks, it is in her fleets and armies; that if the United States can bring her to reason at all, the surest as well as the cheapest means, will be a judicious system of commercial operations; that here the United States are unquestionably an overmatch for Great-Britain.

It must be the ardent prayer of all, that the occasion may not happen for such a test of the consistency and the disposition of those whose counsels were so materially different on the subject of a commercial vindication of our rights. Should it be otherwise ordained, the public judgment will pronounce on which side, the politics were most averse to war, and most anxious for every pacific effort, that might at the same time be an efficient one, in preference to that last and dreadful resort of injured nations.

There remain two subjects belonging to the session of Congress under review, on each of which some comments are made proper by the misrepresentations which have been propagated.

Appendix 3: "Political Observations"

The first is, The naval armament.

The second, The new taxes then established.

As to the first, it appears from the debates and other accounts, to have been urged in favor of the measure, that six frigates of one hundred and eighty four guns, to be stationed at the mouth of the Mediterranean, would be sufficient to protect the American trade against the Algerine pirates, that such a force would not cost more than six hundred thousand dollars, including an out-fit of stores and provisions for six months, and might be built in time to take their station by July or August last; that the expence of this armament would be fully justified by the importance of our trade to the south of Europe; that without such a protection, the whole trade of the Atlantic would be exposed to depredation; nay, that the American coast might not escape the enterprising avarice of these roving Barbarians; that such an effort on the part of the United States, was particularly due to the unfortunate citizens already groaning in chains and pining in despair, as well as to those who might otherwise be involved in the same fate. Other considerations of less influence may have entered into the decision on the same side.

On the other side, it was said, that the force was insufficient for the object; that the expence would be greater than was estimated; that there was a limit to the expence, which could be afforded for the protection of any branch of trade; that the aggregate value of the annual trade, export and import to Spain and Portugal, appeared from authentic documents not to exceed three and an half millions of dollars, that the profit only, on this amount, was to be compared with the expence of the frigates; that if the American vessels engaged in those channels, should give place to vessels at peace with Algiers, they would repair to the channels quitted by the latter vessels; so that it would be rather a change than a loss of employment; that the other distant branches of our trade, would be little affected and our own coast not at all; that the frigates, at so great a distance on a turbulent sea, would he exposed to dangers, as well as attended with expences, not to be calculated; and if stationed where intended, would leave our trade up the Mediterranean as unprotected as it is at present. That in addition to these considerations, the frigates would not be ready by the time stated, nor probably until the war, and the occasion would be over; that if the removal of the Portuguese squadron from the blockade really proceeded, as was alledged from Great-Britain, she would, under some pretext or other, contrive to defeat the object of the frigates; that if Great-Britain was not at the bottom of the measure, the interest which Portugal had in our trade, which supplies her with the necessaries of life, would soon restore the protection she had withdrawn; that it would be more effectual as well as cheaper, to concert arrangements with Portugal, by which the United States would be subjected to an equitable share only, instead of taking on themselves the whole of the burden; that as to our unfortunate citizens in captivity, the frigates could neither be in time nor of force, to relieve them; that money alone could do this, and that a sufficient sum ought to be provided for the purpose: that it was moreover to be considered, that if there were any disposition in Great-Britain, to be irritated into a war with us, or to seek an occasion for it; those, who on other questions had taken that ground of argument, ought to be particularly aware of danger, from the collision of naval armaments, within the sphere of British jealousy, and in the way perhaps of a favorite object.

No undue blame is meant to be thrown on those, who did not yield to this reasoning, however conclusive it may now appear. The vote in favor of the measure was indeed so checquered, that it cannot even be attributed to the influence of party. It is but justice, at the same time, to those who opposed the measure, to remark, that instead of the frigates being at their destined station in July or August last, the keel of one only was laid in December; the timber for the rest being then in the forest, and the whole of the present year stated to be necessary for their completion; that consequently it is nearly certain now, they will not be in service, before the war in Europe will be over, and that in the mean time it has turned out as was foretold, that Portugal has felt sufficient motives to renew the blockade; so that if the frigates had been adapted to the original object, they would not be required for it;

more especially, as it has likewise turned out according to another anticipation, that money would alone be the agent for restoring the captive exiles to their freedom and their country.

It may possibly be said, that the frigates, though not necessary or proper for the service first contemplated, may usefully be applied to the security of our coasts, against Pirates, Privateers, and Smugglers. This is a distinct question. The sole and avowed object of the naval armament was the protection of our trade against the Algerines. To that object the force is appropriated by the law itself. The President can apply it to no other. If any other now presents itself, it may fairly be now discussed, but as it was not the object then, the measure cannot be tested by it now. If there be sufficient reasons of any sort for such a naval establishment, those who disapproved it for an impracticable and impolitic object, may with perfect consistency allow these reasons their full weight. It is much to be questioned, however, whether any good reason could be found for going on with the whole undertaking; besides, that in general the commencement of political measures under one pretext, and the prosecution of them under another, has always an aspect, that justifies circumspection if not suspicion.

With respect to the new taxes, the second remaining subject, a very brief explanation will be sufficient.

From a general view of the proceedings of Congress on this subject, it appears, that the advocates for the new taxes urged them. 1st. On the probability of a diminution of the import for 1794, as an effect of some of the questions agitated in Congress on the amount of exports from Great Britain to the United States. 2dly. On the probability of war with Great Britain, which would still further destroy the revenue, at the same time that it would beget an immense addition to the public expenditures. On the first of these points, those who did not concur in the new taxes, at least in all of them, denied the probability of any material diminution of the import without a war: On the other point, they denied any such probability of a war, as to require what was proposed; and in both these opinions, they have been justified by subsequent experience. War has not taken place, nor does it appear ever to have been meditated, unless in the event of subverting the French Republic, which was never probable; whilst the revenue from the import, instead of being diminished, has very considerably exceeded any former amount.

It will not be improper to remark, as a further elucidation of this subject. 1st. That most, if not all, who refused to concur in some of the new taxes as not justified by the occasion, actually concurred in others which were least objectionable, as an accommodating precaution against contingencies. 2d. That the objection to one of the taxes was its breach of the constitution; an objection insuperable in its nature, and which there is reason to believe, will be established by the judicial authority, if ever brought to that test; and that the objections to others were such as had always had weight with the most enlightened patriots of America. 3. That in the opinions of the most zealous patrons of new Ways and Means, the occasion, critical as they pressed it, did not ultimately justify all the taxes proposed. It appears in particular, that a bill imposing a variety of duties, mostly in the nature of stamp duties, into which, a duty on transfers of stock, had been inserted as an amendment, was in the last stage defeated, by those who had in general, urged the new taxes, and this very bill itself in the earlier stage of it.

These, with the preceding observations, on a very interesting period of Congressional history, will be left to the candid judgement of the public. Such as may not before have viewed the transactions of that period, through any other medium than the misrepresentations which have been circulated, will have an opportunity of doing justice to themselves, as well as to others. And no doubt can be entertained, that in this as in all other cases, it will be found, that truth, however, stifled or perverted for a time, will finally triumph in the detection of calumny, and in the contempt which awaits its authors.

WORKS CITED

Adair, Douglass. "James Madison's Autobiography." *The William and Mary Quarterly* Vol. 2, No. 2 (1945): 191-209.

Bailyn, Bernard, ed. *The Debate on the Constitution: Federalist and Antifederalist Speeches, Articles, and Letters During the Struggle over Ratification.* New York: Library of America, 2015.

Brant, Irving. *James Madison: The Virginia Revolutionist.* New York: The Bobbs-Merrill Co., 1941.

Brookhiser, Richard. "Finally, James Madison Mania." The Daily Beast. April 5, 2015. http://www.thedailybeast.com/articles/2015/04/05/finally-james-madison-mania.html (accessed March 1, 2017).

Farrand, Max. *The Records of the Federal Convention of 1787.* Vol. 3. New Haven: Yale University Press, 1911. http://oll.libertyfund.org/titles/1787

Folsom, Burton, Jr. "Madison's Veto Sets a Precedent." *The Freeman*, January/February 2008, 29-30.

Founders Online. *The Papers of Alexander Hamilton.* National Archives and Records Administration. National Historical Papers and Records Commission. Washington, DC. https://founders.archives.gov/

Founders Online. *The Papers of Thomas Jefferson.* National Archives and Records Administration. National Historical Papers and Records Commission. Washington, DC. https://founders.archives.gov/

Founders Online. *The Papers of James Madison.* National Archives and Records Administration. National Historical Papers and Records Commission. Washington, DC. https://founders.archives.gov/

Founders Online. *The Papers of George Washington.* National Archives and Records Administration. National Historical Papers and Records Commission. Washington, DC. https://founders.archives.gov/

Frisch, Morton J., ed. *The Pacificus-Helvidius Debates of 1793-1794: Toward the Completion of the American Founding.* Indianapolis: Liberty Fund, 2007.

Hamilton, Alexander, James Madison, and John Jay. *The Federalist Papers.* Edited by Clinton Rossiter. New York: New American Library, 1961.

Humphrey, Grace. *Women in American History.* Indianapolis: Bobbs-Merrill Company, 1919.

Hutchinson, William, et al., eds. *The Papers of James Madison.* Chicago and London: University of Chicago Press, 1962-77 (vols. 1-10); Charlottesville: University Press of Virginia, 1977-91 (vols. 11-17).

Jefferson, Thomas. *Notes on the State of Virginia.* New York: Penguin Books, 1999.

Jennings, Paul. *A Colored Man's Reminiscences of James Madison.* Electronic edition. University of North Carolina, 1991.

Kaminski, John P. "Madison's Gift." Review of *Notes of Debates in the Federal Convention of 1787 Reported by James Madison.* New York: W.W. Norton and Co., 1987. http://common-place.org/book/madisons-gift/

Ketcham, Ralph. *James Madison: A Biography.* Charlottesville: The University Press of Virginia, 1990.

Koch, Adrienne. *Jefferson and Madison: The Great Collaboration.* Old Saybrook: Konecky and Konecky, 2004.

Madison, James. *Notes of Debates in the Federal Convention of 1787 Reported by James Madison.* Bicentennial Edition. New York: W.W. Norton and Co., 1987.

Meyers, Marvin, ed. *The Mind of the Founder: Sources of the Political Thought of James Madison*. Revised edition. University Press of New England, 1991.

Miller, William Lee. *The Business of May Next: James Madison & the Founding*. Charlottesville: The University Press of Virginia, 1992.

"Monticello." Thomas Jefferson's Monticello. Accessed 2016. https://www.monticello.org/

"Montpelier." James Madison's Montpelier. Accessed 2016. http://www.montpelier.org/

Shulman, Holly C., ed. *The Papers of Dolley Madison Digital Edition*. Charlottesville: University of Virginia Press, 2008. http://rotunda.upress.virginia.edu/founders/DYMN-01-03-02-0229

Smelser, Marshall. *The Democratic Republic: 1801-1815*. Prospect Heights: Waveland Press, 1992.

Stagg, J.C.A., ed. *The Papers of James Madison Digital Edition*. Charlottesville: University of Virginia Press, 2010. http://rotunda.upress.virginia.edu/founders/JSMN-03-06-02-0006

Thompson, Dennis F. "The Education of a Founding Father: The Reading List for John Witherspoon's Course in Political Theory, as Taken by James Madison," *Political Theory* 4, No. 4 (1976): 523-29. http://www.jstor.org/stable/191140

Washington, George, and W.B. Allen. *George Washington: A Collection*. Indianapolis: Liberty Fund, 1988. Print.

Wood, Gordon S. *Revolutionary Characters: What Made the Founders Different*. New York: Penguin Press, 2006.

Selected Quotations from the Writings of James Madison

AFFLICTION, Moral fortitude and.—Afflictions of every kind are the onerous conditions charged on the tenure of life; and it is a silencing if not a satisfactory vindication of the ways of Heaven to Man, that there are but few who do not prefer an acquiescence in them, to a surrender of the tenure itself.

> Letter to John Jackson, December 28, 1821

AGRICULTURAL SOCIETIES, Praise for.—In my opinion, it would be proper, also, for gentlemen to consider the means of encouraging the great staple of America, I mean agriculture, which I think may justly be styled the staple of the United States; from the spontaneous productions which nature furnishes, and the manifest preference it has over every other object of emolument in this country.

> Speech in Congress, April 9, 1789

The life of the husbandman is pre-eminently suited to the comfort and happiness of the individual. Health, the first of blessings, is an appurtenance of his property and his employment. Virtue, the health of the soul, is another part of his patrimony, and no less favored by his situation. Intelligence may be cultivated in this as well as any other walk of life. If the mind be less susceptible of polish in retirement than in a crowd, it is more capable of profound and comprehensive efforts. Is it more ignorant of some things? It has a compensation in its ignorance of others. Competency is more universally the lot of those who dwell in the country, when liberty is at the same time their lot. The extremes of both want and of waste have other abodes.

National Gazette essay, March 3, 1792

The class of citizens who provide at once their own food and their own raiment, may be viewed as the most truly independent and happy. They are more: they are the best basis of public liberty and the strongest bulwark of public safety. It follows, that the greater the proportion of this class to the whole society, the more free, the more independent, and the more happy must be the society itself.

National Gazette essay, March 3, 1792

AMBITION.—Ambition is so vigilant, and where it has a model always in view as in the present case, is so prompt in seizing its advantages, that it can not be too closely watched, or too vigorously checked.

Letter to Thomas Jefferson, December 25, 1797

AMERICA, The world and.—Is it not the glory of the people of America, that whilst they have paid a decent regard to the opinions of former times and other nations, they have not suffered a blind veneration for antiquity, for custom, or for names, to overrule the suggestions of their own good sense, the knowledge of their own situation, and the lessons of their own experiences? To this manly spirit, posterity will be indebted for the possession, and the world for the example of the possession, and the world for the example of numerous innovations displayed on the American theatre, in favour of private rights and public happiness.

Federalist No. 14, November 30, 1787

All Europe must by degrees be aroused to the recollection and assertion of the rights of human nature. Your good will to Mankind will be gratified with this prospect, and your pleasure as an American be enhanced by the reflection that the light which is chasing darkness and despotism from the old world, is but an emanation from that which has procured and succeeded the establishment of liberty in the new.

Letter to Edmund Pendleton, March 4, 1790

The U.S. are now furnishing models and lessons to all the world, a great, soon to be the most hopeful portion of it, is receiving them with a happy docility; whilst the great European portion is either passively or actively gaining by them. The eyes of the world being thus on our country, it is put the more on its good behavior, and under the greater obligation also, to do justice to the Tree of Liberty by an exhibition of the fine fruits we gather from it.

Letter to James Monroe, December 16, 1824

AMERICA, Politics of.—A government, deriving its energy from the will of the society, and operating by the reason of its measures, on the understanding and interest of the society. Such is the government for which philosophy has been searching, and humanity been sighing, such are the republican governments which it is the glory of America to have invented, and her unrivalled happiness to possess.

National Gazette essay, February 18, 1792

Here [in the United States], we are, on the whole, doing well, and giving an example of a free system, which I trust will be more of a pilot to a good port, than a Beacon, warning from a bad one. We have, it is true, occasional fevers; but they are of a transient kind, flying off through the surface, without preying on the vitals. A government like ours has so many safety-valves, giving vent to overheated passions, that it carries within itself a relief against the infirmities from which the best of human Institutions can not be exempt.

Letter to Marquis de Lafayette, November 25, 1820

AMERICAN REVOLUTION.—Happily for America, happily, we trust, for the whole human race, they pursued a new and more noble course. They accomplished a revolution which has no parallel in the annals of human society.

Federalist No. 14, November 20, 1787

They accomplished a revolution which has no parallel in the annals of human society. They reared the fabrics of governments which have no model on the face of the globe. They formed the design of a great Confederacy, which it is incumbent on their successors to improve and perpetuate.

Federalist No. 14, November 30, 1787

Is it not the glory of the people of America, that whilst they have paid a decent regard to the opinions of former times and other nations, they have not suffered a blind veneration for antiquity, for custom, or for names, to overrule the suggestions of their own good sense, the knowledge of their own situation, and the lessons of their own experience? To this manly spirit, posterity will be indebted for the possession, and the world for the example of the numerous innovations displayed on the American theatre, in favor of private rights and public happiness.

Federalist No. 14, November 30, 1787

ARMS.—Besides, the advantage of being armed forms a barrier against the enterprises of ambition, more insurmountable than any which a simple government of any form can admit of.

Federalist No. 46, January 29, 1788

But ambitious encroachments of the federal government, on the authority of the State governments, would not excite the opposition of a single State, or of a few States only. They would be signals of general alarm. Every government would espouse the common cause. A correspondence would be opened. Plans of resistance would be concerted. One spirit would animate and conduct the whole. The same combinations, in short, would result from an apprehension of the federal, as was produced by the dread of a foreign, yoke; and unless the projected innovations should be voluntarily renounced, the same appeal to a trial of force would be made in the one case as was made in the other.

Federalist No. 46, January 29, 1788

ARTS, The.—Regarding the Arts which it [the Society of Artists of Philadelphia] cherishes, as among the endowments and enjoyments, which characterize human society, under its highest and happiest destinies; it is one of my ardent wishes, that the tendency of our free system of Government may be portrayed as well in what may contribute to embellish the mind and refine the manners, as in those primary blessings, of which it already affords so many grateful proofs and presages.

Letter to Benjamin Henry Latrobe and George Murray, January 28, 1811

AUTOCRACY.—Can any despotism be more cruel than a situation, in which the existence of thousands depends on one will, and that will on the most slight and fickle of all motives, a mere whim of the imagination.

National Gazette essay, March 20, 1792

BANKS.—With regard to banks, they have taken too deep and too wide a root in social transactions, to be got rid of altogether, if that were desirable. In providing a convenient substitute, to a certain extent, for the metallic currency, and a fund of credit, which prudence may turn to good account, they have a hold on public opinion, which alone would make it expedient to aim rather at the improvement, than the suppression of them. As now generally, their advantages whatever they may be, are outweighed by the excess of their paper emissions, and the partialities and corruption with which they are administered.

Rivers Collection, Madison Papers, March 10, 1827

BILL OF RIGHTS.—What use then it may be asked can a bill of rights serve in popular Governments? I answer the two following which though less essential than in other governments, sufficiently recommend the precaution, 1. The political truths declared in that solemn manner acquire by degrees the character of fundamental maxims of free Government, and as they become incorporated with the national sentiment, counteract the impulses of interest and passion. 2. Altho' it be generally true as above stated that the danger of oppression lies in the interested majorities of the people rather than in usurped acts of the government yet there may be occasions on which the evil may spring from the latter sources; and on such, a bill of rights will be a good ground for an appeal to the sense of the community.

Letter to Thomas Jefferson, October 17, 1788

In proportion as Government is influenced by opinion, must it be so by whatever influences opinion. This decides the question concerning a bill of rights, which acquires efficacy as time sanctifies and incorporates it with the public sentiment.

Notes for Essays, December 19, 1791-March 3, 1792

In Europe, charters of liberty have been granted by power. America has set the example and France has followed it, of charters of power granted by liberty. This revolution in the practice of the world, may, with an honest praise, be pronounced the most triumphant epoch of its history, and the most consoling presage of its happiness.

National Gazette essay, January 18, 1792

BOOKS.—With us [in the United States] there are more readers than buyers of Books. In England there are more buyers than Readers. Hence those Gorgeous Editions, which are destined to sleep in the private libraries of the Rich, whose vanity aspires to that species of furniture; or who give that turn to their public spirit and patronage of letters.

Letter to Edward Everett, March 19, 1823

CIVIL LIBERTY.—The civil rights of none, shall be abridged on account of religious belief or worship, nor shall any national religion be established, nor shall the full and equal rights of conscience be in any manner, or on any pretext infringed.

Proposed amendment to the Constitution, given in a speech in the House of Representatives, 1789

In a free government, the security for civil rights must be the same as that for religious rights. It consists in the one case in the multiplicity of interests, and in the other, in the multiplicity of sects.

Federalist No. 51, February 6, 1788

As a man is said to have a right to his property, he may be equally said to have a property in his rights. Where an excess of power prevails, property of no sort is duly respected. No man is safe in his opinions, his person, his faculties, or his possessions.

National Gazette essay, March 27, 1792

CLASSICAL CIVILIZATIONS.—Had every Athenian citizen been a Socrates, every Athenian assembly would still have been a mob.

Federalist No. 55, February 15, 1788

COMMERCE.—Wherever Commerce prevails there will be an inequality of wealth, and wherever the latter does a simplicity of manners must decline.

Letter to Edmund Randolph, September 30, 1783

Every new regulation concerning commerce or revenue; or in any manner affecting the value of the different species of property, presents a new harvest to those who watch the change and can trace its consequences; a harvest reared not by themselves but by the toils and cares of the great body of their fellow citizens. This is a state of things in which it may be said with some truth that laws are made for the few not for the many.

Federalist No. 62, February 27, 1788

I own myself the friend to a very free system of commerce, and hold it as a truth, that commercial shackles are generally unjust, oppressive and impolitic—it is also a truth, that if industry and labour are left to take their own course, they will generally be directed to those objects which are the most productive, and this in a more certain and direct manner than the wisdom of the most enlightened legislature could point out.

Speech in Congress, April 9, 1789

COMMON LAW.—If it be understood that the common law is established by the constitution, it follows that no part of the law can be altered by legislature . . . and the whole code with all its incongruities, barbarisms, and bloody maxims would be inviolably saddled on the good people of the United States.

"The Report of 1800," January 7, 1800

CONGRESS.—In forming the Senate, the great anchor of the Government, the questions as they came within the first object turned mostly on the mode of appointment, and the duration of it.

Letter to Thomas Jefferson, October 24, 1787

For the same reason that the members of the State legislatures will be unlikely to attach themselves sufficiently to national objects, the members of the federal legislature will be likely to attach themselves too much to local objects.

Federalist No. 47, February 1, 1788

The legislative department is everywhere extending the sphere of its activity and drawing all power into its impetuous vortex.

Federalist No. 48, February 1, 1788

The members of the legislative department . . . are numerous. They are distributed and dwell among the people at large. Their connections of blood, of friendship, and of acquaintance embrace a great proportion of the most influential part of the society . . . they are more immediately the confidential guardians of their rights and liberties.

Federalist No. 50, February 5, 1788

I cannot undertake to lay my finger on that article of the Constitution which granted a right to Congress of expending, on the objects of benevolence, the money of their constituents.

James Madison, 1794

The house of representatives ... can make no law which will not have its full operation on themselves and their friends, as well as the great mass of society. This has always been deemed one of the strongest bonds by which human policy can connect the rulers and the people together. It creates between them that communion of interest, and sympathy of sentiments, of which few governments have furnished examples; but without which every government degenerates into tyranny.

Federalist No. 57, February 19, 1788

CONSCIENCE.—Conscience is the most sacred of all property; other property depending in part on positive law, the exercise of that, being a natural and unalienable right. To guard a man's house as his castle, to pay public and enforce private debts with the most exact faith, can give no title to invade a man's conscience which is more sacred than his castle, or to withhold from it that debt of protection, for which the public faith is pledged, by the very nature and original conditions of the social pact.

National Gazette essay, March 27, 1792

CONSTITUTION, Amendments to.—The danger of disturbing the public tranquility by interesting too strongly the public passions, is a still more serious objection against a frequent reference of constitutional questions, to the decision of the whole society. Notwithstanding the success which has attended the revisions of our established forms of government, and which does so much honor to the virtue and intelligence of the people of America, it must be confessed, that the experiments are too ticklish a nature to be unnecessarily multiplied.

Federalist No. 49, February 2, 1788

It may be considered as an objection inherent in the principle, that as every appeal to the people would carry an implication of some defect in the government, frequent appeals would in great measure deprive the government of that veneration which time bestows on everything, and without which perhaps the wisest and freest governments would not possess the requisite stability. If it be true that all governments rest on opinion, it is no less true that the strength of opinion in each individual, and its practical influence on his conduct, depend much on the number which he supposes to have entertained the same opinion. The reason of man, like man himself, is timid and cautious, when left alone; and acquires firmness and confidence, in proportion to the number with which it is associated. When the examples, which fortify opinion, are ancient as well as numerous, they are known to have double effect. In a nation of philosophers, this consideration ought to be disregarded. A reverence for the laws, would be sufficiently inculcated by the voice of an enlightened reason. But a nation of philosophers is as little to be expected as the philosophical race of kings wished for by Plato. And in every other nation, the most rational government will not find it as superfluous advantage to have the prejudices of the community on its side.

Federalist No. 49, February 2, 1788

The Constitution of the United States may doubtless disclose from time to time, faults which call for the pruning or the ingrafting hand. But remedies ought to be applied, not in the paroxysms of party and polar excitements; but with the more leisure and reflection, as the Great Departments of power according to experiences may be successively and alternately in and out of public favour, and as changes hastily accommodated to these vicissitudes would destroy the symmetry and the stability aimed at in our political system.

Letter to John M. Patton, March 24, 1834

CONSTITUTION, Interpretation of.—No axiom is more clearly established in law, or "in reason, than that wherever the end is required," the means are authorized; wherever a general power to do a thing is given, every particular power necessary for doing it, is included.

Federalist No. 44, January 25, 1788

What is to be the consequence, in case the Congress shall misconstrue this part [the necessary and proper clause] of the Constitution and exercise powers not warranted by its true meaning, I answer the same as if they should misconstrue or enlarge any other power vested in them.... The success of the usurpation will depend on the executive and judiciary departments, which are to expound and give effect to the legislative acts; and in a last resort a remedy must be obtained from the people, who can by the elections of more faithful representatives, annul the acts of the usurpers.

Federalist No. 44, January 25, 1788

I acknowledge, in the ordinary course of government, that the exposition of the laws and Constitution devolves upon the judicial. But I beg to know upon what principle it can be contended that any one department draws from the Constitution greater powers than another in marking out the limits of the powers of the several departments.

Speech in the Congress of the United States, June 17, 1789

Nothing has yet been offered to invalidate the doctrine that the meaning of the Constitution may as well be ascertained by the Legislative as by the Judicial authority.

Speech in the Congress of the United States, June 18, 1789

The federal government has been hitherto limited to the Specified powers, by the greatest Champions for Latitude in expounding those powers. If not only the means, but the objects are unlimited, the parchment had better be thrown into the fire at once.

Letter to Henry Lee, January 1, 1792

If Congress can do whatever in their discretion can be done by money, and will promote the general welfare, the Government is no longer a limited one possessing enumerated powers, but an indefinite one subject to particular exceptions. It is to be remarked that the phrase out of which this doctrine elaborated is copied from the old articles of Confederation, where it was always understood as nothing more than a general caption to the specified powers, and it is a fact that it was preferred in the new instrument for that very reason as less liable than any other to misconstruction.

Letter to Edmund Pendleton, January 21, 1792

If Congress can apply money indefinitely to the general welfare, and are the sole and supreme judges of the general welfare, they may take the care of religion into their own hands, they may establish teachers in every state, county, and parish and pay them out of the public treasury, they may take into their own hands the education of children, establishing in like manner schools throughout the union; they may assume the provision for the poor they may undertake the regulation of all roads other than post roads; in short, every thing, from the highest objection of state legislation, down to the most minute object of police, would be thrown under the power of Congress; for every object I have mentioned would admit the application of money, and might be called, if Congress pleased, provisions for the general welfare.

Speech in Congress, February 6, 1792

I, sir, have always conceived—I believe those who proposed the Constitution conceived; it is still more fully known, and more material to observe, those who ratified the constitution conceived, that this is not an indefinite government deriving its powers from the general terms prefixed to the specified powers—but, a limited government tied down to the specified powers, which explain and define the general terms.

> Speech in Congress, February 6, 1792

I cannot undertake to lay my finger on that article of the Constitution which granted a right to Congress of expending, on the objects of benevolence, the money of their constituents.

> James Madison, 1794

It would be absurd to say, first, that Congress may do what they please; and then, that they may do this or that particular thing. After giving Congress power to raise money, and apply it to all purposes which they may pronounce necessary to the general welfare, it would be absurd, to say the least, to superadd a power to raise armies, to provide fleets, &c. In fact, the meaning of the general terms in question must either be sought in subsequent enumerations which limits and details them, or they convert the government from one limited as hitherto supposed, to the enumerated powers, into a government without any limits at all. But, after all, whatever venerations might be entertained for the body of men who formed our constitution, the sense of that body could never be regarded as the oracular guide in the expounding the constitution. As the instrument came from them, it was nothing more than the draught of a plan, nothing but a dead letter, until life and validity were breathed into it by the voice of the people, speaking through the several State conventions. If we were to look therefore, for the meaning of the instrument, beyond the face of the instrument, we must look for it not in the general convention, which proposed, but in the state conventions, which accepted and ratified the Constitution.

> Speech in Congress, April 6, 1796

So far is the political system of the United States distinguishable from that of other countries, by the caution which with powers are delegated and defined; that in one very important case, even of commercial regulation and revenue, the power is absolutely locked up against the hands of both governments. A tax on exports can be laid by no Constitutional Authority whatever.

"The Report of 1800," January 7, 1800

Serious danger seems to be threatened to the genuine sense of the Constitution, not only by an unwarrantable latitude of construction, but by the use made of precedents which can not be supposed to have had in the view of their authors, the bearings contended for, and even where they may have crept thro' inadvertence, into acts of congress, and been signed by the Executive at a midnight hour, in the midst of a group scarcely admitting persual, and under a weariness of mind a little admitting a vigilant attention. Another and perhaps a greater danger is to be apprehended for the influence which the usefulness and popularity of measures may have on questions of their constitutionality.

Letter to James Monroe, February 27, 1817

What is the most importance [in the decision of *McCulloch v. Maryland*] is the high sanction given to a latitude in expounding the Constitution which seems to break down the landmarks intended by a specification of the powers of Congress, and to substitute for a definite connection between means and ends, a Legislative discretion as to the former to which no practical limit can be assigned. In the great system of political economy having for its general object the national welfare, everything is related immediately or remotely to every other thing; and consequently a power over any one thing, if not limited by some obvious and precise affinity, may amount to a power over every other. Ends and means they shift their character at the will and according to the ingenuity of the Legislative Body.

... It could not but happen, and was foreseen at the birth of the Constitution, that difficulties and differences of opinion might occasionally arise and expounding terms and phrases, necessarily used in such a Charter, more especially those which divide legislation between the General and local Governments; and that it might require a regular course of practice, to liquidate and settle the meaning of some of them. But it was anticipated I believe by few if any of the friends of the Constitution, that a rule of construction would be introduced as Broad and as pliant as what has occurred.

Letter to Spencer Roane, September 2, 1819

I entirely concur in the propriety of restoring the sense in which the Constitution was accepted and ratified by the nation. In that sense alone it is a legitimate Constitution. And if that be not the guide in expounding it, there can be no security for a consistent and stable [government], more than for a faithful exercise of its powers. If the meaning of the text be sought in the changeable meaning of the words composing it, it is evident that the shape and attributes of the Government must partake of the changes to which the words and phrases of all living languages are constantly subject. What a metamorphosis would be produced in the code of law if all its ancient phraseology was to be taken in its modern sense. And that the language of our Constitution is already undergoing interpretations unknown to its founders, will I believe appear to all unbiassed and Enquireres into the history of its origin and adoption.

Letter to Henry Lee, June 25, 1824

CONSTITUTION, Ratification of.—Each State, in ratifying the Constitution, is considered as a sovereign body, independent of all others, and only to be bound by its own voluntary act. In this relation, then, the new Constitution will, if established, be a FEDERAL, and not a NATIONAL constitution.

Federalist No. 39, January 1788

CONSTITUTION, Signing of.—Whilst the last members were signing it Doctr. Franklin looking towards the President's chair, at the back of which a rising sun happened to be painted, observed to a few members near him, that Painters had found it difficult to distinguish in their art a rising from a setting sun.

Farrand's *The Records of the Federal Convention of 1787*, September 17, 1787

CONSTITUTION, The miracle of.—The great objects which presented themselves were 1. To unite a proper energy in the Executive and a proper stability in the Legislative departments, with the essential characters of Republican Government. 2. To draw a line of demarcation which would give to the General Government every power requisite for general purposes, and leave to the States every power which might be most beneficially administered by them. 3. To provide for the different parts of the union. 4. To adjust the clashing pretensions of the large and small states. Each of these objects was pregnant with difficulties. The whole of them together formed a task more difficult than can be well conceived by those who were not concerned in the execution of it. Adding to these considerations the natural diversity of human opinions on all new and complicated subjects, it is impossible to consider the degree of concord which ultimately prevailed as less than a miracle.

Letter to Thomas Jefferson, October 24, 1787

The diversity of opinions on so interesting a subject [the Constitution], among men of equal integrity and discernment, is at once a melancholy proof of fallibility of the human judgment, and of the imperfect progress yet made in the science of Government.

Letter to Archibald Stuart, October 24, 1787

The real wonder is that so many difficulties should have been surmounted [in the federal convention], and surmounted with a unanimity almost as unprecedented as it must have been unexpected. It is impossible for any man of candor to reflect on this circumstance without partaking of the astonishment. It is impossible for the man of pious reflection not to perceive in it a finger of that Almighty hand which has been so frequently and signally extended to our relief in the critical stages of the revolution.

Federalist No. 37, January 11, 1788

You ask me why I agreed to the Constitution proposed by the convention at Philadelphia? I answer, because I thought it safe to the liberties of the people, and the best that could be obtained from the jarring interests of States, and the miscellaneous opinions of Politicians; and because experience has proved that the real danger to America and to liberty lies in the defect of energy and stability in the present establishments of the United States.

Letter to Philip Mazzei, October 8, 1788

The happy union of these states is a wonder; their Constitution a miracle; their example the hope of liberty throughout the world. Woe to the ambition that initiates the destruction of either.

"Notes on the Federal Constitution," September 1829

The Constitution of the United States being established by a competent authority, by that of the sovereign people of the several states who were the parties to it; it remains only to enquire what the Constitution is; and here it speaks for itself: It organizes a Government into the usual Legislative, Executive and Judiciary Departments; invests it with specified powers, leaving others to the parties to the Constitution, it makes the Government like other Governments to operate directly on the people; it places at its command the needful physical means of executing its powers; and finally proclaims its supremacy and that of the laws made in pursuance of it, over the Constitution and laws of the States; the powers of the Government being exercised, as in other elective and responsible Governments, under control of its Constituents the people and the legislatures of the States; and subject to the Revolutionary rights of the people in extreme cases. Such is the Constitution of the United States de jure and de facto; and the name whatever it may be, that may be given to it, can make it nothing more or less than it actually is.

Letter to Daniel Webster, March 15, 1833

You give me a credit to which I have no claim in calling me 'the writer of the Constitution of the United States.' This was not, like the fabled Goddess of Wisdom, the offspring of a single brain. It ought to be regarded as the work of many heads and many hands.

Letter to William Cogswell, March 10, 1834

Whatever may be the judgment pronounced on the competency of the architects of the Constitution, or whatever may be the destiny of the edifice prepared by them, I feel it a duty to express my profound and solemn conviction . . . that there never was an assembly of men, charged with a great and arduous trust, who were more pure in their motives, or more exclusively or anxiously devoted to the object committed to them.

James Madison, circa 1835

Happily for America, happily, we trust, for the whole human race, they pursued a new and more noble course. They accomplished a revolution which has no parallel in the annals of human society.

Federalist No. 14, November 30, 1787

They accomplished a revolution which has no parallel in the annals of human society. They reared the fabrics of governments which have no model on the face of the globe. They formed the design of a great Confederacy, which it is incumbent on their successors to improve and perpetuate.

Federalist No. 14, November 30, 1787

Is it not the glory of the people of America, that whilst they have paid a decent regard to the opinions of former times and other nations, they have not suffered a blind veneration for antiquity, for custom, or for names, to overrule the suggestions of their own good sense, the knowledge of their own situation, and the lessons of their own experience? To this manly spirit, posterity will be indebted for the possession, and the world for the example of the numerous innovations displayed on the American theatre, in favor of private rights and public happiness.

Federalist No. 14, November 30, 1787

CONSTITUTIONAL CONVENTION(S).—The danger of disturbing the public tranquility by interesting too strongly the public passions is a still more serious objection against a frequent reference of constitutional questions, to the decision of the whole society... We are to recollect that all the existing constitutions were formed in the midst of a danger which repressed the passions most unfriendly to order and concord; of an enthusiastic confidence of the people in their patriotic leaders, which stifled the ordinary diversity of opinions on great national questions; of a universal ardor for new and opposite forms, produced by a universal resentment and indignation against the ancient government; and whilst no spirit of party, connected with the changes to be made, or the abuses to be reformed, could mingle its leaven in the operation. The future situations in which we must expect to be usually placed, do not present any equivalent security against the danger which is apprehended.

Federalist No. 49, February 2, 1788

CORPORATIONS.—There is an evil which ought to be guarded against in the indefinite accumulation of property from the capacity of holding it in perpetuity by ecclesiastical corporations. The power of all corporations, ought to be limited in this respect. The growing wealth acquired by them never fails to be a source of abuses.

Detached Memoranda, post-1817

Incorporated Companies, with proper limitations and guards, may in particular cases, be useful, but they are at best a necessary evil only. Monopolies and perpetuities are objects of just abhorrence. The former are unjust to the existing, the latter usurpations on the rights of future generations. Is it not strange that the law which will not permit an individual to bequeath his property to the descendants of his own loins for more than a short and strictly defined term, should authorize an associated few, to entail perpetual and indefeasible appropriations; and that, not only to objects visible and tangible, but to particular opinions, consisting, sometimes, of the most metaphysical niceties; as is the case of Ecclesiastical Corporations.

Letter to James K. Paulding, March 10, 1827

CREDIT.—The experience of European Merchants who have speculated in our trade will probably check in a great measure our opportunities of consuming beyond our resources; but they will continue to credit us as far as our coin in addition to our productions will extend, and our experience here teaches us that our people will extend their consumption as far as credit can be obtained.

Letter to James Monroe, April 9, 1786

DEATH.—Nothing more than a change of mind, my dear.

Madison's last words, June 28, 1836

DEBATE.—When I alluded to the proceedings of this day [in Congress], I contemplated the manner in which the business was conducted; and though I acknowledge that a majority ought to govern, yet they have no authority to deprive the minority of a constitutional right; they have no authority to debar us the right of free debate. An important and interesting question being under consideration, we ought to have time allowed for its discussion. Facts have been stated on one side, and members ought to be indulged on the other with an opportunity of collecting and ascertaining other facts. We have a right to bring forward all the arguments which we think can, and ought to have an influence on the decision.

Speech in Congress, September 3, 1789

He [Madison] was sorry that it almost always happened, whenever any question of general policy and advantage to the union was before the House, when gentlemen found themselves at a loss for general arguments, they commonly resorted to local views; and at all times as well as at present, when there was most occasion for members to act with the utmost coolness, when their judgments ought to be the least biassed—it was to be regretted that at those times they suffered their feelings, passions and prejudices to govern their reason. Thus it is that the most important points are embarrassed, the northern and southern interests are held up, every local circumstance comes into view, and every idea of liberality and candor is banished.

Speech in Congress, December 19, 1791

DECLARATION OF INDEPENDENCE.—On the distinctive principles of the Government . . . of the U. States, the best guides are to be found in . . . The Declaration of Independence, as the fundamental Act of Union of these States.

Letter to Thomas Jefferson, February 8, 1825

DEFICIT.—I think it would be a powerful and unanswerable objection against assuming the state debts at this time, that we did not see or are not prepared to decide on the means for providing them. There is not a more important and fundamental principle in legislation, than that the ways and means ought always to face the public engagements; that our appropriations should ever go hand-in-hand with our promises. To say that the United States should be answerable for twenty-five millions of dollars without knowing whether the ways and means can be provided, and without knowing whether those who are to succeed us will think with us on the subject, would be rash and unjustifiable. Sir, in my opinion, it would be hazarding the public faith in a manner contrary to every idea of prudence.

Speech in Congress, April 22, 1790

That the most productive system of finance will always be the least burdensome.

Federalist No. 39, January 18, 1788

DIET.—Horticulture is a valuable and interesting section of Agriculture, the main resource of human subsistence. Apart from the ornamental, the scientific, and experimental uses, which it may embrace, it affords a cheap and wholesome substitute for the disproportionate consumption of animal food, which has long been a habit of our Country, resulting from the exuberant supply it has enjoyed of this article. In promoting a reform of this habit, horticultural Societies can not fail of a happy tendency.

Letter to George Watterson, March 8, 1824

DIPLOMACY.—It is a nice task to speak of war, so as to impress our own people with a dislike of it, and not impress foreign Governments with the idea that they may take advantage of the dislike.

Letter to Thomas Jefferson, September 7, 1808

DISTRICT OF COLUMBIA.—If any state had the power of legislation over the place where congress should fix the general government; this would impair the dignity, and hazard the safety of congress. If the safety of the union were under the control of any particular state, would not foreign corruption probably prevail in such a state, to induce it to exert its controlling influence over the members of the general government?

Speech in Virginia Ratifying Convention, June 6, 1788

DIVINE INTERVENTION.—The real wonder is that so many difficulties should have been surmounted [in the federal convention], and surmounted with a unanimity almost as unprecedented as it must have been unexpected. It is impossible for any man of candor to reflect on this circumstance without partaking of the astonishment. It is impossible for the man of pious reflection not to perceive in it a finger of that Almighty hand which has been so frequently and signally extended to our relief in the critical stages of the revolution.

Federalist No. 37, January 11, 1788

DRUGS AND ALCOHOL.—A compleat suppression of every species of stimulating indulgence, if attainable at all, must be work of peculiar difficulty, since it has to encounter not only the force of habit, but a propensity in human nature. In every age and nation, some exhilarating or exciting substance seems to have been sought for, as a relief from the languor of idleness, or the fatigues of labor. In the rudest state of Society, whether in hot or cold climates, a passion for ardent spirit is in a manner universal. In the progress of refinement, beverages less intoxicating, but still of an exhilarating quality, have been more or less common. And where all these sources of excitement have been unknown, or been totally prohibited by a religious faith, substitutes have been found in opium, in the nut of the betel, the root of the Ginseng, or the leaf of the Tobacco plant. It would doubtless be a great point gained for our Country... if ardent spirits could be made only to give way to malt liquors, to those afforded by the apple and the pear, and to the lighter and cheaper varieties of wine. It is remarkable that in the Countries where the grape supplies the common beverage, habits of its of intoxication are rare; and in some places almost without example.

Letter to Thomas Hertell, December 20, 1819

EDUCATION.—If Congress can apply money indefinitely to the general welfare, and are the sole and supreme judges of the general welfare, they may take the care of religion into their own hands, they may establish teachers in every state, county, and parish and pay them out of the public treasury, they may take into their own hands the education of children, establishing in like manner schools throughout the union; they may assume the provision for the poor they may undertake the regulation of all roads other than post roads; in short, every thing, from the highest object of state legislation, down to the most minute object of police, would be thrown under the power of Congress; for every object I have mentioned would admit the application of money, and might be called, if Congress pleased, provisions for the general welfare.

Speech in Congress, February 6, 1792

Whilst it is universally admitted that a well instructed people alone, can be permanently a free people; and whilst it is evident that the means of diffusing and improving useful knowledge, form so small a proportion of the expenditures for national purposes, I cannot presume it to be unseasonable, to invite your attention to the advantages of superadding, to the means of Education provided by the several States, a Seminary of Learning, instituted by the national Legislature, within the limits of their exclusive jurisdiction; the expence of which might be defrayed, or reimbursed, out of the vacant grounds which have accrued to the Nation, within those limits. Such an Institution, tho' local in its legal character, would be universal in its beneficial effects. By enlightening the opinions, by expanding the patriotism; and by assimilating the principles, the sentiments and the manners of those who might resort to this Temple of Science, to be redistributed, in due time, through every part of the community; sources of jealousy and prejudice would be diminished, the features of national character would be multiplied, and greater extent given to Social harmony. But above all, a well constituted Seminary, in the center of the nation, is recommended by the consideration, that the additional instruction emanating from it, would contribute not less to strengthen the foundations, than to adorn the structure, of our free and happy system of Government.

        Annual Message to Congress, December 5, 1810

Learned Institutions ought to be favorite objects with every free people. They throw that light over the public mind which is the best security against crafty and dangerous encroachments on the public liberty. They are nurseries of skillful Teachers for the schools distributed throughout the Community. They are themselves Schools for the particular talents required for some of the public Trusts, on the able execution of which the welfare of the people depends. They multiply the educated individuals from among whom the people may elect a due portion of their public agents of every description; more especially of those who are to frame the laws; by the perspicuity, the consistency, and the stability, as well as by the just and equal spirit of which the great social purposes are to be answered.... What spectacle can be more edifying or more seasonable, than that of Liberty and Learning, each leaning on the other for their mutual and surest support?

        Letter to William T. Barry, August 4, 1822

Your old friend Mr. Jefferson still lives, and will close his illustrious career, by bequeathing to his Country a Magnificent Institute for the advancement and diffusion of Knowledge, which is the only Guardian of true liberty, the great cause to which his life has been devoted.

        Letter to George Thomas, June 30, 1825

I congratulate you on the foundation thus laid for a general System of Education, and hope it presages a superstructure, worthy of the patriotic forecast which has commenced the Work. The best service that can be rendered to a Country, next to that of giving it liberty, is in diffusing the mental improvement equally essential to the preservation, and the enjoyment of the blessing.

> Letter to Littleton Dennis Teackle, March 29, 1826

No feature in the aspect of our Country is more gratifying, than the increases and variety of Institutions for educating the several ages and classes of the rising generation, and the meritorious patriotism which improving on their most improved forms extends the benefit of them to the sex heretofore, sharing too little of it. Considered as at once the fruits of our free System of Government, and the true means of sustaining and recommending it, such establishments are entitled to the best praise that can be offered.

> Letter to Gulian C. Verplanck, February 14, 1828

ELECTIONS.—An auxiliary desideratum for the melioration of the Republican form is such a process of elections as will most certainly extract from the mass of the Society the purest and noblest characters which it contains; such as will at once feel most strongly the proper motives to pursue the end of their appointment, and be most capable to devise the proper means of attaining it.

> "Vices of the Political System of the United States," April 1787

I go on this great republican principle, that the people will have virtue and intelligence to select men of virtue and wisdom. Is there no virtue among us? If there be not, we are in a wretched situation. No theoretical checks—no form of government can render us secure. To suppose that any form of government will secure liberty or happiness without any virtue in the people, is a chimerical idea, if there be sufficient virtue and intelligence in the community, it will be exercised in the selection of these men. So that we do not depend on their virtue, or put confidence in our rulers, but in the people who are to choose them.

The Debates in the Several State Conventions on the Adoption of the Federal Constitution, vol 3, pp. 536-37

I am now pressed by some of my friends to repair to Virginia as a requisite expedient for counteracting the machinations against my election into the House of Representatives. To this again I am extremely disinclined for reasons additional to the one above mentioned. It will have an electioneering appearance which I always despised and wish to shun.

Letter to Edmund Randolph, November 23, 1788

In the election of Delegates to the Legislature for the ensuing year (1777), he was an unsuccessful candidate. Previous to the Revolution the election of the Country Representatives, was as in England, septennial, and it was as there the usage for the Candidates to recommend themselves to the voters, not only by personal solicitation, but by the corrupting influence of spirituous liquors, and other treats, having a like tendency. Regarding these as equally inconsistent with the purity of moral and of republican principles; and anxious to promote, by his example, the proper reform, he trusted to the new views of the subject which he hoped would prevail with the people; whilst his competitors adhered to the old practice. The consequence was that the election went against him; his abstinence being represented as the effect of pride or parsimony.

Madison's Autobiography, 1831

EQUALITY.—Equal laws protecting equal rights—the best guarantee of loyalty and love of country.

Letter to Jacob de la Motta, August 1820

EXECUTIVE BRANCH.—The constitution supposes, what the History of all Governments demonstrates, that the Executive is the branch of power most interested in war, and most prone to it.

> Letter to Thomas Jefferson, April 2, 1798

[T]o exclude foreign intrigues and foreign partialities, so degrading to all countries and so baneful to free ones; to foster a spirit of independence too just to invade the rights of others, too proud to surrender our own, too liberal to indulge unworthy prejudices ourselves and too elevated not to look down upon them in others; to hold the union of the States on the basis of their peace and happiness; to support the Constitution, which is the cement of the Union, as well in its limitations as in its authorities; to respect the rights and authorities reserved to the States and to the people as equally incorporated with and essential to the success of the general . . . as far as sentiments and intentions such as these can aid the fulfillment of my duty, they will be a resource which can not fail me.

> Second Inaugural Address, March, 1813

I cannot feel all the alarm you express at the prospect for the future, as reflected from the mirror of the past. It will be a rare case that the Presidential contest will not issue in a choice that will not discredit the Station, and not be acquiesced in by the unsuccessful party, foreseeing as it must do, the appeal to be again made at no very distant day, to the will of the nation. As long as the Country shall be exempt from a Military force powerful in itself, and combined with a powerful faction, liberty and peace will find safeguards in the Elective resource, and spirit of the people.

> Letter to James Hillhouse, May 17, 1830

FACTIONS.—The latent causes of faction are thus sown in the nature of man; and we see them every where brought into different degrees of activity, according to the different circumstances of civil society. A zeal for different opinions concerning religion, concerning government, and many other points, as well of speculation as of practice; an attachment to different leaders ambitiously contending; for pre-eminence and power; or to persons of other descriptions whose fortunes have been interesting to the human passions, have in turn divided mankind into parties, inflamed them with mutual animosity, and rendered them much more disposed to vex and oppress each other, than to co-operate for their common good.

The Federalist Nos. 10 and 22, November, 1787

Within the local limits, parties generally exist, founded on the different sorts of property, even sometimes on division by streets or little streams; frequently on political and religious differences. Attachments to rival individuals, are not seldom a source of the same divisions. In all these cases, the party animosities are the more violent as the compass of the Society may more easily admit of the contagion and collision of the passions; and according to that violence is the danger of oppression by one party on the other; by the majority on the minority.

Detached Memoranda, post-1817

In a society under the forms of which the stronger faction can readily unite and oppress the weaker, anarchy may as truly be said to reign as in a state of nature.

Federalist No. 52, February 8, 1788

FEDERAL GOVERNMENT, Powers and limitations of.—In the first place, it is to be remembered, that the general government is not to be charged with the whole power of making and administering laws: its jurisdiction is limited to certain enumerated objects, which concern all the members of the republic, but which are not to be attained by the separate provisions of any.

Federalist No. 14, November 30, 1787

Each State, in ratifying the Constitution, is considered as a sovereign body, independent of all others, and only to be bound by its own voluntary act. In this relation, then, the new Constitution will, if established, be a FEDERAL, and not a NATIONAL constitution.

Federalist No. 39, January 1788

The powers delegated by the proposed Constitution to the federal government are few and defined. Those which are to remain in the State governments are numerous and indefinite.

Federalist No. 45, January 26, 1788

The operations of the federal government will be most extensive and important in times of war and danger; those of the State governments, in times of peace and security.

Federalist No. 45, January 26, 1788

The accumulation of all powers, legislative, executive, and judiciary, in the same hands, whether of one, a few, or many, and whether hereditary, self-appointed, or elective, may justly be pronounced the very definition of tyranny.

Federalist No. 47, January 30, 1788

I do not conceive that power is given to the President and Senate to dismember the empire, or to alienate any great, essential right.

I do not think the whole legislative authority have this power. The exercise of the power must be consistent with the object of the delegation.

> Debate in Virginia Ratifying Convention,
> Elliot 3:499-515. June 18, 1788

I consider it . . . as subverting the fundamental and characteristic principle of the Government . . . and as bidding defiance to the sense in which the Constitution is known to have been proposed, advocated, and adopted. If Congress can do whatever in their discretion can be done by money, and will promote the General Welfare, the Government is no longer a limited one.

> Letter to Edmund Pendleton, January 21, 1792

I cannot undertake to lay my finger on that article of the Constitution which granted a right to Congress of expending, on the objects of benevolence, the money of their constituents.

> James Madison, 1794

[T]he government of the United States is a definite government, confined to specified objects. It is not like the state governments, whose powers are more general. Charity is no part of the legislative duty of the government.

> Speech in the House of Representatives, January 10, 1794

That this Assembly doth explicitly and peremptorily declare, that it views the powers of the federal government, as resulting from the compact, to which the states are parties; as limited by the plain sense and intention of the instrument constituting the compact; as no further valid than they are authorized by the grants enumerated in that compact; and that in case of a deliberate, palpable, and dangerous exercise of other powers, not granted by the said compact, the states who are parties thereto, have the right, and are in duty bound, to interpose for arresting the progress of the evil, and for maintaining within their respective limits, the authorities, rights and liberties appertaining to them.

Virginia Resolutions, December 24, 1798

FEDERAL LANDS.—You request an answer at length to the claim of the new States to the Federal lands within their limits.... I have always viewed the claim as so unfair & unjust, so contrary to the certain & notorious intentions of the parties to the case, and so directly in the teeth of the condition in which the lands were ceded to the Union, that if a technical title could be made out by the claimants, it ought in Conscience & honour to be waived. But the title in the people of the U. S. rests on a foundation too just & solid to be shaken by any technical or metaphysical arguments whatever. The Known and acknowledged intentions of the parties at the time, with a prescriptive sanction of so many years, consecrated by the intrinsic principle of equity, would over-rule even the most explicit terms; as has been done, without the aid of that principle, in the case of the slaves who remain such in spight of the express declarations that all men are born equally free.

Letter to Edward Coles, June 28, 1831

FEDERALISM.—In the American Constitution The general authority will be derived entirely from the subordinate authorities. The Senate will represent the States in their political capacity; the other House will represent the people of the States in their individual capacity. The former will be accountable to their constituents at moderate, the latter at short periods. The President also derives his appointment from the states, and is periodically accountable to them. This dependence of the General, on the local authorities, seems effectually to guard the latter against any dangerous encroachments of the former: Whilst the latter, within their respective limits, will be continually sensible of the abridgment of their power, and be stimulated by ambition to resume the surrendered portion of it. We find the representatives of Counties and corporations in the Legislatures of the States, much more disposed to sacrifice the aggregate interest, and even authority, to the local views of their Constituents: than the latter to the former. I mean not by these remarks to insinuate that an esprit de corps will not exist in the national Government or that opportunities may not occur, of extending its jurisdiction in some points. I mean only that the danger of encroachments is much greater from the other side, and that the impossibility of dividing powers of legislation, in such a manner, as to be free from, different constructions by different interests, or even from ambiguity in the judgment of the impartial, requires some such expedient as I contend for.

Letter to Thomas Jefferson, October 24, 1787

That this Assembly doth explicitly and peremptorily declare, that it views the powers of the federal government, as resulting from the compact to which the states are parties; as limited by the plain sense and intention of the instrument constituting that compact; as no farther valid than they are authorised by the grants enumerated in that compact, and that in case of a deliberate, palpable and dangerous exercise of other powers not granted by the said compact, the states who are parties thereto have the right, and are in duty bound, to interpose for arresting the progress of the evil, and for maintaining within their respective limits, the authorities, rights and liberties appertaining to them.

Virginia Resolutions, December 24, 1798

My prolonged life has made me a witness of the alternate popularity, and unpopularity of each of the great branches of the Federal Government. I have witnessed, also, the vicissitudes, in the apparent tendencies in the Federal and State Governments, to encroach each on the authorities of the other, without being able to infer with certainty, what would be the final operation of the causes as heretofore existing; whilst it is far more difficult to calculate, the mingled and checkered influences, on the future from an expanding territorial Domain: from the multiplication of the parties to the Union, from the great and growing power of not a few of them, from the absence of external danger; from combinations of states in some quarters, and collisions in others, and from questions, incident to a refusal of the unsuccessful party to abide by the issue of controversies judiciously decided. To these uncertainties, may be added, the effects of a dense population and the multiplication, and the varying relations of the classes composing it. I am far however from desponding of the great political experiment in the hands of the American people.

> Letter to an unidentified correspondent,
> March 1836

FOREIGN AFFAIRS.—The means of defense against foreign danger historically have become the instruments of tyranny at home.

> Speech at the Constitutional Convention,
> June 29, 1787

The management of foreign relations appears to be the most susceptible of abuse of all the trusts committed to a Government, because they can be concealed or disclosed, or disclosed in such parts and at such times as will best suit particular views; and because the body of the people are less capable of judging, and are more under the influence of prejudices, on that branch of their affairs, than of any other. Perhaps it is a universal truth that the loss of liberty at home is to be charged to provisions against danger, real or pretended, from abroad.

> Letter to Thomas Jefferson, 1798

GOVERNMENT, Abuses of.— Enlightened statesmen will not always be at the helm.

Federalist No. 10, November 23, 1787

The apportionment of taxes on the various descriptions of property is an act which seems to require the most exact impartiality; yet there is, perhaps, no legislative act in which greater opportunity and temptation are given to a predominant party to trample on the rules of justice. Every shilling which they overburden the inferior number is a shilling saved to their own pockets.

Federalist No. 10, November 23, 1787

It may be a reflection on human nature that such devices [as Constitutional limits on power] should be necessary to control the abuses of government. But what is government itself but the greatest of all reflections on human nature? . . . If angels were to govern men, neither external nor internal controls on government would be necessary. [But lacking these] in framing a government which is to be administered by men over men, the great difficulty lies in this: You must first enable the government to control the governed; and in the next place oblige it to control itself.

Federalist No. 51, February 8, 1788

Wherever the real power in a Government lies, there is the danger of oppression.

Letter to Thomas Jefferson, October 17, 1788

There is not a more important and fundamental principle in legislation, than that the ways and means ought always to face the public engagements; that our appropriations should ever go hand in hand with our promises. To say that the United States should be answerable for twenty-five millions of dollars without knowing whether the ways and means can be provided, and without knowing whether those who are to succeed us will think with us on the subject, would be rash and unjustifiable. Sir, in my opinion, it would be hazarding the public faith in a manner contrary to every idea of prudence.

Speech in Congress, April 22, 1790

Where an excess of power prevails, property of no sort is duly respected. No man is safe in his opinions, his person, his faculties, or his possessions.

National Gazette essay, March 27, 1792

The management of foreign relations appears to be the most susceptible of abuse of all the trusts committed to a Government, because they can be concealed or disclosed, or disclosed in such parts and at such times as will best suit particular views; and because the body of the people are less capable of judging, and are more under the influence of prejudices, on that branch of their affairs, than of any other. Perhaps it is a universal truth that the loss of liberty at home is to be charged to provisions against danger, real or pretended, from abroad.

Letter to Thomas Jefferson, 1798

The essence of Government is power; and power, lodged as it must be in human hands, will ever be liable to abuse.

Speech in the Virginia constitutional convention, December 2, 1829

It has been said that all Government is an evil. It would be more proper to say that the necessity of any Government is a misfortune. This necessity however exists; and the problem to be solved is, not what form of Government is perfect, but which of the forms is least imperfect.

Letter to an unidentified correspondent, 1833

GOVERNMENT, Criticism of.—It must be seen that no two principles can be either more indefensible in reason, or more dangerous in practice—than that 1. arbitrary denunciation may punish, what the law permits, & what the Legislature has no right, by law, to prohibit—and that 2. the Government may stifle all censures whatever on its misdoings; for if it be itself the Judge it will never allow any censors to be just, and if it can suppress censures flowing from one lawful source, it may those flowing from any other—from the press and from individuals as well as from Societies.

Letter to James Monroe, December 4, 1794

GOVERNMENT, Distrust of.—Complaints are every where heard from our most considerate and virtuous citizens, equally the friends of public and private faith, and of public and personal liberty; that our governments are too unstable; that the public good is disregarded in the conflicts of rival parties; and that measures are too often decided, not according to the rules of justice, and the rights of the minor party; but by the superior force of an interested and overbearing majority. . . . It will be found indeed, on a candid review of our situation, that some of the distresses under which we labour, have been erroneously charged on the operation of our governments; but it will be found at the same time, that other causes will not alone account for many of our heaviest misfortunes; and particularly, for that prevailing and increasing distrust of public engagements, and alarm for private rights, which are echoed from one end of the continent to the other. These must be chiefly, if not wholly, effects of the unsteadiness and injustice, with which a factious spirit has tainted our public administration.

Federalist No. 10, November 22, 1787

The house of representatives . . . can make no law which will not have its full operation on themselves and their friends, as well as the great mass of society. This has always been deemed one of the strongest bonds by which human policy can connect the rulers and the people together. It creates between them that communion of interest, and sympathy of sentiments, of which few governments have furnished examples; but without which every government degenerates into tyranny.

Federalist No. 57, February 19, 1788

Nothing is so contagious as opinion, especially on questions which, being susceptible of very different glosses, beget in the mind a distrust of itself.

Letter to Benjamin Rush, March 7, 1790

GOVERNMENT, Encroachment of.—It is proper to take alarm at the first experiment on our liberties. We hold this prudent jealousy to be the first duty of citizens and one of the noblest characteristics of the late Revolution. The freemen of America did not wait till usurped power had strengthened itself by exercise and entangled the question in precedents.

"Memorial and Remonstrance Against Religious Assessments," June 20, 1785

The great desideratum in Government is, so to modify the sovereignty as that it may be sufficiently neutral between different parts of the Society to control one part from invading the rights of another, and at the same time sufficiently controlled itself, from setting up an interest adverse to that of the entire Society.

Letter to Thomas Jefferson, October 24, 1787

What is to be the consequence, in case the Congress shall misconstrue this part [the necessary and proper clause] of the Constitution and exercise powers not warranted by its true meaning, I answer the same as if they should misconstrue or enlarge any other power vested in them. . . . The success of the usurpation will depend on the executive and judiciary departments, which are to expound and give effect to the legislative acts; and in a last resort a remedy must be obtained from the people, who can by the elections of more faithful representatives, annul the acts of the usurpers.

Federalist No. 44, January 25, 1788

Resuming the subject of the last paper, I proceed to inquire whether the federal government or the State governments will have the advantage with regard to the predilection and support of the people. Notwithstanding the different modes in which they are appointed, we must consider both of them as substantially dependent on the great body of the citizens of the United States. I assume this position here as it respects the first, reserving the proofs for another place. The federal and State governments are in fact but different agents and trustees of the people, constituted with different powers, and designed for different purposes. The adversaries of the Constitution seem to have lost sight of the people altogether in their reasonings on this subject; and to have viewed these different establishments, not only as mutual rivals and enemies, but as uncontrolled by any common superior in their efforts to usurp the authorities of each other. These gentlemen must here be reminded of their error. They must be told that the ultimate authority, wherever the derivative may be found, resides in the people alone, and that it will not depend merely on the comparative ambition or address of the different governments, whether either, or which of them, will be able to enlarge its sphere of jurisdiction at the expense of the other.

Federalist No. 46, January 29, 1788

The passions, therefore, not the reason, of the public would sit in judgment. But it is the reason, alone, of the public, that ought to control and regulate the government. The passions ought to be controlled and regulated by the government.

Federalist No. 49, February 5, 1788

If men were angels, no government would be necessary. If angels were to govern men, neither external nor internal controls on government would be necessary. In framing a government which is to be administered by men over men, the great difficulty lies in this: you must first enable the government to control the governed; and in the next place, oblige it to control itself.

Federalist No. 51, February 8, 1788

Since the general civilization of mankind, I believe there are more instances of the abridgment of the freedom of the people by gradual and silent encroachments of those in power, than by violent and sudden usurpations; but, on a candid examination of history, we shall find that turbulence, violence, and abuse of power, by the majority trampling on the rights of the minority, have produced factions and commotions, which, in republics, have, more frequently than any other cause, produced despotism. If we go over the whole history of ancient and modern republics, we shall find their destruction to have generally resulted from those causes.

Speech at the Virginia Ratifying Convention, June 6, 1788

[T]he great security against a gradual concentration of the several powers in the same department consists in giving to those who administer each department the necessary constitutional means and personal motives to resist encroachment of the others.

Federalist No. 10, November 23, 1787

We are teaching the world the great truth that Governments do better without Kings & Nobles than with them. The merit will be doubled by the other lesson that Religion Flourishes in greater purity, without than with the aid of Government.

Letter to Edward Livingston, July 10, 1822

GOVERNMENT, Integrity of.—There is not a more important and fundamental principle in legislation, than that the ways and means ought always to face the public engagements; that our appropriations should ever go hand in hand with our promises. To say that the United States should be answerable for twenty-five millions of dollars without knowing whether the ways and means can be provided, and without knowing whether those who are to succeed us will think with us on the subject, would be rash and unjustifiable. Sir, in my opinion, it would be hazarding the public faith in a manner contrary to every idea of prudence.

Speech in Congress, April 22, 1790

[T]o exclude foreign intrigues and foreign partialities, so degrading to all countries and so baneful to free ones; to foster a spirit of independence too just to invade the rights of others, too proud to surrender our own, too liberal to indulge unworthy prejudices ourselves and too elevated not to look down upon them in others; to hold the union of the States on the basis of their peace and happiness; to support the Constitution, which is the cement of the Union, as well in its limitations as in its authorities; to respect the rights and authorities reserved to the States and to the people as equally incorporated with and essential to the success of the general . . . as far as sentiments and intentions such as these can aid the fulfillment of my duty, they will be a resource which can not fail me.

Second Inaugural Address, March, 1813

GOVERNMENT, Purpose of.—The great desideratum in Government is, so to modify the sovereignty as that it may be sufficiently neutral between different parts of the Society to control one part from invading the rights of another, and at the same time sufficiently controlled itself, from setting up an interest adverse to that of the entire Society.

Letter to Thomas Jefferson, October 24, 1787

The diversity in the faculties of men from which the rights of property originate, is not less an insuperable obstacle to a uniformity of interests. The protection of these faculties is the first object of government.

Federalist No. 10, November 23, 1787

In the first place, it is to be remembered, that the general government is not to be charged with the whole power of making and administering laws: its jurisdiction is limited to certain enumerated objects, which concern all the members of the republic, but which are not to be attained by the separate provisions of any.

Federalist No. 14, November 30, 1787

It is too early for politicians to presume on our forgetting that the public good, the real welfare of the great body of the people, is the supreme object to be pursued; and that no form of government whatever has any other value than as it may be fitted for the attainment of this object.

Federalist No. 45, January 26, 1788

Energy in government is essential to that security against external and internal danger and to that prompt and salutary execution of the laws which enter into the very definition of good government. Stability in government is essential to national character and to the advantages annexed to it, as well as to that repose and confidence in the minds of the people, which are among the chief blessings of civil society.

Federalist No. 37, January 11, 1788

Justice is the end of government. It is the end of civil society. It ever has been and ever will be pursued until it be obtained, or until liberty be lost in the pursuit.

Federalist No. 51, February 8, 1788

If individuals be not influenced by moral principles; it is in vain to look for public virtue; it is, therefore, the duty of legislators to enforce, both by precept and example, the utility, as well as the necessity of a strict adherence to the rules of distributive justice.

In response to Washington's first
Inaugural address, May 18, 1789

[T]he government of the United States is a definite government, confined to specified objects. It is not like the state governments, whose powers are more general. Charity is no part of the legislative duty of the government.

Speech in the House of Representatives,
January 10, 1794

Government is instituted to protect property of every sort. . . . This being the end of government, that alone is a *just* government which *impartially* secures to every man, whatever is his *own*. . . . That is not a just government, nor is property secure under it, where the property which a man has in his personal safety and personal liberty is violated by arbitrary seizures of one class of citizens for the service of the rest. [Emphasis in original.]

"Property" Essay, March 29, 1792

It is sufficiently obvious, that persons and property are the two great subjects on which Governments are to act; and that the rights of persons, and the rights of property, are the objects, for the protection of which Government was instituted. These rights cannot well be separated.

> Speech at the Virginia Constitutional Convention, December 2, 1829

GOVERNMENT SPENDING.—There is not a more important and fundamental principle in legislation, than that the ways and means ought always to face the public engagements; that our appropriations should ever go hand in hand with our promises. To say that the United States should be answerable for twenty-five millions of dollars without knowing whether the ways and means can be provided, and without knowing whether those who are to succeed us will think with us on the subject, would be rash and unjustifiable. Sir, in my opinion, it would be hazarding the public faith in a manner contrary to every idea of prudence.

> Speech in Congress, April 22, 1790

JEFFERSON, THOMAS.—[He] will live in the memory and gratitude of the wise & good, as a luminary of Science, as a votary of liberty, as a model of patriotism, and as a benefactor of human kind.

> Letter to Nicholas P. Trist, July 6, 1826

He was certainly one of the most learned men of the age. It may be said of him as has been said of others that he was a "walking Library," and what can be said of but few such prodigies, that the Genius of Philosophy ever walked hand in hand with him.

> Letter to Samuel Harrison Smith, November 4, 1826

JUDICIARY.—As the courts are generally the last in making the decision, it results to them, by refusing or not refusing to execute a law, to stamp it with its final character. This makes the Judiciary department paramount in fact to the Legislature, which was never intended, and can never be proper.

Observations on Thomas Jefferson's Draft of a Constitution for Virginia, October 15, 1788

I acknowledge, in the ordinary course of government, that the exposition of the laws and Constitution devolves upon the judicial. But I beg to know upon what principle it can be contended that any one department draws from the Constitution greater powers than another in marking out the limits of the powers of the several departments.

Speech in the Congress of the United States, June 17, 1789

JUSTICE.—No man is allowed to be a judge in his own cause, because his interest would certainly bias his judgment, and, not improbably, corrupt his integrity.

Federalist No. 10, November 23, 1787

LAWS.—Every new regulation concerning commerce or revenue; or in any manner affecting the value of the different species of property, presents a new harvest to those who watch the change and can trace its consequences; a harvest reared not by themselves but by the toils and cares of the great body of their fellow citizens. This is a state of things in which it may be said with some truth that laws are made for the few not for the many.

Federalist No. 62, February 27, 1788

LEGISLATIVE DEPARTMENT.—The legislative department

is everywhere extending the sphere of its activity and drawing all power into its impetuous vortex.

Federalist No. 48, February 1, 1788

The members of the legislative department . . . are numerous. They are distributed and dwell among the people at large. Their connections of blood, of friendship, and of acquaintance embrace a great proportion of the most influential part of the society . . . they are more immediately the confidential guardians of their rights and liberties.

Federalist No. 50, February 5, 1788

Such an institution may be sometimes necessary as a defense to the people against their own temporary errors and delusions.

Federalist No. 63, March 1, 1788

LEISURE.—Let me recommend the best medicine in the world: a long journey, at a mild season, thro' a pleasant Country, in easy stages.

Letter to Horatio Gates, February 23, 1794

LIBERTY.—Justice is the end of government. It is the end of civil society. It ever has been and ever will be pursued until it be obtained, or until liberty be lost in the pursuit.

Federalist No. 51, February 8, 1788

What spectacle can be more edifying or more seasonable, than that of Liberty and Learning, each leaning on the other for their mutual & surest support?

Letter to W.T. Barry, August 4, 1822

MAJORITY, Power of.—There is no maxim in my opinion which is more liable to be misapplied, and which therefore needs elucidation than the current one that the interest of the majority is the political standard of right and wrong. . . . In fact it is only reestablishing under another name and a more specious form, force as the measure of right.

Letter to James Monroe, October 5, 1786

If we resort for a criterion to the different principles on which different forms of government are established, we may define a republic to be, or at least may bestow that name on, a government which derives all its powers directly or indirectly from the great body of the people, and is administered by persons holding their offices during pleasure for a limited period, or during good behavior.

Federalist No. 39, January 18, 1788

Nothing is so contagious as opinion, especially on questions which, being susceptible of very different glosses, beget in the mind a distrust of itself.

Letter to Benjamin Rush, March 7, 1790

MONARCHY.—We have heard of the impious doctrine in the old world, that the people were made for kings, not kings for the people. Is the same doctrine to be revived in the new, in another shape—that the solid happiness of the people is to be sacrificed to the views of political institutions of a different form? It is too early for politicians to presume on our forgetting that the public good, the real welfare of the great body of the people, is the supreme object to be pursued; and that no form of government whatever has any other value than as it may be fitted for the attainment of this object.

Federalist No. 45, January 26, 1788

We are teaching the world the great truth that Governments do better without Kings & Nobles than with them. The merit will be doubled by the other lesson that Religion Flourishes in greater purity, without than with the aid of Government.

> Letter to Edward Livingston, July 10, 1822

NULLIFICATION.—It becomes all therefore who are friends of a Government based on free principles to reflect, that by denying the possibility of a system partly federal and partly consolidated, and who would convert ours into one either wholly federal or wholly consolidated, in neither of which forms have individual rights, public order, and external safety, been all duly maintained, they aim a deadly blow at the last hope of true liberty on the face of the Earth.

> "Notes on Nullification," 1835

OFFICE, Appointment to.—In forming the Senate, the great anchor of the Government, the questions as they came within the first object turned mostly on the mode of appointment, and the duration of it.

> Letter to Thomas Jefferson, October 24, 1787

The appointment to offices is, of all the functions of Republican and perhaps every other form of government, the most difficult to guard against abuse. Give it to a numerous body, and you at once destroy all responsibility, and create a perpetual source of faction and corruption. Give it to the Executive wholly, and it may be made an engine of improper influence and favoritism.

> *Observations on Thomas Jefferson's Draft of a Constitution for Virginia*, October 15, 1788

The dispension to office, tho' among the most important, is likewise among the most simple of public duties. One solitary principle governs every case: 'That the man appointed to an office shall be irreproachable in point of morality, and in other respects well qualified to discharge its duties with credit to himself and advantage to his country.' The most ordinary capacity may comprehend the principle, and know what should be done. Talents of the more elevated kind are only requisite to enable those trustees of this portion of the public confidence, in the range of faculties, and judiciously to distinguish between men, and to select those best suited for the stations to which they shall be destined. To apply, in short, the most expedient means for the attainment of given ends. If appointments, from the highest to the lowest grade, will bear the test of enquiry by this criterion, those who confer them may rest contented: they have nothing to apprehend from the reproach of their own consciences, or the censure of the public.

For Dunlap's American Daily Advertiser, October 20, 1792

PATRIOTISM.—Every man who loves peace, every man who loves his country, every man who loves liberty ought to have it ever before his eyes that he may cherish in his heart a due attachment to the Union of America and be able to set a due value on the means of preserving it.

Federalist No. 41, January 1788

PEACE.—The operations of the federal government will be most extensive and important in times of war and danger; those of the State governments, in times of peace and security.

Federalist No. 45, January 26, 1788

It is a principle incorporated into the settled policy of America, that as peace is better than war, war is better than tribute.

Letter to the Dey of Algiers, August, 1816

PEOPLE, Arming of.—Besides, the advantage of being armed forms a barrier against the enterprises of ambition, more insurmountable than any which a simple government of any form can admit of. The governments of Europe are afraid to trust the people with arms. If they did, the people would certainly shake off the yoke of tyranny, as America did.

Federalist No. 46, January 29, 1788

Besides the advantage of being armed, which the Americans possess over the people of almost every other nation. . . . Notwithstanding the military establishments in the several kingdoms of Europe, which are carried as far as the public resources will bear, the governments are afraid to trust the people with arms.

Federalist No. 46, January 29, 1788

PEOPLE, Government responsibility to.—Energy in government is essential to that security against external and internal danger and to that prompt and salutary execution of the laws which enter into the very definition of good government. Stability in government is essential to national character and to the advantages annexed to it, as well as to that repose and confidence in the minds of the people, which are among the chief blessings of civil society.

Federalist No. 37, January 11, 1788

We have heard of the impious doctrine in the old world, that the people were made for kings, not kings for the people. Is the same doctrine to be revived in the new, in another shape—that the solid happiness of the people is to be sacrificed to the views of political institutions of a different form? It is too early for politicians to presume on our forgetting that the public good, the real welfare of the great body of the people, is the supreme object to be pursued; and that no form of government whatever has any other value than as it may be fitted for the attainment of this object.

Federalist No. 45, January 26, 1788

Such will be the relation between the House of Representatives and their constituents. Duty, gratitude, interest, ambition itself, are the cords by which they will be bound to fidelity and sympathy with the great mass of the people.

Federalist No. 57, February 19, 1788

PEOPLE, Privacy of.—The invasion of private rights is chiefly to be apprehended, not from acts of Government contrary to the sense of its constituents, but from acts in which the Government is the mere instrument of the major number of the Constituents.

Letter to Thomas Jefferson, October 17, 1788

PEOPLE, Rights of.—The diversity in the faculties of men from which the rights of property originate, is not less an insuperable obstacle to a uniformity of interests. The protection of these faculties is the first object of government.

Federalist No. 10, November 23, 1787

Every new regulation concerning commerce or revenue; or in any manner affecting the value of the different species of property, presents a new harvest to those who watch the change and can trace its consequences; a harvest reared not by themselves but by the toils and cares of the great body of their fellow citizens. This is a state of things in which it may be said with some truth that laws are made for the few not for the many.

Federalist No. 62, February 27, 1788

The right of freely examining public characters and measures, and of free communication among the people thereon . . . has ever been justly deemed the only effectual guardian of every other right.

Virginia Resolutions, December 24, 1798

It is sufficiently obvious, that persons and property are the two great subjects on which Governments are to act; and that the rights of persons, and the rights of property, are the objects, for the protection of which Government was instituted. These rights cannot well be separated.

Speech at the Virginia Constitutional Convention, December 2, 1829

PEOPLE, Virtue and intelligence of.—Is it not the glory of the people of America, that whilst they have paid a decent regard to the opinions of former times and other nations, they have not suffered a blind veneration for antiquity, for custom, or for names, to overrule the suggestions of their own good sense, the knowledge of their own situation, and the lessons of their own experience? To this manly spirit, posterity will be indebted for the possession, and the world for the example of the numerous innovations displayed on the American theatre, in favor of private rights and public happiness.

Federalist No. 14, November 30, 1787

If we resort for a criterion to the different principles on which different forms of government are established, we may define a republic to be, or at least may bestow that name on, a government which derives all its powers directly or indirectly from the great body of the people, and is administered by persons holding their offices during pleasure for a limited period, or during good behavior.

Federalist No. 39, January 18, 1788

Every man who loves peace, every man who loves his country, every man who loves liberty ought to have it ever before his eyes that he may cherish in his heart a due attachment to the Union of America and be able to set a due value on the means of preserving it.

Federalist No. 41, January 19, 1788

If individuals be not influenced by moral principles; it is in vain to look for public virtue; it is, therefore, the duty of legislators to enforce, both by precept and example, the utility, as well as the necessity of a strict adherence to the rules of distributive justice.

In response to Washington's first Inaugural address, May 18, 1789

Public opinion sets bounds to every government, and is the real sovereign in every free one.

"Public Opinion" Essay December 19, 1791

I go on this great republican principle, that the people will have virtue and intelligence to select men of virtue and wisdom. Is there no virtue among us? If there be not, we are in a wretched situation. No theoretical checks—no form of government can render us secure. To suppose that any form of government will secure liberty or happiness without any virtue in the people, is a chimerical idea, if there be sufficient virtue and intelligence in the community, it will be exercised in the selection of these men. So that we do not depend on their virtue, or put confidence in our rulers, but in the people who are to choose them.

Speech at Virginia Ratifying Convention, June 20, 1788

POLITICAL PARTIES.—The latent causes of faction are thus sown in the nature of man; and we see them every where brought into different degrees of activity, according to the different circumstances of civil society. A zeal for different opinions concerning religion, concerning government, and many other points, as well of speculation as of practice; an attachment to different leaders ambitiously contending; for pre-eminence and power; or to persons of other descriptions whose fortunes have been interesting to the human passions, have in turn divided mankind into parties, inflamed them with mutual animosity, and rendered them much more disposed to vex and oppress each other, than to co-operate for their common good.

Federalist Nos. 10 and 22, November, 1787

In a society under the forms of which the stronger faction can readily unite and oppress the weaker, anarchy may as truly be said to reign as in a state of nature.

Federalist No. 52, February 8, 1788

In every political society, parties are unavoidable. A difference of interests, real or supposed, is the most natural and fruitful source of them. The great object should be to combat the evil: 1. By establishing a political equality among all. 2. By withholding unnecessary opportunities from a few, to increase the inequality of property, by an immoderate, and especially an unmerited, accumulation of riches. 3. By the silent operation of laws, which, without violating the rights of property, reduce extreme wealth towards a state of mediocrity, and raise extreme indigence towards a state of comfort. 4. By abstaining from measures which operate differently on different interests, and particularly such as favor one interest at the expence of another. 5. By making one party a check on the other, so far as the existence of parties cannot be prevented, nor their views accommodated. If this is not the language of reason, it is that of republicanism.

"Parties" Essay, January 23, 1792

In all political societies, different interests and parties arise out of the nature of things, and the great art of politicians lies in making them checks and balances to each other. Let us then increase these natural distinctions by favoring an inequality of property; and let us add to them artificial distinctions, by establishing kings, and nobles, and plebeians. We shall then have the more checks to oppose to each other: we shall then have the more scales and the more weights to perfect and maintain the equilibrium. This is as little the voice of reason, as it is that of republicanism.

"Parties" Essay, January 23, 1792

POWER, Balance of.—What is to be the consequence, in case the Congress shall misconstrue this part [the necessary and proper clause] of the Constitution and exercise powers not warranted by its true meaning, I answer the same as if they should misconstrue or enlarge any other power vested in them. . . . The success of the usurpation will depend on the executive and judiciary departments, which are to expound and give effect to the legislative acts; and in a last resort a remedy must be obtained from the people, who can by the elections of more faithful representatives, annul the acts of the usurpers.

Federalist No. 44, January 25, 1788

It will not be denied that power is of an encroaching nature and that it ought to be effectually restrained from passing the limits assigned to it. After discriminating, therefore, in theory, the several classes of power, as they may in their nature be legislative, executive, or judiciary, the next and most difficult task is to provide some practical security for each, against the invasion of the others.

Federalist No. 48, February 1, 1788

[I]n the next place, to show that unless these departments be so far connected and blended as to give to each a constitutional control over the others, the degree of separation which the maxim requires, as essential to a free government, can never in practice be duly maintained.

Federalist No. 48, February 1, 1788

[I]t is the reason alone, of the public, that ought to control and regulate the government.

Federalist No. 49, February 5, 1788

The passions, therefore, not the reason, of the public would sit in judgment. But it is the reason, alone, of the public, that ought to control and regulate the government. The passions ought to be controlled and regulated by the government.

Federalist No. 49, February 5, 1788

It may be considered as an objection inherent in the principle, that as every appeal to the people would carry an implication of some defect in the government, frequent appeals would in great measure deprive the government of that veneration which time bestows on every thing, and without which perhaps the wisest and freest governments would not possess the requisite stability.

Federalist No. 49, February 5, 1788

But the great security against a gradual concentration of the several powers in the same department, consists in giving to those who administer each department, the necessary constitutional means, and personal motives, to resist encroachments of the others. The provision for defence must in this, as in all other cases, be made commensurate to the danger of attack. Ambition must be made to counteract ambition. The interest of the man must be connected with the constitutional rights of the place. It may be a reflection on human nature, that such devices should be necessary to control the abuses of government. But what is government itself but the greatest of all reflections on human nature? If men were angels, no government would be necessary. If angels were to govern men, neither external nor internal controls on government would be necessary. In framing a government which is to be administered by men over men, the great difficulty lies in this: You must first enable the government to control the governed; and in the next place, oblige it to control itself. A dependence on the people is no doubt the primary control on the government; but experience has taught mankind the necessity of auxiliary precautions.

Federalist No. 51, February 6, 1788

Had every Athenian citizen been a Socrates, every Athenian assembly would still have been a mob.

Federalist No. 55, February 15, 1788

If it be asked what is to restrain the House of Representatives from making legal discriminations in favor of themselves and a particular class of the society? I answer, the genius of the whole system, the nature of just and constitutional laws, and above all the vigilant and manly spirit which actuates the people of America, a spirit which nourishes freedom, and in return is nourished by it.

Federalist No. 57, February 19, 1788

I acknowledge, in the ordinary course of government, that the exposition of the laws and Constitution devolves upon the judicial. But I beg to know upon what principle it can be contended that any one department draws from the Constitution greater powers than another in marking out the limits of the powers of the several departments.

Speech in the Congress of the United States, June 17, 1789

Nothing has yet been offered to invalidate the doctrine that the meaning of the Constitution may as well be ascertained by the Legislative as by the Judicial authority.

Speech in the Congress of the United States, June 18, 1789

PRESS, The.—To the press alone, checkered as it is with abuses, the world is indebted for all the triumphs which have been gained by reason and humanity over error and oppression.

Report on the Virginia Resolutions, January 1800

The right of electing the members of the government, constitutes more particularly the essence of a free and responsible government. The value and efficacy of this right, depends on the knowledge of the comparative merits and demerits of the candidates for public trust; and on the equal freedom, consequently, of examining and discussing these merits and demerits of the candidates respectively.

Report of 1800, January 1800

The people, not the government, possess the absolute sovereignty. The legislature, no less than the executive, is under limitations of power. Encroachments are regarded as possible from the one, as well as from the other. Hence, in the United States, the great and essential rights of the people are secured against legislative, as well as against executive ambition. They are secured, not by laws paramount to prerogative, but by constitutions paramount to laws. This security of the freedom of the press requires, that it should be exempt, not only from previous restraint by the executive, as in Great Britain, but from legislative restraint also; and this exemption, to be effectual, must be an exemption not only from the previous inspection of licensers, but from the subsequent penalty of laws.

Report of 1800, January 1800

PROPERTY.—Where an excess of power prevails, property of no sort is duly respected. No man is safe in his opinions, his person, his faculties, or his possessions.

"Property" Essay, March 29, 1792

Government is instituted to protect property of every sort. . . . This being the end of government, that alone is a *just* government which *impartially* secures to every man, whatever is his *own*. . . . That is not a just government, nor is property secure under it, where the property which a man has in his personal safety and personal liberty is violated by arbitrary seizures of one class of citizens for the service of the rest. [Emphasis in original.]

"Property" Essay, March 29, 1792

This term in its particular application means "that dominion which one man claims and exercises over the external things of the world, in exclusion of every other individual."

In its larger and juster meaning, it embraces every thing to which a man may attach a value and have a right; and which leaves to every one else the like advantage.

"Property" Essay, March 29, 1792

If the United States mean to obtain or deserve the full praise due to wise and just governments, they will equally respect the rights of property, and the property in rights: they will rival the government that most sacredly guards the former; and by repelling its example in violating the latter, will make themselves a pattern to that and all other governments.

"Property" Essay, March 29, 1792

If there be a government then which prides itself in maintaining the inviolability of property; which provides that none shall be taken directly even for public use without indemnification to the owner, and yet directly violates the property which individuals have in their opinions, their religion, their persons, and their faculties; nay more, which indirectly violates their property, in their actual possessions, in the labor that acquires their daily subsistence, and in the hallowed remnant of time which ought to relieve their fatigues and soothe their cares, the influence will have been anticipated, that such a government is not a pattern for the United States.

"Property" Essay, March 29, 1792

It is sufficiently obvious, that persons and property are the two great subjects on which Governments are to act; and that the rights of persons, and the rights of property, are the objects, for the protection of which Government was instituted. These rights cannot well be separated.

Speech at the Virginia Constitutional Convention, December 2, 1829

PUBLIC OPINION.—Public opinion sets bounds to every government, and is the real sovereign in every free one.

"Public Opinion" Essay, December 19, 1791

RELIGION.—Religious bondage shackles and debilitates the mind and unfits it for every noble enterprize, every expanded prospect.

Letter to William Bradford, April 1, 1774

It is the duty of every man to render to the Creator such homage and such only as he believes to be acceptable to him. This duty is precedent, both in order of time and in degree of obligation, to the claims of Civil Society.

> "Memorial and Remonstrance Against
> Religious Assessments," June 20, 1785

The civil rights of none, shall be abridged on account of religious belief or worship, nor shall any national religion be established, nor shall the full and equal rights of conscience be in any manner, or on any pretext infringed.

> Proposed amendment to the Constitution,
> given in a speech in the House of Representatives, 1789

We are teaching the world the great truth that Governments do better without Kings & Nobles than with them. The merit will be doubled by the other lesson that Religion Flourishes in greater purity, without than with the aid of Government.

> Letter to Edward Livingston, July 10, 1822

More sparingly should this praise be allowed to a government, where a man's religious rights are violated by penalties, or fettered by tests, or taxed by a hierarchy. Conscience is the most sacred of all property; other property depending in part on positive law, the exercise of that, being a natural and unalienable right. To guard a man's house as his castle, to pay public and enforce private debts with the most exact faith, can give no title to invade a man's conscience which is more sacred than his castle, or to withhold from it that debt of protection, for which the public faith is pledged, by the very nature and original conditions of the social pact.

> "Property" Essay, March 29, 1792

SELF-GOVERNMENT, Uniqueness of.—Is it not the glory of

the people of America, that whilst they have paid a decent regard to the opinions of former times and other nations, they have not suffered a blind veneration for antiquity, for custom, or for names, to overrule the suggestions of their own good sense, the knowledge of their own situation, and the lessons of their own experience? To this manly spirit, posterity will be indebted for the possession, and the world for the example of the numerous innovations displayed on the American theatre, in favour of private rights and public happiness.

Federalist No. 14, November 30, 1787

. . . Democracies have ever been spectacles of turbulence and contention; have ever been found incompatible with personal security, or the rights of property; and have in general been as short in their lives as they are violent in their deaths.

Federalist No. 10, November 29, 1787

Here [in the United States], we are, on the whole, doing well, and giving an example of a free system, which I trust will be more of a pilot to a good port, than a beacon, a warning from a bad one. We have, it is true, occasional fevers; but they are of the transient kind, flying off through the surface, without preying on the vitals. A government like ours has so many safety-valves, giving vent to overheated passions, that it carries within itself a relief against the infirmities from which the best of human institutions cannot be exempt.

Letter to Marquis de Lafayette, November 25, 1820

I entirely concur in the propriety of resorting to the sense in which the Constitution was accepted and ratified by the nation. In that sense alone it is the legitimate Constitution. And if that is not the guide in expounding it, there may be no security.

Letter to Henry Lee, June 25, 1824

The United States are now furnishing models and lessons to all the world, a great, soon to be the most hopeful portion of it, is receiving them with a happy docility; whilst the great European portion is either passively or actively gaining by them. The eyes of the world being thus on our country, it is put the more on its good behavior, and under the greater obligation also, to do justice to the Tree of Liberty by an exhibition of the fine fruits we gather from it.

Letter to James Monroe, December 16, 1824

The free system of government we have established is so congenial with reason, with common sense, and with a universal feeling that it must produce approbation and a desire of imitation, as avenues may be found for truth to the knowledge of nations.

Letter to Pierre E. Duponceau, January 23, 1826

It has been said that all Government is an evil. It would be more proper to say that the necessity of any Government is a misfortune. This necessity however exists; and the problem to be solved is, not what form of Government is perfect, but which of the forms is least imperfect.

Letter to an unidentified correspondent, 1833

SLAVERY.—We have seen the mere distinction of color made in the most enlightened period of time, a ground of the most oppressive dominion ever exercised by man over man.

Speech at the Constitutional Convention, June 6, 1787

[The Convention] thought it wrong to admit in the Constitution the idea that there could be property in men.

Records of the Convention, August 25, 1787

It ought to be considered as a great point gained in favor of humanity, that a period of twenty years may terminate forever, within these States, a traffic which has so long and so loudly upbraided the barbarism of modern policy; that within that period, it will receive a considerable discouragement from the federal government, and may be totally abolished, by a concurrence of the few States which continue the unnatural traffic, in the prohibitory example which has been given by so great a majority of the Union. Happy would it be for the unfortunate Africans, if an equal prospect lay before them of being redeemed from the oppressions of their European brethren!

Federalist No. 42, January 22, 1788

In a society under the forms of which the stronger faction can readily unite and oppress the weaker, anarchy may as truly be said to reign as in a state of nature.

Federalist No. 52, February 8, 1788

The United States, having been the first to abolish within the extent of their authority the transportation of the natives of Africa into slavery, by prohibiting the introduction of slaves and by punishing their citizens participating in the traffic, can not but be gratified at the progress made by concurrent efforts of other nations toward a general suppression of so great an evil. They must feel at the same time the greater solicitude to give the fullest efficacy to their own regulations. With that view, the interposition of Congress appears to be required by the violations and evasions which it is suggested are chargeable on unworthy citizens who mingle in the slave trade under foreign flags and with foreign ports, and by collusive importations of slaves into the United States through adjoining ports and territories. I present the subject to Congress with a full assurance of their disposition to apply all the remedy which can be afforded by an amendment of the law. The regulations which were intended to guard against abuses of a kindred character in the trade between the several States ought also to be rendered more effectual for their humane object.

>Eighth Annual Message to Congress, December 3, 1816

It is due to justice; due to humanity; due to truth; to the sympathies of our nature; in fine, to our character as a people, both abroad and at home, that they should be considered, as much as possible, in the light of human beings, and not as mere property. As such, they are acted upon by our laws, and have an interest in our laws.

>Speech to the Virginia Constitutional
>Convention, December 2, 1829

STATES, Governments of.—In the first place, it is to be remembered, that the general government is not to be charged with the whole power of making and administering laws: its jurisdiction is limited to certain enumerated objects, which concern all the members of the republic, but which are not to be attained by the separate provisions of any.

>*Federalist* No. 14, November 30, 1787

Each State, in ratifying the Constitution, is considered as a sovereign body, independent of all others, and only to be bound by its own voluntary act. In this relation, then, the new Constitution will, if established, be a FEDERAL, and not a NATIONAL constitution.

>*Federalist* No. 39, January 18, 1788

The powers delegated by the proposed Constitution to the federal government are few and defined. Those which are to remain in the State governments are numerous and indefinite.

>*Federalist* No. 45, January 26, 1788

The operations of the federal government will be most extensive and important in times of war and danger; those of the State governments, in times of peace and security.

Federalist No. 45, January 26, 1788

For the same reason that the members of the State legislatures will be unlikely to attach themselves sufficiently to national objects, the members of the federal legislature will be likely to attach themselves too much to local objects.

Federalist No. 47, February 1, 1788

That this Assembly doth explicitly and peremptorily declare, that it views the powers of the federal government, as resulting from the compact, to which the states are parties; as limited by the plain sense and intention of the instrument constituting the compact; as no further valid than they are authorized by the grants enumerated in that compact; and that in case of a deliberate, palpable, and dangerous exercise of other powers, not granted by the said compact, the states who are parties thereto, have the right, and are in duty bound, to interpose for arresting the progress of the evil, and for maintaining within their respective limits, the authorities, rights and liberties appertaining to them.

Virginia Resolutions, December 24, 1798

The resolution having taken this view of the federal compact, proceeds to infer, "that in case of a deliberate, palpable, and dangerous exercise of other powers not granted by the said compact, the states who are parties thereto, have the right, and are in duty bound to interpose for arresting the progress of the evil, and for maintaining within their respective limits, the authorities, rights and liberties appertaining to them."

It appears to your committee to be a plain principle, founded in common sense, illustrated by common practice, and essential to the nature of compacts; that where resort can be had to no tribunal superior to the authority of the parties, the parties themselves must be the rightful judges in the last resort, whether the bargain made, has been pursued or violated. The constitution of the United States was formed by the sanction of the states, given by each in its sovereign capacity. It adds to the stability and dignity, as well as to the authority of the constitution, that it rests on this legitimate and solid foundation. The states then being the parties to the constitutional compact, and in their sovereign capacity, it follows of necessity, that there can be no tribunal above their authority, to decide in the last resort, whether the compact made by them be violated; and consequently that as the parties to it, they must themselves decide in the last resort, such questions as may be of sufficient magnitude to require their interposition.

The Report of 1800, January 1800

It becomes all therefore who are friends of a Government based on free principles to reflect, that by denying the possibility of a system partly federal and partly consolidated, and who would convert ours into one either wholly federal or wholly consolidated, in neither of which forms have individual rights, public order, and external safety, been all duly maintained, they aim a deadly blow at the last hope of true liberty on the face of the Earth.

"Notes on Nullification," 1835

TAXES.—The apportionment of taxes on the various descriptions of property is an act which seems to require the most exact impartiality; yet there is, perhaps, no legislative act in which greater opportunity and temptation are given to a predominant party to trample on the rules of justice. Every shilling which they overburden the inferior number is a shilling saved to their own pockets.

Federalist No. 10, November 23, 1787

TYRANNY.—The means of defense against foreign danger historically have become the instruments of tyranny at home.

> Speech at the Constitutional Convention, June 29, 1787

Besides, the advantage of being armed forms a barrier against the enterprises of ambition, more insurmountable than any which a simple government of any form can admit of. The governments of Europe are afraid to trust the people with arms. If they did, the people would certainly shake off the yoke of tyranny, as America did.

> *Federalist* No. 46, January 29, 1788

The accumulation of all powers, legislative, executive, and judiciary, in the same hands, whether of one, a few, or many, and whether hereditary, self-appointed, or elective, may justly be pronounced the very definition of tyranny.

> *Federalist* No. 47, January 30, 1788

One hundred and seventy-three despots would surely be as oppressive as one.

> *Federalist* No. 48, February 1, 1788

The house of representatives . . . can make no law which will not have its full operation on themselves and their friends, as well as the great mass of society. This has always been deemed one of the strongest bonds by which human policy can connect the rulers and the people together. It creates between them that communion of interest, and sympathy of sentiments, of which few governments have furnished examples; but without which every government degenerates into tyranny.

> *Federalist* No. 57, February 19, 1788

Wherever the real power in a Government lies, there is the danger of oppression.

Letter to Thomas Jefferson, October 17, 1788

It seems agreed on all hands now that the bank is a certain & gratuitous augmentation of the capitals subscribed, in a proportion of not less than 40 or 50 [per cent] and if the deferred debt should be immediately provided for in favor of the purchasers of it in the deferred shape, & since the unanimous vote that no change [should] be made in the funding system, my imagination will not attempt to set bounds to the daring depravity of the times. The stock-jobbers will become the pretorian band of the Government, at once its tool & its tyrant; bribed by its largesses, & overawing it by clamours & combinations.

Letter to Thomas Jefferson, August 8, 1791

UNION, Preservation of.—Every man who loves peace, every man who loves his country, every man who loves liberty ought to have it ever before his eyes that he may cherish in his heart a due attachment to the Union of America and be able to set a due value on the means of preserving it.

Federalist No. 41, January 1788

VIRTUE.—I go on this great republican principle, that the people will have virtue and intelligence to select men of virtue and wisdom. Is there no virtue among us? If there be not, we are in a wretched situation. No theoretical checks—no form of government can render us secure. To suppose that any form of government will secure liberty or happiness without any virtue in the people, is a chimerical idea, if there be sufficient virtue and intelligence in the community, it will be exercised in the selection of these men. So that we do not depend on their virtue, or put confidence in our rulers, but in the people who are to choose them.

> Speech at the Virginia Ratifying Convention, June 20, 1788

WAR.—The means of defense against foreign danger historically have become the instruments of tyranny at home.

> Speech at the Constitutional Convention, June 29, 1787

How could a readiness for war in time of peace be safely prohibited, unless we could prohibit, in like manner, the preparations and establishments of every hostile nation?

> *Federalist* No. 41, January 19, 1788

The operations of the federal government will be most extensive and important in times of war and danger; those of the State governments, in times of peace and security.

> *Federalist* No. 45, January 26, 1788

Of all the enemies to public liberty, war is, perhaps, the most to be dreaded, because it comprises and develops the germ of every other. War is the parent of armies; from these proceed debts and taxes; and armies, and debts, and taxes are the known instruments for bringing the many under the domination of the few. . . . No nation could preserve its freedom in the midst of continual warfare. In war too, the discretionary power of the Executive is extended; its influence in dealing out offices, honours, and emoluments is multiplied; and all the means of seducing the minds, are added to those of subduing the force, of the people.

> Political Observations, April 20, 1795

To render the justice of the war on our part the more conspicuous, the reluctance to commence it was followed by the earliest and strongest manifestations of a disposition to arrest its progress. The sword was scarcely out of the scabbard before the enemy was apprised of the reasonable terms on which it would be resheathed.

> Second Inaugural Address, March, 1813

It is a principle incorporated into the settled policy of America, that as peace is better than war, war is better than tribute.

> Letter to Omar Bashaw, the Dey of Algiers, August, 1816

WAR OF 1812.—To render the justice of the war on our part the more conspicuous, the reluctance to commence it was followed by the earliest and strongest manifestations of a disposition to arrest its progress. The sword was scarcely out of the scabbard before the enemy was apprised of the reasonable terms on which it would be resheathed.

> Second Inaugural Address, March, 1813

WAR, Power to declare.—The Constitution expressly and exclusively vests in the Legislature the power of declaring a state of war [and] the power of raising armies. . . . A delegation of such powers [to the President] would have struck, not only at the fabric of our Constitution, but at the foundation of all well organized and well checked governments. The separation of the power of declaring war from that of conducting it, is wisely contrived to exclude the danger of its being declared for the sake of its being conducted.

> Political Observations, April 20, 1795

In time of actual war, great discretionary powers are constantly given to the Executive Magistrate. Constant apprehension of War, has the same tendency to render the head too large for the body. A standing military force, with an overgrown Executive will not long be safe companions to liberty. The means of defence against foreign danger have been always the instruments of tyranny at home. Among the Romans it was a standing maxim to excite a war, whenever a revolt was apprehended. Throughout all Europe, the armies kept up under the pretext of defending, have enslaved the people.

> Speech at the Constitutional
> Convention, June 29, 1787

It would be of little use to enter far into the first source of information, not only because our own reason and our own constitution, are the best guides; but because a just analysis and discrimination of the powers of government, according to their executive, legislative, and judiciary qualities, are not to be expected in the works of the most received jurists, who wrote before a critical attention was paid to those objects, and with their eyes too much on monarchical governments, where all powers are confounded in the sovereignty of the prince. It will be found, however, I believe, that all of them, particularly Wolsius, Burlemaqui, and Vatel, speak of the powers to declare war, to conclude peace, and to form alliances, as among the highest acts of the sovereignty; of which the legislative power must at least be an integral and preeminent part.

> "Helvidius" No. 1, August 24, 1793

If we consult, for a moment, the nature and operation of the two powers to declare war and to make treaties, it will be impossible not to see, that they can never fall within a proper definition of executive powers.

> "Helvidius" No. 1, August 24, 1793

In the general distribution of powers, we find that of declaring war expressly vested in the congress, where every other legislative power is declared to be vested; and without any other qualification than what is common to every other legislative act. The constitutional idea of this power would seem then clearly to be, that it is of a legislative and not an executive nature.

"Helvidius" No. 1, August 24, 1793

Those who are to conduct a war cannot in the nature of things, be proper or safe judges, whether a war ought to be commenced, continued, or concluded. They are barred from the latter functions by a great principle in free government, analogous to that which separates the sword from the purse, or the power of executing from the power of enacting laws.

"Helvidius" No. 1, August 24, 1793

The declaring of war is expressly made a legislative function. The judging of the obligations to make war, is admitted to be included as a legislative function.

"Helvidius" No. 2, August 31, 1793

The power to judge of the causes of war, as involved in the power to declare war, is expressly vested, where all other legislative powers are vested, that is, in the congress of the United States. It is consequently determined by the constitution to be a legislative power.

"Helvidius" No. 2, August 31, 1793

Neutrality means peace, with an allusion to the circumstances of other nations being at war. The term has no reference to the existence or nonexistence of treaties or alliances between the nation at peace and the nations at war. The laws incident to a state of neutrality, are the laws incident to a state of peace, with such circumstantial modifications only as are required by the new relation of the nations at war: until war therefore be duly authorized by the United States, they are as actually neutral when other nations are at war, as they are at peace (if such a distinction in the terms is to be kept up) when other nations are not at war. The existence of eventual engagements which can only take effect on the declaration of the legislature, cannot, without that declaration, change the actual state of the country, any more in the eye of the executive than in the eye of the judiciary department. The laws to be the guide of both, remain the same to each, and the same to both.

"Helvidius" No. 2, August 31, 1793

The power of the legislature to declare war, and judge of the causes for declaring it, is one of the most express and explicit parts of the constitution. To endeavour to abridge or affect it by strained inferences, and by hypothetical or singular occurrences, naturally warns the reader of some lurking fallacy.

"Helvidius" No. 3, September 7, 1793

Every just view that can be taken of this subject, admonishes the public of the necessity of a rigid adherence to the simple, the received, and the fundamental doctrine of the constitution, that the power to declare war, including the power of judging of the causes of war, is fully and exclusively vested in the legislature; that the executive has no right, in any case, to decide the question, whether there is or is not cause for declaring war; that the right of convening and informing congress, whenever such a question seems to call for a decision, is all the right which the constitution has deemed requisite or proper; and that for such, more than for any other contingency, this right was specially given to the executive.

"Helvidius" No. 4, September 14, 1793

War is in fact the true nurse of executive aggrandizement. In war, a physical force is to be created; and it is the executive will, which is to direct it. In war, the public treasures are to be unlocked; and it is the executive hand which is to dispense them. In war, the honours and emoluments of office are to be multiplied; and it is the executive patronage under which they are to be enjoyed. It is in war, finally, that laurels are to be gathered; and it is the executive brow they are to encircle. The strongest passions and most dangerous weaknesses of the human breast; ambition, avarice, vanity, the honourable or venial love of fame, are all in conspiracy against the desire and duty of peace.

"Helvidius" No. 4, September 14, 1793

Index

Adams, John, 8, 53, 59, 164-165, 167, 227, 240, 275
Adams, John Quincy, 153, 208, 279
Adams, Samuel, 113
Alien and Sedition Acts, 165-167, 169, 281
American Experiment, vi
American Whig Society, 17-19
Annapolis Convention, xi, 48, 50
Anti-Federalists, 109, 111, 116, 130
Antony, Marc, 53
Aristotle, 183
Articles of Confederation, viii, 30-31, 45-48, 78-80, 82, 85, 144, 298, 312-313, 363
Athens, 55-56, 61-62, 142

Barry, W.T. (William), 249, 264, 397
Biddle, Nicholas, 307
Bill of Rights, xi, 5, 19, 119-121, 128, 130, 132, 135-136, 138-140, 142, 144, 183, 200-201, 257, 356
Bonaparte, Napoleon (see Napoleon Bonaparte)

Bradford, William, 14-16, 18, 23-26, 40, 42, 411
Brandywine, battle of, 262
USS *Brandywine*, 264
Brutus, Marcus Junius, 53, 55-56, 93
Burr, Aaron, 175, 177-178

Cabell, William, 2, 22, 41
Cabell, Joseph, 304
Caesar, Julius, 3, 7, 53
Calhoun, John, 250
Campaigning for Office, 123, 280
Carrington, Edward, 302
Carroll, Daniel, 59
Catiline, conspiracy of, 55
U.S.S. *Chesapeake*, 215-217, 222
Cicero, Marcus Tullius, 6, 10, 52-53, 55, 67-68, 109
Clark, George Rogers, 7
Clinton, George, 219
Cliosophic Society, 17
Coles, Edward, 221, 383
Coles, Isaac, 177
Compact of the States, viii, 45, 80-81, 168, 186, 309, 313, 382-384, 417-418

Confederation Congress, viii, xi, 30-31, 48, 69, 88, 121, 154-155, 157, 229
Conscience, Freedom of, 28, 33, 35, 39-40, 133, 136-137, 241
Conscience, as Property, 296-297, 412
Constitution of the United States, 89, 91, 118, 168, 196, 251-252, 361, 368-369, 418
Constitutional Convention, Philadelphia 1787, xi, 5, 50, 56, 66, 68, 72-74, 77, 83, 90, 127-128, 139, 157-159, 168, 170, 233, 246, 281, 414, 421
Continental Congress, First, viii, xi, 23-25, 27-28, 30, 45, 47
Conway, Sir Edward, 5
Cutts, Anna Payne, 179
Cutts, Richard, 221, 294

Declaration of Independence, 7, 28, 152, 189-190, 192, 217, 235, 237, 248, 266-267, 275-276, 372
Defence of the Constitutions of the United States (John Adams), 53
Democracy, dangers of, 52, 67
Demosthenes, 62

Ellsworth, Oliver, 154-155
Enquirer (Richmond), 272

Essay Concerning Human Understanding (John Locke), vi, 8
Executive Power, 333, 423
Eustis, William, 142, 306

Federal Convention, 77, 83, 95, 118, 281, 347-348, 367-368, 374
Federalism, 252, 383
The Federalist (Alexander Hamilton, James Madison, John Jay), ix, xi, 10, 48, 50, 52, 93-108, 109, 130, 160, 168, 195, 201, 257, 348, 380
Federalists, 119, 129-130, 222, 231
France, 16, 32, 45, 71, 135, 158, 161, 163, 165-166, 179, 208-212, 215, 222, 225, 227, 231-232, 261, 264, 310, 326, 334-335, 340-341, 357
Franklin, Benjamin, 45, 70-73, 158, 286
Freneau, Philip, 15-18, 184-185, 298, 302

Gallatin, Albert, 209, 233-234, 236, 258-259
Gates, Horatio, 397
General Welfare Clause, 252
Gerry, Elbridge, 139
Giles, William Branch, 302-303
Grayson, William, 33
Greece, 6, 22, 40, 51-52, 55-56, 58, 70, 93

Hamilton, Alexander, ix, 10, 48, 59-60, 82, 87, 93, 95, 119, 146, 154, 160-161, 184, 254, 257, 281, 286, 301, 306, 347-348
Henry, Patrick, 30, 33-34, 44, 101, 109-120, 280
Herodotus, 7, 58
Hume, David, 67-68

"Idea of a Perfect Commonwealth" (David Hume), 67
Interposition, 296, 415, 418

Jackson, Andrew, 237, 253-255, 262, 306
Jay, John, ix, 93, 257, 298, 300, 341, 348
Jefferson, Thomas, viii, xi, 16, 19-20, 30, 32-33, 41, 45, 48, 50, 60, 62, 68-69, 72, 74, 76, 89-90, 123-124, 127, 135, 149, 151-172, 173, 179, 181-182, 184, 202-212, 215, 217, 219-222, 227-228, 231, 233, 240, 257, 260, 262, 268-270, 273, 275-276, 280, 285-286, 288, 298, 300, 302, 306, 352, 356, 359, 367, 372-373, 376, 379, 384-387, 393, 395-396, 402, 420
Jennings, Paul, 276, 282, 284, 348
Jones, Joseph, 298, 300, 302-303

Julian Calendar, 3

Kentucky Resolutions, 164, 168
Key, Francis Scott, 238
King, Rufus, 301

Lafayette, Georges, 262
Lafayette, Marquis de, 32-33, 90, 261-263, 354, 413
Lee, Henry, 363, 366, 413
Lee, Richard Henry, 33
H.M.S. *Leopard*, 215-217, 222
Levasseur, Auguste, 262, 264
Livingston, Edward, 392, 399, 412
Livingston, Robert, 206-207, 209
Livy, 58
Locke, John, vi, viii, 8, 37, 95-98, 266-267
Louisiana Purchase, 206-207, 209, 211, 257
Lycurgus, 53, 55-56

Maddison, John, 4, 282
Madison, Ambrose, 2, 4
Madison, Dolley Payne Todd, 22, 173-182, 205, 221, 224, 234, 236-237, 257, 259-260, 262, 264, 276, 278
Madison, Frances Taylor, 4
Madison, James
    "Advice to My Country", 289
    American Revolution (see

War of Independence)
Ancestry, 4
Assembly of Virginia, 168
Bill of Rights, sponsorship of, 5, 19, 201
Birth, xi,
College of New Jersey (see Princeton)
Commonplace Book, 8-9, 43, 51
Constitutional Convention, Philadelphia 1787
   As "Miracle", 90
   Correspondence with George Washington, 300
   Preparation for, 63, 76, 85
   Record keeper, 76-81, 83, 89-90
   Speaker, 73, 282
   Supper with Key Figures, 71
   Virginia Plan, vi, 68, 71-72, 78, 86, 257
Constitutional Convention, Virginia 1829-1830, 270-271
Continental Congress, viii, xi, 23, 27-28, 30, 45
Death, 275-284, 286-287
Declaration of Independence, 7, 28, 152, 189, 192, 276
Declaration of Rights, Virginia, 27-28, 34, 43, 72
Diplomacy, 211, 212
Early Education, vi

Essays (In defense of Republican policies)
   "Population and Immigration", 186
   "Property," 199, 394, 410-412
Family and Eulogies, 278
Friends, 128, 158, 388
Gravestone, 287
Health, 6, 19, 23, 26, 76, 203, 295-296, 307
Hebrew, study of, 19, 294
History, study of, x, 6, 8, 15, 45, 50, 56-59, 63, 268, 391
House of Representatives, vii, xi, 15, 81, 83, 127, 131, 138, 140, 147, 209, 245, 251, 254, 257
Law, plan to study, 21
Marriage, 173-182
"Memorial and Remonstrance Against Religious Assessments," 34-39, 44, 389, 412
Militia Service, 26-27, 112, 245-247
Ministry, plan to enter, 15
Montpelier, xi, 9, 21-22, 31-32, 63, 124, 179-182, 203-205, 221, 224, 255, 278, 284, 288
Nullification, 399, 418
Orange County Committee of Safety, xi, 25
Presidency, 88, 163, 187, 221, 240

Princeton (College of New Jersey), vii, xi, 9-21, 138, 157, 294
Ratification of Constitution of 1787, 69, 93-108
Republican Party (also known as the Democratic-Republicans), 219
Religion, 27, 34-44
Retirement, 257-274
Secretary of State, vi, viii, xi, 184, 202, 203-218, 257, 305
Siblings' Tutor, 20-21, 23
Social Life, 151
Teachers, iv-viii
Union, Devotion to, 111, 128, 154, 171, 219, 284
University of Virginia, xi, 41, 170, 264-270, 288
Virginia Declaration of Rights, 27-28, 34, 43, 72
Virginia Executive Committee, 27
Virginia Ratifying Convention, xi, 50, 59, 109, 112, 116, 131, 167, 280, 374, 382, 391, 404, 421
Virginia Resolutions, 168, 170, 257, 383-384, 403, 409, 417
War of Independence, 7, 14-15, 26-27, 45-46, 64, 154, 206, 262, 279
War of 1812, xi, 2, 227-242, 245, 247, 257, 422

White House, burning of, 243
Williamsburg, 296
Madison, Nelly Conway, 7
Madison, William, 2
Marshall, John, 219, 271
Martin, Reverend Thomas, vii, 11, 294
Martineau, Harriet, 278
Mason, George, 34, 72, 297, 299
Mazzei, Philip, 368
"Memorial and Remonstrance Against Religious Assessments," 34-39, 44, 389, 412
Mobocracy, 68, 358, 408
Monroe, James, 33, 121, 123-125, 179, 206-207, 209, 211, 213-214, 217-219, 271, 353, 365, 371, 388, 398, 414
Montesquieu, Baron de, vi, ix, 8, 68, 98
Monticello, 157, 167, 179, 205, 208, 227, 260, 262, 288
Montpelier, xi, 9, 21-22, 31-32, 63, 124, 179-182, 203-205, 221, 224, 255, 257-275, 278, 284, 288
Morris, Gouverneur, Robert, 74, 338
Mount Vernon Conference, 46

Napoleon Bonaparte, 206, 212, 224, 227, 262
National Gazette, 15-16, 184-186, 188, 199, 201, 298, 302, 352-357, 360, 387

Necessary and Proper Clause, 145-149, 362, 390, 406
Nicholas, Wilson Cary, 303
Notes of Debates in the Federal Convention of 1787, 77, 83
"Notes on Ancient and Modern Confederacies," 50, 68
"Notes on Commentary on the Bible," 41
"Notes on Nullification," 399, 418
"Notes on the Federal Constitution," 368
Notes on the State of Virginia, 265
Nullification, 399, 418

"Of Ancient and Modern Confederacies," 50, 195, 391

Pacificus-Helvidius articles (Alexander Hamilton and James Madison), 160, 281
Paine, Thomas, 299
Paper Money, 31, 299, 310, 316
Paterson, William, 12, 78-80
Payne, John, 174-175, 179, 221
Payne, Mary, 179, 260
Peloponnesian War, 60
Pendleton, Edmund, 34, 300, 306, 353, 363, 382
Philip of Macedonia, 52, 61-62
Pickering, Thomas, 305
Pinckney, Charles, 206
Pinckney, Charles Cotesworth, 219-220, 323, 338

Plutarch, v, 7, 52, 55-56, 58, 93
Polybius, 58
Princeton (College of New Jersey), vii, xi, 9-21, 138, 157, 294
Publius, xi, 92-95, 257, 301

Randolph, Edmund, 16, 31-32, 66, 68, 71-72, 147, 298, 302, 306, 358, 378
Randolph, John, of Roanoke, 231
Report on Manufactures (Alexander Hamilton), 183-184
Republican party, 202
Republicanism, 96, 98, 103, 153, 245, 328, 405-406
Rives, William Cabell, 2, 22, 41
Roane, Spencer, 306, 366
Robertson, Donald, vi, vii, 6-9, 12, 17, 294
Rome, 6, 22, 51-52, 55-58, 70, 86, 88, 93, 95, 142
Rush, Benjamin, 223-224, 299, 307, 389, 398

Sallust, 58-59
Second Treatise of Government (John Locke), 96-98
Separation of Powers, ix, 106, 196, 209
Sherman, Roger, 89
Sidney, Algernon, viii, 266
Slavery, 52, 62, 263, 311, 414-415

432

Smith, Robert, 306
Smith, Samuel Harrison, 307, 395
Socrates, 72, 358, 408
Solon, 53, 55-56
Sparta, 55, 142
The Spirit of the Laws (Baron de Montesquieu), vi, 8
State Governments, 69, 110-114, 154, 170, 187, 196, 252-253, 321, 329, 355, 381-382, 385, 390, 394, 400, 416-417, 421

Tacitus, 7, 58-59
Talleyrand, 206, 209
Taylor, John, of Caroline, 7, 219, 231
Thucydides, 8, 60-61, 183
Todd, John, 174
Todd, John Payne, 174, 179, 221
Tucker, St. George, 229-230, 276
Tyranny, ix, 35-36, 52, 56, 62-63, 86, 93, 157, 170, 189, 200, 262, 360, 381, 385, 389, 401, 419, 421, 423

Union, 99-104, 118, 137, 159-160, 164, 168, 240, 245, 249, 266, 273, 282, 289, 310-313, 372, 379, 383, 385, 392, 400, 404, 415, 420
University of Virginia, xi, 41, 170, 264-270, 288

"Vices of the Political System of the United States" (James Madison), 68, 309-317, 377
Virginia Convention of 1776, 43
Virginia Constitutional Convention of 1829-1830, 270-271, 374
Virginia Plan (see Constitutional Convention Philadelphia 1787)
Virginia Resolutions, 168, 170, 257, 383-384, 403, 409, 417

War, xi, 2, 5, 17-18, 212, 227-241, 245, 247, 257, 345, 422
War of Independence, 7, 14-15, 26-27, 45-46, 64, 154, 206, 227-241, 262, 279
Washington, George, 8, 14, 26, 31, 46, 53, 57, 63-72. 76, 82-83, 90, 123-124, 127-128, 161, 177, 184, 212, 220, 224, 235, 237, 240, 254, 262, 266, 275, 281, 286, 300, 332, 394, 404
Washington, Martha, 173
Washington, D.C., 181-182, 203-205, 234, 236, 238, 243, 248, 259-260, 278, 305
Webster, Daniel, 260, 283, 369
Willis, Nelly Conway Madison, 1, 3, 4, 22
Wilson, James, 74, 86-88
Witherspoon, John, vii, 10, 12, 16, 19-20, 294-295
Wythe, George, 33, 72, 305

Index

The Official Store of The John Birch Society

To order extra copies of this book, go to ShopJBS.org or call 1-800-342-6491

How Can I Make a Difference?

GETTING STARTED IS AS EASY AS 1,2,3

1 **Sign up for JBS news and action alerts**
- Stay informed with free content
- Visit www.JBS.org/e-newsletter to sign up now

2 **Contact your elected representatives**
- Local, state, and federal officials represent you
- Visit www.JBS.org/act-now for contact information

3 **Join The John Birch Society**
- National concerted action multiplies your impact
- Visit www.JBS.org/join to apply for membership today

The John Birch Society

P.O. Box 8040
Appleton, WI 54912-8040
(920) 749-3780 • **JBS.org**

"Less government, more responsibility,
and — with God's help — a better world."

www.ingramcontent.com/pod-product-compliance
Lightning Source LLC
Chambersburg PA
CBHW020321170426
43200CB00006B/235